Start Your Own

IMPORT/
EXPORT
BUSINESS

D1257426

Additional titles in *Entrepreneur's* Startup Series

Start Your Own

Arts and Crafts Business

Automobile Detailing Business

Bar and Club

Bed and Breakfast

Blogging Business

Business on eBay

Car Wash

Child-Care Service

Cleaning Service

Clothing Store and More

Coaching Business

Coin-Operated Laundry

Construction and Contracting Business

Consulting Business

Day Spa and More

e-Business

Event Planning Business

Executive Recruiting Business

Fashion Accessories Business

Florist Shop and Other Floral Businesses

Food Truck Business

Freelance Writing Business and More

Freight Brokerage Business

Gift Basket Service

Grant-Writing Business

Graphic Design Business

Green Business

Hair Salon and Day Spa

Home Inspection Service

Import/Export Business

Information Marketing Business

Kid-Focused Business

Lawn Care or Landscaping Business

Mail Order Business

Medical Claims Billing Service

Net Services Business

Online Coupon or Daily Deal Business

Online Education Business

Personal Concierge Service

Personal Training Business

Pet Business and More

Pet-Sitting Business and More

Photography Business

Public Relations Business

Restaurant and More

Retail Business and More

Self-Publishing Business

Seminar Production Business

Senior Services Business

Travel Business and More

Tutoring and Test Prep Business

Vending Business

Wedding Consultant Business

Wholesale Distribution Business

Entrepreneur
MAGAZINE'S

startup

4TH EDITION

Start Your Own

IMPORT/
EXPORT
BUSINESS

Your Step-by-Step
Guide to Success

Entrepreneur Press and Krista Turner

EP
Entrepreneur
PRESS®

FOUNTAINDALE PUBLIC LIBRARY
300 West Briarcliff Road
Bolingbrook, IL 60440-2894
(630) 759-2102

Entrepreneur Press, Publisher
Cover Design: Beth Hansen-Winter
Production and Composition: Eliot House Productions

© 2014 by Entrepreneur Media, Inc.
All rights reserved.
Reproduction or translation of any part of this work beyond that permitted by Section 107
or 108 of the 1976 United States Copyright Act without permission of the copyright owner
is unlawful. Requests for permission or further information should be addressed to the Business Products Division, Entrepreneur Media Inc.

This publication is designed to provide accurate and authoritative information in regard to
the subject matter covered. It is sold with the understanding that the publisher is not
engaged in rendering legal, accounting or other professional services. If legal advice or other
expert assistance is required, the services of a competent professional person should be
sought.

Library of Congress Cataloging-in-Publication Data
  Turner, Krista.
  Start your own import/export business: your step-by-step guide to success / Entrepreneur
    Press and Krista Turner.—4th ed.
    pages cm.—(Startup series)
    Includes index.
    ISBN–13: 978-1-59918-523-3 (paperback)
    ISBN–10: 1-59918-532-6 (paperback)
    1. Trading companies—United States—Management. 2. Imports—United States.
  3. Exports—United States 4. New business enterprises—United States—Management.
  5. International trade. I. Turner, Krista. II. Entrepreneur Press. III. Title.
  HF1416.5.T87 2014
  658.8'4--dc23   2014012020

Printed in the United States of America

18 17 16 15 14   10 9 8 7 6 5 4 3 2

Contents

Chapter 4
Tricks of the Trade: Startup Basics 59

▲

Chapter 5

Trade Routes: Daily Operations 75

Chapter 6

Rituals and Red Tape 107

Chapter 7

Charting Your Trade Route: Market Research **133**

Chapter 8

Trade Dollars: What a Haul! **153**

Chapter 11°
The Trader's Trumpet: Advertising and Marketing 197

▲

Preface

You're holding this book either in your hands, on your lap, or on your desk—possibly near a spillable cup of coffee—because you're one of those people who likes to live on the edge. You're contemplating starting your own business.

This is one of the most exhilarating things you can do for yourself and your family. It's also one of the scariest. Owning your own business means you're the boss, the big cheese, the head honcho. You make the rules. You lay down the law. It also means you can't call in sick (especially when you are also the only employee), you can't let somebody else worry about making enough to cover payroll and expenses, and you can't defer that cranky client or intimidating IRS representative to a higher authority. You're it.

We're assuming you've picked up this particular book on starting and running an import/export business for one or more of the following reasons:

- You have a background in the import/export field.
- You're an avid fan of the *Travel Channel*, your passport is close at hand even when you're just going to the supermarket, and you think international trade is a glamorous and exciting business.
- You have a background in sales or distribution and feel that sales is sales, no matter where in the world you are.
- You have no background or interest in any of the above but believe import/export is a hot opportunity and are willing to take a chance.

Which did you choose? (Didn't know it was a test, did you?)

There is, of course, no wrong answer. Any of these responses is entirely correct as long as you realize they all involve a lot of learning and hard work. They can also be a heck of a lot of fun as well as providing personal and professional satisfaction.

Our goal here is to tell you everything you need to know to decide whether an import/export business is the right business for you, and then, assuming it is, to do the following:

- get your business started successfully,
- keep your business running successfully, and
- make friends and influence people. (Which is actually part of Chapter 11, advertising and marketing.)

We've attempted to make this book as user-friendly as possible. We've interviewed lots of people out there on the front lines of the industry—all around the world—to find out how the import/export business really works and what makes it tick. And we've set aside places for them to tell their own stories and share their own hard-won advice and suggestions, which creates a sort of round-table discussion group with you right in the thick of things. (For a listing of these successful business owners, see the Appendix.) We've broken our chapters into manageable sections on every aspect of startup and operations. And we've left some space for your own creativity to work.

The pages are packed with helpful addresses, phone numbers, and websites so you can get up and running on your new venture as quickly as possible. And we've provided a resource section crammed with even more contacts and sources. Here's a tip: You'll find a complete listing of the sources mentioned throughout the book in the Appendix.

So sit back—don't spill that coffee!—get reading, and get ready to become an import/export pro.

International Trade
Passport to Success

International trade is one of the hot industries of the millennium. But it's not new. Think Marco Polo. Think the great caravans of the Biblical Age with their cargoes of silks and spices. Think even further back to prehistoric man trading shells and salt with distant tribes. Trade exists because one group or country has a supply of some commodity or merchandise that is in demand by another. And as the world becomes more and more technologically advanced, as we shift in subtle and not so subtle ways toward one-world modes of thought, international trade becomes more and more rewarding, both in terms of profit and personal satisfaction.

This chapter explores the flourishing business of international trade from both the import and export sides of the fence. Think of this chapter as an investigative report—like those TV news magazine shows, but without the commercials. We'll delve into the steadily rising economic importance of the field and dip into the secrets of the United State's, and the world's, import/export industry.

The International Adventurer

The stereotypical importer rides around in his battered jeep, bargaining for esoteric goods in exotic markets amid a crescendo of foreign tongues. If that's your idea of an international trader, you're absolutely right. You're also dead wrong.

Importing is not just for those lone footloose adventurer types who survive by their wits and the skin of their teeth. It's big business these days—to the tune of an annual $2.3 trillion in goods and services, according to the U.S. Department of Commerce. Exporting is also big. In one year alone, American companies exported $2.2 trillion in goods and services to more than 150 foreign countries. Everything from beverages to commodes to computer consulting services—and a staggering list of other products and services you might never imagine as global merchandise—are fair game for the savvy trader. And these goods and services are bought, sold, represented, and distributed somewhere in the world on a daily basis.

But the import/export field is not the sole purview of the conglomerate corporate trader. While large companies exported 70 percent of the value of all exports, according to the U.S. Department of Commerce, the big guys make up only about 3 percent of all exporters. Which means that the other 97 percent of exporters, the lion's share, are small outfits like yours will be—when you're new, at least.

Stat Fact

According to the office of the U.S. Trade Representative, the U.S.'s recent annual exports of goods and services to Western Hemisphere nations totaled more than $817 billion in U.S. imports.

Champagne and Caviar

Why are imports such big business in the United States and around the world? There are lots of reasons, but the three main ones boil down to:

1. *Availability*. There are some things you just can't grow or make in your home country. Bananas in Alaska, for example, mahogany lumber in Maine, or Ball Park Franks in France.

2. *Cachet*. A lot of things, like caviar and champagne, pack more cachet, more of an "image," if they're imported rather than homegrown. Think Scandinavian furniture, German beer, French perfume, Egyptian cotton. Even when you can make it at home, it all seems classier when it comes from distant shores.

3. *Price*. Some products are cheaper when brought in from out of the country. Korean toys, Taiwanese electronics, and Mexican clothing, to rattle off a few, can often be manufactured or assembled in foreign factories for far less money than if they were made on the domestic front.

Aside from cachet items, countries typically export goods and services that they can produce inexpensively and import those that are produced more efficiently somewhere else. What makes one product less expensive for a nation to manufacture than another? Two factors: resources and technology. Resources are natural products, such as timber and minerals, as well as human ones, such as low-cost labor and highly skilled workers. Technology is the knowledge and tools to process raw resources into finished products. A country with extensive oil resources and the technology of a refinery, for example, will export oil but may need to import clothing.

The United States has long been a major import destination for other nations. Canada, China, Mexico, Japan, and Germany are the top foreign sellers. We Americans like variety, low prices, and year-round availability in our goods, and importing has allowed us to achieve these goals.

Although the United States is an experienced exporter of its services (e.g., travel services and technical, financial, and legal expertise), the exportation of U.S. goods represents a virtually untapped field of endeavor—one into which few companies have ventured.

Surprisingly, most of those daring exporters are smaller firms. According to a recent report from the U.S. Census Bureau, companies with fewer than 100 employees accounted for about 90 percent of all exporters, while approximately 97 percent of the total exporters were small or medium-sized companies (meaning they employ fewer than 500 people). Also surprisingly, most exporters, over 90 percent, shipped goods to fewer than ten countries. The top five export destinations, in order of preference, were Canada, Mexico, China, Japan, and the United Kingdom.

Import/Export—The Prequel

OK, you may be thinking, sounds good. But what exactly does an international trader do? In the simplest terms, he or she is a salesperson. Instead of peddling domestically manufactured products on his or her home turf, a trader deals in more exotic merchandise, materials that are foreign to somebody on some far shore. The importer/exporter also acts as a sort of international matchmaker, pairing up buyers and sellers of products in different countries. He can operate as a middleman, purchasing merchandise directly from the manufacturer and selling to retailers or wholesalers in another country. Or he may have his own network of retail distribution representatives selling on commission. As a third permutation, he might hire an outside company to find sales for him. And as a fourth version, he might serve as a consultant for foreign countries that want to export their products but don't know how.

> **Fun Fact**
>
> Premier international trade merchant Marco Polo, who's also the man responsible for the European image of the Far East until the late 19th century, was only 17 when he first set out for China.

Let's back up a little and take this one step at a time. When you're wearing your import hat, you'll be bringing goods into the United States. When you've got on your export cap, you'll be shipping things out of the country, into foreign markets.

Let's say, for example, that you've decided to import Guatemalan handcrafts. You might have spotted them at an outdoor market while you were traveling through Central America, or maybe you became involved by answering a trade lead, a "want ad" placed by a local artisan group desperately seeking U.S. representation. In either case, you swing into action. You get hold of a price list and some samples and then, here in America, you ferry the samples around to wholesalers or retailers, generate interest through your top-notch salesmanship, and book orders. Once you've made a predetermined number of sales, you purchase the handcrafts from the artisans, have them shipped to your buyers, and then those buyers pay you.

This may sound complicated, with you busily purchasing merchandise and having it sent on to third parties who haven't yet coughed up a dime, but there are ways to protect yourself that you'll learn as we go along in this book. And this won't be the only way you'll structure deals. You might, for example, work off a commission as a representative, negotiating payments directly between artisans and buyers, so that you don't put up any money yourself. But we'll discuss all this later, too. For now, let's say that you'll learn how to make it work.

Ice Chests to Siberia

You'll also learn how to export merchandise. You might, for example, decide to sell ice chests in Siberia. (Well, why not? It isn't icy there all the time.) You may have seen the manufacturer's advertisement seeking a sales or distribution representative. But in this instance, let's say you came up with this idea on your own after spotting the sporty items in a local store and figuring that the really American-looking country-western decals on the product would give it a certain "imported" cachet in the target country. You approach the manufacturer, who may very well be astounded by the idea of exporting her product—this is still a novel idea to most companies. But you explain why you think she has a hot ticket for a cold climate, and you offer to purchase the ice chests at her factory price, leaving the selling to you. All you need from her is a price list, some samples and figures on what quantities you can order, and how long it will take her to fill your Siberian orders.

The manufacturer agrees and you're off and running. Your first task is to determine just how to generate sales in Siberia and how to price the ice chests to cover expenses (including shipping costs, taxes, and tariffs) and still make a profit. Next, you find a foreign partner to distribute your product in Siberia. You send him some samples and a price list, and he gets busy selling.

As you predicted, the American ice chests are a smash hit. Your sales representative generates oodles of sales from Siberian retailers and sends the orders to you along with letters of credit from the buyers. (A letter of credit is an agreement from the buyer's bank to release the buyer's funds into your local bank account. More on this later.) So with your orders and letter of credit in hand, you purchase enough ice chests to fill the orders and have them picked up by the shipping company directly from the manufacturer. Then you take the shipping documents showing that you've fulfilled your part of the deal by sending out the merchandise and the letters of credit to your bank. Bingo! The money goes into your account. As a final step, you send your Siberian sales representative his commission.

And in a very basic way that's how the international trade business works. It can appear daunting, with convoluted components like customs, trade barriers and tariffs, currency fluctuations, exclusive/nonexclusive distribution rights, and packing and shipping plights, not to mention cultural and communication twists. It can also be exciting, rewarding, and profitable. And not at all daunting once you've done your homework.

Back to the Future

It's no wonder that international trade is a growing industry. In spite of the recent global financial crisis and the resulting slowdown in world economies (see Chapter 3 for more discussion of this and other world events), the emergence of free market ideas around the globe has created a stimulating environment for international trade opportunities.

As the world faces the challenges of global recession and financial shake-ups, nations dust themselves off and respond to those challenges. Huge, rapidly expanding markets like China and India are expected to become increasingly important due to their large populations and the expansion of their middle classes. On the other side of the International Date Line, Mexico has become one of the United States' biggest trading partners, and Brazil is emerging as a trading force. Chapter 3 discusses key global economic and political factors, and provides a snapshot of the most promising trading partner countries.

> **Fun Fact**
>
> Never heard of Comoros, Niue, or Kiribati? Well, some United States exporters have. The U.S. Department of Commerce counts these obscure places among the 200-plus countries and territories that import American-made goods.

Counting Your Coconuts

What can you expect to make as an international trader? The amount's entirely up to you, depending only on how serious you are and how willing you are to expand. Annual gross revenues for the industry range from $40,000 to $300,000 and beyond, with an average of about $85,000. Some traders work from home, supplementing 9-to-5 incomes with their trading expertise. Others have launched thriving full-time businesses that demand constant care and feeding.

In Maryland, Wahib Wahba heads an export company that, with a staff of five, oversees multimillion-dollar contracts.

"There are tons and tons of opportunity for [export] trade," says Wahib. "U.S. manufacturers are behind the clock in exporting." So the potential for growth is entirely up to you, as long as you're willing to put in the time. "Be prepared to work long hours!" advises Jan Herremans, a trader in Belgium. "It takes a lot of work," agrees Sam Nelson, a North Carolina export trader. "You have to try with all your energy," says Bruno Carlier, an export manager in France. And Wahib echoes this sentiment. "Just keep doing your job," he counsels. "Work on it all the time."

"Do not expect immediate or short-term success," adds Lloyd Davidson, a Florida export manager. "Be willing to work around the international clock, if you will; take discourtesies, both foreign and domestic, in stride; maintain the highest standard of personal and business ethics in dealing with your principal and buyer; learn from your mistakes; and keep a supply of antidepressants nearby."

Crank-Up Costs

One of the catch-22s of being in business for yourself is that you need money to make money—in other words, you need startup funds. These costs range from less than $5,000 to more than $25,000 for the import/export business. You can start out homebased, which means you won't need to worry about leasing office space. You don't need to purchase a lot of inventory and you probably won't need employees.

Your basic necessities will be a computer, printer, fax machine, and internet service. If you already have these items, then you're off and running. Several of the traders we talked with started from ground zero. "I just had a computer," says Sam Nelson. "I started from my house." "We started from nothing," says Wahib Wahba, "but once we got a large project, that was all it took."

The Rock of Gibraltar

In addition to profits and startup costs, two other important areas to consider are risk and stability. You want a business that, like the Rock of Gibraltar, is here to stay. In import/export, consistency and effort matter. The risk factor is relatively low, providing you're willing to work for your rewards. Michael Richter, an international trade consultant in Seekirch, Germany, advises, "Look at the markets, the pricing, the trends. Look to your customers' wishes, target your market, and you will never, ever fail, so long as you do all this thoroughly and earnestly."

The Right Stuff

So you've decided running an import/export business is potentially profitable for you. You're willing to invest your money and also the time it'll take to establish your business. What else should you consider?

Personality. Not everybody is cut out to be an international trader. This is not, for example, a career for the salesphobic. If you're one of those people who would rather trim your lawn a blade at a time than sell Girl Scout cookies, then you don't want to be in import/export. This is also not a career for the organizationally challenged. If you're one of those let-the-devil-handle-the-details types whose idea of follow-up is waiting to see what happens next, you should think twice about international trading.

If, on the other hand, you're an enthusiastic salesperson and a dynamo at tracking things like invoices and shipping receipts, then import/export could be for you. And if your

> **Bright Idea**
> Check out the International Small Business Consortium at all-business.com. It boasts more than 30,000 members from more than 130 countries. You can get help from and develop business connections with people all over the world.

Traits of the Trade

Hey, kids! Take this fun quiz and find out if you've got what it takes to become an ace international trader.

1. *My idea of a fun evening is:*
   a. Watching James Bond movies on television. He's my idea of an agent!
   b. Kicking back with a piña colada, a copy of *Export Today* magazine, and a Spanish for Gringos tape on my headset.
   c. Cruising around town singing "American Pie."

2. *When I send Christmas gifts to relatives who live out of state, I usually:*
   a. Wait until December 24, stuff the gifts into old grocery bags with the addresses scribbled in crayon, then rush to the post office and stand in a huge, snaky line with all the other procrastinators and hope my gifts arrive on time and intact.
   b. Wrap my gifts carefully in specially selected packaging no later than December 10, call my predesignated FedEx or UPS courier (I've already checked to see which is cheaper and faster), then follow up to make sure the gifts arrive on time and intact.
   c. Hope no one notices I forgot to send gifts.

3. *I consider myself to be a "people" person because:*
   a. Even though I have to force myself, I'm able to interact with people so long as it's not more than once a day.
   b. I love working with all kinds of folks!
   c. I know all the words to the Barbra Streisand song "People."

4. *If I could spend one week a month in a foreign country, I would:*
   a. Go to the nearest McDonald's and stay there until it's time to go home.
   b. Try to meet all kinds of people so I could see the world from different perspectives and learn about other cultures.
   c. Try not to breathe in case I picked up some sort of weird foreign germs.

Scoring: If you chose "b" for each answer, you passed with flying colors! You've got what it takes to become an international trader. You're self-motivated, detail-oriented, and eager to work with people all over the world on their own terms.

It's No Secret

It certainly helps to have a background in import/export. But if you don't, should you forget a career in the industry? No. It's entirely possible to start from scratch. You simply offset your deficit in international trade with your assets in a business you already know. If you're a computer whiz, start out importing or exporting computers. (Or maybe even exporting computer services.) If your turf is landscape materials, go green. Launch your import/export business with those same materials. Go with what you already understand.

And don't let the mechanics of international trade, like letters of credit, scare you away. "You have to know what you're doing," advises Wahib Wahba. "Otherwise, you may send a shipment and never get your money just because you spell a name wrong."

For your first few forays, he suggests you hire a customs broker or freight forwarder to handle the paperwork for you. After that, you can do it on your own. "It's no secret at all," he says. "It's just a trick."

idea of heaven is seeing where new ideas and new products will take you and talking with people from different cultures along the way, then this is the career for you.

The Trade Bug

Michael Richter, the German trade consultant, let his enchantment with the world be his entrée into the industry. "I was simply interested in the worldwide markets and their cultural and personal relationships," he explains, "and I started from being an apprentice—right from the beginning—mostly in investment and construction goods and projects." Now, over 35 years later, Michael is still in the business—and still enjoying it.

For Jan Herremans, an importer/exporter in Belgium, just living in Western Europe was enough to open the door to international trade. So how did he get started? "I don't really know," he says. "It's an instinct. Belgium is such

Smart Tip
International business discussion groups are full of information for the SME. Just what is this entity? What you're about to become—a small or medium enterprise.

▲

a small country that one has to look around. And I love to travel the world, especially warm countries."

Spin-Off

Wahib Wahba, a native of Egypt, started out as a mechanical engineer for Caterpillar, the world's leading manufacturer of construction and mining equipment, working overseas. In 1985, he arrived in the United States, where he promptly started in on both an MBA degree and a position with a company that sold runway lights and navigational aids for airports. When the company became too heavily involved in domestic sales to handle the international work, Wahib formed a company to take up the slack. The new company also began selling other types of construction projects, from wooden telephone pole installation to railroads, supplying materials, construction services, or both. Soon business was so good that he was able to buy out his former employer.

Wahib stresses that his success developed from his prior experience in the field. "Nobody becomes an exporter overnight from nothing," he says. "You have to be coming from somewhere."

Take John Laurino, an international business services provider in São Paulo, Brazil. John learned the ins and outs of import/export as an international purchasing manager for a large company before striking out on his own in 1994.

And in Florida, Lloyd Davidson worked in the operations sector of international banking before making the move to his own company. "I decided to expand into export management and export trading," he explains, "relying on my previous experience in an international environment to support my new endeavors."

Here You Are

Bruno Carlier, who makes his home in Derchigny Graincourt, France, studied international trade at universities in France and Spain and completed his schooling in South America by teaching import and export strategy and techniques to others. He then went on to the college of real life. "One of my first jobs after my studies was in one of the . . . major French supermarket groups as an import assistant," Bruno says. "I can say that in four months [there], I learned much more than in four years of studies."

But that wasn't enough to get him a job in international trade. Despite a year of teaching in Ecuador and his supermarket job, he lacked hands-on training. "Therefore," Bruno continues, "because I was not considered to have enough experience to work in the [international trade] department of a medium-sized company, I decided to create my own business. And here I am."

Here, too, are you—on the brink of an exciting new course of action, starting your own import/export business. As you can see, there are many paths you can take toward your own niche in the field, many roads that lead to success. Keep in mind, however, that they all require dedication, hard work, and, especially for those who are newbies in the field, a great deal of learning.

Future Forecast

Perhaps the import/export business looks like the perfect fit for you—at least, on paper. There is, however, one more thing to take into consideration: the industry prognosis. Will international trading be around for the next 100 years and beyond?

The odds are good. We may live in challenging times, but they are also interesting times. The world has already experienced world wars, natural disasters, and global financial crises, and we—and our trading partners—are still alive and kicking. And, in many cases, even thriving.

So fasten your seatbelt, hang on tightly, and let's start your learning curve.

Trader's View

Wahib Wahba advises the newbie trader to focus on a country in which he or she already has direct experience. "I see a lot of [traders] who were in the American military overseas," Wahib says, "or who have an ethnic background from another country and have family or contacts overseas. Personal contact is a very strong [asset]."

Import/Export 101

Some international traders do very well importing or exporting services, which can mean a variety of things. As a contractor, you export services and sometimes equipment when your company builds bridges, airports, or telecommunications facilities in a foreign country. As a consultant, you're exporting a service when you supply your knowledge to a foreign firm. And you're importing a service when you purchase the licensing to open your franchise of a pub that started in England.

In this book, we're talking mainly about importing and exporting products. If you are trading in services, some of our information should still be useful to you (especially Chapter 3). You may also want to consult Entrepreneur's *Start Your Own Consulting Service*.

Global trade of any kind involves nations. Where there are nations there is government. And government means red tape—miles of it! So where on this big blue marble do you start? At the beginning, of course, with the people who will help you through that red tape.

> ## Fun Fact
> Although the United States has a large trade deficit, it is a top exporter of services, ranging from tourist services to professional and technical services.

Most international traders use freight forwarders or customs brokers to handle all the details of shipping and documentation. These people earn their living by sorting out government rules, regulations, forms, and assorted red tape—both foreign and domestic—but they're also excellent sources of advice on freight costs, port charges, consular fees, and insurance.

Even if you use their services and leave the form filling to them, you should have a working knowledge of what goes on behind the scenes. This chapter, therefore, takes you on a whirlwind tour of the import/export world.

The Players

First off, let's take a look at the players. While they can be divided in broad strokes into importers and exporters, there are many variations on the main theme:

- *Export management company (EMC)*. An EMC handles export operations for a domestic company that wants to sell its product overseas but doesn't know how (and perhaps doesn't want to know how). The EMC does it all—hiring dealers, distributors, and representatives; handling advertising, marketing, and promotions; overseeing marking and packaging; arranging shipping; and sometimes arranging financing. In some cases, the EMC even takes title to (purchases) the goods, in essence becoming its own distributor. EMCs usually specialize by product, foreign market, or both, and—unless they've taken title—are paid by commission, salary, or retainer plus commission.

- *Export trading company (ETC)*. While an EMC has merchandise to sell and is using its energies to seek out buyers, an ETC attacks the other side of the trading coin. It identifies what foreign buyers want to spend their money on and then hunts down domestic sources willing to export, thus becoming a pseudo-EMC. An ETC sometimes takes title to the goods and sometimes works on a commission basis.

- *Import/export merchant.* This international entrepreneur is a sort of free agent. He has no specific client base, and he doesn't specialize in any one industry or line of products. Instead, he purchases goods directly from a domestic or foreign manufacturer and then packs, ships, and resells the goods on his own. This means, of course, that unlike his compatriot, the EMC, he assumes all the risks (as well as all the profits).

More Players

Let's say you're an exporter with a really hot product to sell. Who do you look for? A buyer, otherwise known as an importer. Here's the rundown on the various types:

- *Commission agents.* These are intermediaries commissioned by foreign firms searching for domestic products to purchase.
- *Commission representatives.* Similar to independent sales reps in the United States, these folks usually work on a commission basis, and because they don't purchase (take title to) the product, they don't assume any risk or responsibility.
- *Country-controlled buying agents.* These foreign government agencies or quasi-governmental firms are charged with the responsibility of locating and purchasing desired products.
- *Foreign distributors.* Similar to wholesale distributors in the United States, these merchants buy for their own account, taking title to and responsibility for the merchandise.
- *State-controlled trading companies.* Some countries have government-sanctioned and controlled trading entities. These agencies often deal in raw materials, agricultural machinery, manufacturing equipment, and technical instruments.

The Major Players

There are, of course, more players than just the importers, exporters, and their cast of distributors and representatives. You'll also be dealing with the major players in the game: the government entities.

▲

I've Grown Accustomed

Two important goals of the U.S. Customs Facilitation and Trade Enforcement Reauthorization Act of 2009 are enhancement of supply chain security and enhancement of trade facilitation. Toward those goals, the U.S. government created the U.S. Customs and Border Protection Agency (CBP) and the U.S. Immigration and Customs Enforcement Agency (ICE). You may already know customs officers as those people who fix you and your luggage with a beady eye as you trudge through the airport on your way home from a foreign vacation. But together these two agencies take on many more tasks than just checking for contraband souvenirs. According to their websites, they also

- assess and collect customs duties, excise taxes, fees, and penalties due on imported merchandise.
- intercept and seize contraband, including narcotics and other illegal drugs.
- process people, baggage, cargo, and mail.
- administer certain navigation laws.
- protect American business, labor, and intellectual property rights by enforcing U.S. laws designed to prevent illegal trade practices, including provisions related to quotas and the marking of imported goods.
- enforce the Anti-Dumping Act.
- provide customs records for copyrights, patents, and trademarks.
- enforce import and export restrictions and prohibitions, including the export of technology used to make weapons of mass destruction.
- protect against money laundering.
- collect import/export data to translate into international trade statistics
- secure the national borders.

> **Smart Tip** *Tip...*
>
> The "dump" in the Anti-Dumping Act refers to the practice of flooding a market with an imported product that's far cheaper than a comparable domestic one (see "Can We Quota You?" on page 22).

Lend Me Your EAR

The Bureau of Industry and Security, also known as BIS, is another entity that governs the exportation of sensitive materials—the Dr. No. stuff, like defense systems, plutonium, and encrypted software. Headed up by the Department of Commerce, BIS administers export controls, coordinates Department of Commerce security activities, and oversees defense trade. BIS manages the export of most merchandise through the Export Administration Regulations, also known as EAR.

Say "Cheese"

Of course, because the federal government is involved, it's not quite that simple. Beyond CBP, ICE, and BIS, various agencies regulate the importation of sundry products, some of which even a Trivial Pursuit champ couldn't guess. If you're planning on importing, for example, Cleopatra's magic milk bath, lucky Chinese crickets, cereals, fur coats, or parrots, you'd better check with the agency in charge. Here is a sampling of what you can expect:

1. *Cheese, milk, and other dairy products.* Cheese and cheese products are subject to the vagaries of the Food and Drug Administration (FDA) and the Department of Agriculture. You must have an import license to bring in most cheeses, which are usually subject to quotas administered by the Department of Agriculture's Foreign Agricultural Service. Milk and cream fall under the aegis of the Food, Drug, and Cosmetic Act (maybe milk baths make milk a cosmetic!) and the Federal Import Milk Act, and cannot be imported unless you have a permit from the Department of Agriculture, the FDA's Office of Food Labeling, and other agencies.

2. *Fruits, vegetables, and nuts.* Some fresh produce items (including fresh tomatoes, avocados, mangoes, limes, oranges, grapefruit, green peppers, Irish potatoes, cucumbers, eggplants, dry onions, walnuts, filberts, processed dates, prunes, raisins, and olives in tins) must meet import requirements relating to size, quality, and maturity. All these tidbits must have an inspection certificate indicating importation compliance issued by the Agricultural Marketing Service of the Department of Agriculture. For questions, contact the Agricultural Marketing Service. You may also have to deal with additional restrictions imposed by the department's Animal and Plant Health Inspection Service, otherwise known as APHIS, or by the FDA's Division of Import Operations and Policy.

3. *Plant and plant products.* If you've got a green thumb and want to import garden goodies, be sure you check with the Department of Agriculture first. The agency regulates plants and plant products (including nursery stock, bulbs, roots, and seeds), certain materials (including cotton and lumber), and soil.

Fun Fact

Historically, U.S. Customs has parented a host of other agencies. Customs officers once administered military pensions (Department of Veterans Affairs), collected import and export statistics (Census Bureau), supervised revenue cutter ships (Coast Guard), collected hospital dues to help sick and disabled seamen (Public Health Service), and came up with a system of standard weights and measures (National Bureau of Standards).

4. *Radio frequency devices*. Radios, stereos, tape recorders, televisions, CB radios, and other radio frequency devices are subject to the radio emission standards of the Federal Communications Commission (FCC). If you import these little sound blasters, you'll need to make sure they comply with FCC standards.

5. *Foods and cosmetics*. Before you import that European miracle fat-melting pill or the Asian wonder longevity lozenge, you'd best check with the FDA to make sure you're not unintentionally bringing in articles that can be considered "misbranded," that is, making false or misleading claims.

That's APHIS, Not Aphids

Other products that fall under some agency's thumb are:

- *Insects*. Animal and Plant Health Inspection Service (APHIS, not to be confused with aphids), Department of Agriculture

- *Livestock and animals*. APHIS.

- *Meat and meat products*. APHIS.

- *Poultry and poultry products*. APHIS.

- *Arms, ammunition, explosives, and implements of war*. In a word, no, except with the express permission of the Bureau of Alcohol, Tobacco, and Firearms, which falls under the Treasury Department.

- *Radioactive materials and nuclear reactors*. In another word, nope, unless you have a permission slip from the Nuclear Regulatory Commission.

- *Household appliances*. Includes refrigerators, dishwashers, clothes dryers, room air conditioners, and kitchen ranges and ovens. Department of Energy, Office of Codes and Standards, and/or the Federal Trade Commission (FTC), Division of Enforcement.

- *Flammable fabrics*. Consumer Product Safety Commission.

- *Radiation-producing products*. Includes those that produce sonic radiation, that is, TV receivers, microwave ovens, X-ray equipment, laser products, ultrasound equipment, and sunlamps. FDA's Center for Devices and Radiological Health

- *Seafood*. FDA and the National Marine Fisheries Service.

- *Biological drugs*. FDA.

Don't stop reading! You're halfway through the list.

- *Biological materials and vectors*. Think "Andromeda Strain." Think killer bees. Prohibited except with special license from the Secretary of the Department of Health and Human Services, and then with a sample of the licensed product forwarded by the port director of customs to the FDA's Center for Biologics

Evaluation and Research in Rockville, Maryland. Plus, you must obtain a permit from the Centers for Disease Control in Atlanta to import any insect, animal, or plant capable of being a vector of human disease.

- *Narcotic drugs and derivatives.* Need we say NO?!!! Unless you're trying for something like hospital-use morphine, in which case you need to get the OK from the Drug Enforcement Administration, which falls under the Department of Justice.

- *Drug paraphernalia.* Another major no.

- *Gold and silver.* To ensure that precious metals meet quality standards, talk with U.S. Customs and the FBI.

- *Caustic or corrosive substances for household use.* Office of Hazardous Materials Transportation, which falls under the Department of Transportation.

- *Furs.* FTC.

- *Textiles.* FTC.

- *Wildlife and pets.* U.S. Fish and Wildlife Service, Assistant Regional Director for Law Enforcement, for the state in which you're located. For birds, cats, dogs, monkeys, and turtles, check with the Centers for Disease Control in Atlanta as well as APHIS.

- *Petroleum and petroleum products.* Department of Energy.

- *Alcoholic beverages.* Bureau of Alcohol, Tobacco, and Firearms and the Treasury Department.

> **Tip...**
>
> ### Smart Tip
>
> Hop onto customs.gov and search under "Trade Publications" for a copy of *Importing Into the United States.* Although it's not what you'd call a fun read, it's (surprisingly) clear, understandable, and chock-full of import rules, regulations, and tidbits. And it's free! You can also check cbp.gov for all the latest rules and regulations concerning customs information.

Don't let this list keep you from treading into international trade waters. Chances are that you're not going to be dealing in most of this merchandise anyway. But if any of these goods are where your particular interests lie, you'll know who to call for more detailed information. And remember, as the Customs Service people like to say, "Know before you go." If you have any questions at all, ask! There's no charge for asking, and answers are free.

Guided Tour

Depending on whether you're importing or exporting, you can also get answers to your pesky procedure questions from a customs broker or a freight forwarder.

The customs broker (sometimes called a customhouse broker) is the importer's pal. It's his or her job to know the ins and outs of importing in intimate detail and to handle them for you. Some brokers are small outfits consisting of a single owner-operator at a single port of entry; others are corporate types with lots of employees and offices in many ports. The Treasury Department licenses them all.

When you hire a customs broker, she acts as your agent during the entry process. She prepares and files the entry documents, acquires any necessary bonds, deposits any required duties, gets the merchandise released into her custody or yours, arranges delivery to the site you've chosen, and obtains any drawback refunds.

A customs broker is not a legal necessity, but a good one will make your life considerably easier.

While the customs broker is the importer's best friend, the freight forwarder is the exporter's pal. Acting as the exporter's agent, the international freight forwarder uses his expertise with foreign import rules and regulations as well as domestic export laws to move cargo to overseas destinations.

Freight forwarders can assist with an order from the get-go by advising you of freight costs, port charges, consular fees, special documentation charges, and insurance costs. They can recommend the proper type of packing to protect your merchandise in transit, arrange to have the goods packed at the port or containerized, quote shipping rates, and then book your merchandise onto a plane, train, truck, or cargo ship. Like a concierge in a really good hotel, they can get anything you've got anywhere you want it to go. "There's nothing we say 'no' to," says Ray Tobia, president of Air Sea International Forwarding. "We try to offer everybody everything, provided it's legal."

Like customs brokers, freight forwarders are licensed, but in this case, by the International Air Transport Association (IATA) and Federal Maritime Commission (for ocean freight). You don't have to use the freight forwarder's services to transport your goods, and not all exporters rely on such services, but they're a definite plus.

Swimming the Trade Channel

Now that you're familiar with the players, you'll need to take a swim in the trade channel, the means by which the merchandise travels from manufacturer to end user. A manufacturer who uses a middleman who resells to the consumer is paddling around in a three-level channel of distribution. The middleman can be a merchant who purchases the goods and then resells them, or she can be an agent who acts as a broker but doesn't take title to the stuff.

Who your fellow swimmers are will depend on how you configure your trade channel. We'll discuss this more in Chapter 11, but for now, let's just get acquainted with the group:

- *Manufacturer's representative.* This is a salesperson who specializes in a type of product or line of complementary products; for example, home electronics:

televisions, radios, CD players, and sound systems. He often provides additional product assistance, such as warehousing and technical service.

- *Distributor or wholesale distributor.* A company that buys the product you have imported and sells it to a retailer or other agent for further distribution until it gets to the end user.

- *Representative.* A savvy salesperson who pitches your product to wholesale or retail buyers, then passes the sale on to you; differs from the manufacturer's rep in that she doesn't necessarily specialize in a particular product or group of products.

- *Retailer.* This is the tail end of the trade channel where the merchandise smacks into the consumer. As yet another variation on a theme, if the end user is not Joan Q. Public but an original equipment manufacturer (OEM), you don't need to worry about the retailer because the OEM becomes your end of the line. (Think Dell purchasing a software program to pass along to its personal computer buyer as part of the goodie package.)

The Rules

Now that you know all the players and their channels, let's look at some of the rules of the import/export game. As you already know, countries typically export goods and services that they can produce inexpensively and import those that are produced more efficiently somewhere else. But, as usual, when governments are involved, it's not quite that simple. Countries also have a tendency to block and counterblock sundry items of each other's products in a sort of giant, industrial-sized game of Risk.

Those Tetchy Trade Barriers

Trade barriers are set up by national governments to protect certain domestic industries from hefty foreign competition. If the shoe industry in the Land of Oz, for example, makes ruby slippers for $2 a pair, and the Land of Nod manufactures them for only $1 a pair, then Oz might put a tariff trade barrier on any ruby slippers brought in-country from Nod, charging, say, $1.50 per pair in import tax, or duty. Because this extra charge will have to be passed on to the consumer for the Nod people to make a profit, the Oz government figures it can keep its native slippers competitive in the marketplace.

Most trade barriers take the form of tariffs, but they can be camouflaged as quotas on foreign goods or as maximum-frustration builders, like excessive marking and labeling requirements, excessive pollution control regulations, and unfair classification of imports for customs duties. These nontax barriers can be just as costly as the tariff kind; the cost of getting products qualified for all these special requirements still has to be passed along to the end user.

Recently, world economists have been pushing the idea that in the long run, trade barriers only hurt our global economy. And governments have listened, thus the recent trend toward free marketplace initiatives, even during the global recession (see Chapter 3).

Can We Quota You?

An import quota is a limit on the quantity of a particular product that can be brought into the country over a specified period of time. The

Beware!

Before you decide whether you can trade profitably with a particular country, you need to know what tariffs or other barriers might stand in your way. For imports, check with the U.S. Customs Service. For exports, ask for help at your local Department of Commerce office or the commerce department of the country you're interested in. Or ask your freight forwarder.

Cruising the Caribbean

Under the Caribbean Basin Initiative (CBI), designated beneficiary countries in (surprise!) the Caribbean receive duty-free entry of certain merchandise into the United States, typically most goods produced in the Caribbean Basin region. Although the countries on the list change from time to time, you can generally count on the following being there:

- ○ Antigua and Barbuda
- ○ Aruba
- ○ The Bahamas
- ○ Barbados
- ○ Belize
- ○ British Virgin Islands
- ○ Dominica
- ○ Grenada
- ○ Guyana
- ○ Haiti
- ○ Jamaica
- ○ Montserrat
- ○ Netherlands Antilles
- ○ Panama
- ○ Saint Kitts and Nevis
- ○ Saint Lucia
- ○ Saint Vincent and the Grenadines
- ○ Trinidad and Tobago

You'll need to consult the newest edition of the *Harmonized Tariff Schedule* (see Chapter 6 for the complete skinny on this) to make sure the country you want to work with is a CBI beneficiary. Or better yet, ask your customs broker to do it for you.

Land of Oz, for example, might put a limit on the number of ruby slippers that can be brought into the country each year, say, 10,000 pairs between January 1 and December 31. If a few really zealous slipper salesmen fill that quota by February 15, then it's tough luck for anybody else who might be importing ruby slippers for the rest of the year.

The United States divides its import quotas into two types: tariff rate and absolute. Under the tariff rate banner, quota goods can be imported at a sort of "sale" price; you pay a reduced tariff or duty during a given period. There's no quantity limit, so you can bring in as much as you want, but when the special period ends, you pay a higher duty.

Absolute quotas are the quantitative ones. Once the limit's been bagged on the product, no more are let into the country until the next time period. Some absolute quotas apply to every country in the world, while others are aimed at certain nations.

Some absolute quotas become filled within moments of the period's official opening time, which is usually at noon on the designated effective date. To deal with this port rush, customs releases everybody's merchandise in prorated portions, based on a ratio between the quota limit and the total amount offered for entry. In this way, each importer gets an equitable chunk of the quota.

Andes Are Dandy

The Andean Trade Promotion and Drug Eradication Act, formerly known as the Andean Trade Preference Act, or ATPA, is another piece of legislation that allows for duty-free entry to U.S. markets of approximately 5,600 products from certain countries. In this case, the favored nations are those in the Andes mountain region of South America, specifically Bolivia, Colombia, Ecuador, and Peru. Enacted in 1991, the act was passed to deter drug production and trafficking in these countries and help them to establish legitimate businesses.

Most of these countries' products are duty-free, with certain exceptions, including textiles and clothing that are subject to textile agreements, some footwear, preserved tuna in airtight containers (sorry, Charlie!), petroleum products, watches, and watch parts subject to other duty rates, various sugar products, rum, and tafia (which is essentially the cheap version of rum).

Be sure to check the Harmonized Tariff System for the fine-print details on these products.

The Buddy System

Countries, like children, often play favorites. A country with "normal trade relations" with the United States is one that enjoys trade with Americans without additional barriers or duties. France, for example, is an American trading partner, or buddy, and therefore its imports get the standard rate on most products.

Some countries even get duty-free entry for most types of merchandise. Under a variety of programs, some developing nations receive the freebie treatment as a means of contributing to their economic growth.

To qualify for duty-free trade preferences, your merchandise must meet several conditions, including the following:

- Merchandise must be imported directly from the beneficiary country into U.S. Customs territory (no side trips or detours).

- Merchandise must have been produced in the beneficiary country, meaning that 1) it's entirely the growth, product, or manufacture of that country, or 2) it's been substantially transformed into a new and different product in that country.

- At least 35 percent of the appraised value of the article must consist of the cost or value of materials produced in the beneficiary country and/or the direct costs of processing operations that were carried out in that country.

Kibbutzing Around

The United States-Israel Free Trade Area (FTA) agreement provides duty-free entry for certain Israeli products. Lest you think these goods are restricted to lemons and grapefruit off the kibbutz, think again. Kibbutzes (communal farms) export other items as well, including radiators for Mercedes and other upscale automobiles. According to the Jewish Virtual Library, a division of the American/Israeli Cooperative Enterprise, kibbutzes have a 36 percent export rate, and they provide over 8 percent of Israel's exports. Plastic and rubber products, metals, and food are all popular kibbutz products. And Israel is making a name for itself as a premier manufacturer of computers and computer peripherals.

Because some aspects of the FTA agreement differ slightly from the Caribbean and Andean schedules, make sure you check the rules before you buy to make sure you're within the program.

Because the rules may vary slightly from one trade initiative or pact to another, be sure to check with your customs broker or the director of the port of entry or district where your merchandise will make landfall in the United States.

Smart Tip

Tip...

If your goods hit port after a quota has been filled, you're not stuck and out of luck. You can store them in a foreign trade zone (see Chapter 6) until the next quota period rolls around.

World Tour

Countries that have trading treaties with the U.S. make good candidates for import/export partners. So do countries with high populations and emerging economies. These are the topics of the next chapter.

3

The World Stage
The Roles of Politics and the Global Economy

We're beginning to realize that our planet belongs to all of us. The powers that be—and the importers and exporters out in the field—are moving toward a one-world economy. How are they accomplishing this? International traders contribute by working with (and, in many cases, making lifelong friends of) people all over the globe.

Governments contribute by writing policies that make importing and exporting easier and more profitable for everyone involved.

The state of the world's economy also greatly affects international trade, and vice-versa. The global financial crisis of 2007–2010 had a large impact, but governments have taken numerous measures to aid in the global recovery.

In this chapter we'll discuss trade agreements between nations, the global recession's effect on international trade, the world community's responses to the challenges of recessions, and the current forecast for international trade. We'll also focus on the Big Emerging Markets (BEMs) and the United State's largest trading partners on a country-by-country basis.

Club WTO

The grandfather of modern trade policy is the General Agreement on Tariffs and Trade, or GATT, an international agreement designed to reduce trade barriers between countries. First instituted in 1947 when World War II was still a fresh wound in millions of minds, it remains the primary international trade instrument used around the globe, now under the auspices of the World Trade Organization (WTO).

The WTO was formed in 1995. Its over 150 members account for more than 97 percent of all world trade. Currently, more than 25 countries are negotiating membership.

Based in Geneva, the WTO has a secretariat, a Ministerial General, a General Council that acts as a dispute settler, a Goods Council, a Services Council, and an Intellectual Property Council, as well as a host of committees.

The WTO's prime directive is to ease trade barriers around the world, help developing nations pull themselves up into the mainstream, and give smaller businesses in all nations more opportunities to join the world marketplace. The precepts it upholds are the following:

- Trade should be conducted without discrimination.
- Domestic industry should be protected only through tariffs and not through restrictive policies.
- All parties should reduce tariffs through negotiations.
- Members should work together to overcome trade problems.

Members of the World Trade Organization meet in sessions called "rounds" to negotiate agreements. Unlike a square dance round, a WTO round can last for years.

Beware!
"Intellectual property" refers to patented, trademarked, or copyrighted products. Books, music, and inventions are only a few examples of products protected by law. You can't import this merchandise without permission any more than you can sell U.S. intellectual property.

WTO negotiations center on topics related to service industries, investments, government procurement policies, research subsidies, patents and other intellectual properties, and telecommunications.

One such round, the Doha Development Round, has been ongoing since 2001. Undertaken by the WTO Group of 20 (G20), which is comprised of countries with the largest economies, this negotiating round of the WTO seeks a global trade agreement to lower trade barriers and help developing countries compete in the global marketplace.

Free Trade Frenzy

The last two decades have seen the adoption of many Free Trade Agreements (FTAs). We'll touch on the main agreements involving the United States.

North American Free Trade Agreement (NAFTA)

If you've been adult, conscious, and living in the United States within the last 20 years or so, you've heard at least something about NAFTA, the North American Free Trade Agreement. This 15-year plan to phase out all barriers to trading goods and services among Canada, the United States, and Mexico took effect amid much fanfare on January 1, 1994. A similar agreement between Canada and the United States had already been in operation since 1989.

NAFTA's prime directives are to eliminate barriers to trade, promote fair competition, increase investment opportunities, and provide adequate protection for intellectual property rights. It specifically establishes trade rules for textiles and apparel, automotive goods, agricultural products, and energy and petrochemicals. It also defines standards for technical information and transportation among member nations.

Many Americans feared that since labor is so much cheaper in Mexico, NAFTA would have a super-Drano effect on domestic manufacturing jobs, sending them swirling down the proverbial drain. As yet, this hasn't happened, and it doesn't seem likely to. Instead, U.S. exports to Canada and Mexico have increased dramatically.

No-Barrier North America

Thanks to NAFTA, merchandise traded between the United States, Canada, and Mexico is fast becoming duty-free. With a few exceptions, this no-tariff status applies only to goods that originate in the NAFTA region. What exactly does that mean? Well, according to Article 401 of the agreement, the term "originate" is basically defined as:

○ merchandise entirely obtained or produced in the territory of one or more NAFTA parties

○ unassembled merchandise that hasn't been entirely obtained or produced in the NAFTA region but contains a 50 percent (if using the net cost method) to 60 percent (if using the transaction value method) regional value content

If you monkey around with your officially originating goods—if you transport them outside the NAFTA region and do anything more than unload or reload them for safer shipment—you lose the originating status.

Also, you can't try to beat the system by bringing a nonoriginating product into a NAFTA nation and then "transshipping" it on (see Chapter 5). It won't qualify as a duty-free NAFTA product. To ease your mind and confirm all the down-and-dirty details of origination, learn more about NAFTA at export.gov.

Republic of Korea-U.S. Free Trade Agreement (KORUS FTA)

KORUS is the largest bilateral trade initiative since NAFTA, and it has been almost as controversial. This agreement entered into force on March 15, 2012. Under KORUS FTA, almost 80 percent of U.S. exports to Korea are now duty free. Many remaining tariffs will be eliminated in the coming years, and by March 15, 2017, bilateral trade with Korea is expected to be 95 percent duty free.

Although there is general consensus that the KORUS agreement will increase U.S. exports to South Korea, economists disagree on other ramifications of the agreement. Some point out that in the first year after ratification, the U.S. lost 40,000 jobs and showed a sharp increase in its trade deficit with South Korea. Other economists argue that because not all aspects of the agreement are yet in force, and because companies require time to adjust to new rules and to expand their sales networks within South Korea, it is too early to tell what the overall effect of KORUS will be.

Other Free Trade Agreements

The U.S. also currently has FTAs in force with the following countries: Australia, Bahrain, Chile, Costa Rica, Dominican Republic, El Salvador, Guatemala, Honduras, Israel, Jordan, Morocco, Nicaragua, Oman, Peru, and Singapore. Pending agreements, besides the KORUS FTA, include the Colombia FTA and the Panama FTA.

Another possible future agreement is the Free Trade Area of the Americas (FTAA), which would create a free trade zone throughout both North and South America, with Cuba excluded. This agreement has not even been signed, however, and talks have stalled. So stay tuned.

African Growth and Opportunity Act (AGOA)

While it's not a free trade treaty, the African Growth and Opportunity Act (AGOA) offers incentives to African nations to create free markets and open their economies. Signed into law in 2000, this act opens American markets to eligible countries. Eligibility is determined annually, and there are currently 41 AGOA-eligible countries.

Nigeria and Angola are the largest exporters under AGOA, while South Africa's exports are the most diverse. According to the U.S. Department of Commerce, sub-Saharan Africa is "poised for tremendous growth."

War—What Is It Good For?

Absolutely nothing, so the classic song says. And it's not so great for trade, either. Wartime can challenge even the hardiest of traders, causing hiccups (sometimes lasting decades) to everyday trade functions and operations. And, keep in mind, it does not have to be your home country at war that will bring woe to your bottom line. If, for example, you trade with two countries that are at war, this puts you in the middle of a battle on the world stage. Try as you might to keep your two trading worlds separate, the import/export world is getting smaller every day, and your clients may find out about other deals and question your loyalty to both them and their adversary.

War also can halt production of your import goods. What if you have a trade partner in a country where all metal resources are now required to go to the production of munitions? So much for the metal windchimes you were buying by the gross. Your beautiful windchimes have been melted to make the belly of an airplane.

Stat Fact

United States sanctions are currently in place for the following countries: Balkans, Belarus, Burma, Côte d'Ivoire (Ivory Coast), Cuba, Democratic Republic of the Congo, Iran, Iraq, Lebanon, Liberia, Libya, North Korea, Russia, Somalia, Sudan, Syria, Yemen, and Zimbabwe. Log on to ustreas.gov/offices/enforcement/ofac/programs/ for the most detailed and latest information.

Sanctions

One of the biggest effects war can have on your business is trade sanctions. *Merriam-Webster's Collegiate Dictionary* defines a sanction as, "an economic or military coercive measure adopted usually by several nations in concert for forcing a nation violating international law to desist or yield to adjudication." That's a fancy way of saying that a country can bar imports to and exports from any country deemed to be breaking the international law. This can be a direct result of war, a conflict, or a country's actions toward its own people that are considered cruel and unnecessary. For example, the United States leveled sanctions on the Ivory Coast in 2006 due to "numerous violations of human rights and international humanitarian law," according to the president's executive order. U.S. sanctions are currently in effect for several countries, so be sure to check with the Treasury Department before you start shipping those baseball caps to North Korea.

Global Recession

It turns out that a global recession doesn't do much for trade, either. Big surprise, right?

Leading economists have called the global financial crisis of 2007-2010 the worst financial crisis since the Great Depression of the 1930s. The collapse of the global housing bubble sent the values of all securities connected to the real estate market plummeting. Financial institutions failed. Available credit declined. Businesses failed. Investor confidence hit an all-time low, which in turn shook up the global stock markets. The collapse of U.S. investment bank Lehman Brothers led to an intensified global crisis as trade finance increased in cost and became less available. World consumer wealth declined by trillions of U.S. dollars. Economies slowed worldwide and international trade declined.

Ernst & Young, a leading professional services organization, points out that while the global financial crisis significantly affected world trade, these effects were not consistent from country to country. In other words, some were hit much harder than others. Our nation-by-nation look at the current and future potential of U.S. trading partners includes information on each country's status in the wake of the crisis.

Global Responses to the Crisis

Within a few months of the beginning of the crisis (2007), the World Bank reported that 17 of the 20 largest industrialized nations had adopted new trade restriction measures. As overall trade volumes decreased, the complexity of conducting trade increased. Trade disputes also increased. The International Money Fund estimates that from 2008 to 2009, global trade fell by 12 percent. Between Spring 2008 and Spring 2009, U.S. international trade in goods and services decreased by 17 percent.

Fortunately for international trade, governments of the major world economies soon realized that protectionist measures (all too common during the Great Depression) were not the way to go. In addition to enacting national stimulus packages and institutional bailouts at home, the international community responded to the crisis with a number of measures.

Members of the World Trade Organization's G20 held a 2009 London Summit to plan a coordinated response to the global economic crisis. They agreed to refrain from enacting any new trade barriers or export restrictions. They also agreed not to constrain capital flow and to commit to the conditions of the Doha Round, which would boost world trade by $150 billion annually. An additional action was the adoption of the G20 Trade Package, which provides for an injection of $250 billion in trade financing over two years.

The International Finance Corporation (IFC), a member of the World Bank group, expanded its already-existing Global Trade Finance Program (GTFP) to $3 billion. This program offers guarantees and risk mitigation to banks that finance companies operating in new or challenging markets.

The IFC launched the Global Trade Liquidity Program, a coordinated global initiative undertaken by governments, development financing institutions, and private sector banks to provide funds for developing countries. The IFC jump-started the program with $1 billion dollars. Public sector banks have added $5 billion. Recently China, among other countries, has committed funds to the program.

The International Money Fund (IMF) and the World Bank made more trade financing available through their debt relief programs for the world's poorest countries.

U.S. Response

Besides providing a variety of economic stimulus packages, the U.S. government authorized its Export-Import Bank (Ex-Im) to increase direct lending to financial institutions that use those funds to finance export businesses. In addition, the National Export Initiative, unveiled in 2010, increased the budget of the International Trade Administration by 20 percent to allow it to increase efforts to advocate abroad for

American companies. This initiative also called on the Ex-Im bank to increase financing for small and medium businesses.

Recovery

According to the Office of the U.S. Trade Representative (USTR), the United States is showing signs of recovery and economic growth, and export-oriented growth can be a "pillar of opportunity." The USTR's figures show that exports recently accounted for more than 14 percent of Gross Domestic Product, the largest share since 1929. The Organization for Economic Cooperation and Development predicts that over the next few years, as the global economy recovers, U.S. exports will continue to increase.

And what about other nations' recoveries? Given the aforementioned lack of uniformity in recession experiences, these details will be covered on a country-by-country basis. So let's get started by taking a look at U.S. trading partners.

The European Union

In general, the U.S. trades separately with European countries. However, many trade issues arise with the European Union as a block, so it's worth a closer look at this entity.

The European Union (EU) affords Western Europe what NAFTA provides for North America: a single marketplace for the goods and transactions of its member nations. The 27-member European Union roster includes the following countries:

1. Austria
2. Belgium
3. Bulgaria
4. Cypress
5. Czech Republic
6. Denmark
7. Estonia
8. Finland
9. France
10. Germany
11. Greece
12. Hungary

13. Ireland
14. Italy
15. Latvia
16. Lithuania
17. Luxembourg
18. Malta
19. Netherlands
20. Poland
21. Portugal
22. Romania
23. Slovakia
24. Slovenia
25. Spain
26. Sweden
27. United Kingdom

Stat Fact
According to the U.S. Department of Agriculture, the European Union has led imports of prepared or preserved vegetables to the United States since 2005.

These European Union buddy countries, some working together since the late 1960s, have developed a common tariff for countries outside the union and have "harmonized" (or developed a single system for) most internal tariffs and other rules relating to the "four freedoms": free movement of goods, services, people, and capital. According to the European Union's website (europa.eu), its aim is "peace, prosperity and freedom for its 498 million citizens in a fairer, safer world."

Also according to its website, the EU has achieved frontier-free travel and trade, a common currency (the euro), safer food and a greener environment, better living conditions in poorer regions, coordinated action on crime and terror, less expensive phone calls, and opportunities for study abroad.

The Trade Hit Parade

Before we analyze potential trade partners and what they can do for us, let's consider what the United States itself offers as a trading nation. To put into perspective the economic statistics provided in this chapter for the various foreign countries, here are a few for the United States. Economic statistics are provided by the Department of State and are for 2012. GDP figures are estimates—see our GDP Stat Fact on page 40.

The United States of America

Population: 314 million

Median Age: 37

GDP: $15.94 trillion

Annual growth in GDP: 2.2 percent

Per Capita GDP: $50,700

Total Annual Exports: $2.19 trillion (aircraft, chemicals, cars, agricultural products, scientific equipment)

Total Annual Imports: $2.33 trillion (crude oil, machines, electronics, vehicles, medical equipment, clothing, telecommunications equipment, agricultural products)

The United States has a varied topography and climate zones ranging from permafrost in northern Alaska to tropical conditions in southern Florida. It is the fourth largest country geographically. (Russia, Canada, and China are all bigger.) Its population ranks third, behind China and India.

U.S. natural resources include coal, copper, lead, molybdenum, phosphates, uranium, bauxite, gold, iron, silver, petroleum, natural gas, and timber.

The United States has the largest national economy (highest GDP) in the world. It is the world's number-two exporter and the world's top importer. High dependence on foreign oil makes it a huge importer and creates trillions of dollars in deficits with its trading partners.

In the wake of the global financial crisis, the U.S. has made more of a recovery than many European nations, although its economy remains sluggish. According to the USTR, exports play an increasingly important role in economic growth.

Trading Up (and Down and Over and Across)

Now we move on to U.S. trading partners. According to the International Trade Administration (ITA), the top ten countries providing imports to the U.S. (in order of largest import dollars to smallest) are the following:

1. Canada
2. China
3. Mexico
4. Japan
5. Germany
6. United Kingdom
7. Saudi Arabia

8. Venezuela

9. Republic of Korea (South Korea)

10. France

The list of countries that spend top dollar on U.S. goods exports is quite similar, with a couple of differences. They are (in order of largest export dollars to smallest):

1. Canada

2. Mexico

3. China

4. Japan

5. United Kingdom

6. Germany

7. Republic of Korea (South Korea)

8. Brazil

9. Netherlands

10. Singapore

According to the U.S. Census, these countries are collectively responsible for approximately 65 percent of recent U.S. imports and 62 percent of exports. Nevertheless, you needn't, of course, confine yourself to trade deals with importers and exporters in countries on the Top-10 list. There are many other intriguing possibilities available. Chief among them are the fastest-growing emerging markets. These are Brazil, Russia, India, and China—the BRIC Union countries. All four are extremely populous countries with rapidly developing economies. You'll notice China has already made both Top-5 trading partner lists, and Brazil is a top export destination for the United States. India and Russia may not be far behind.

So we'll begin our country-by-country discussion with the BRIC nations, followed by those nations appearing on our Top-10 lists. Finally, we'll explore more emerging markets, those designated either Big Emerging Markets (BEMs) or Advanced Emerging Markets. (See Sorting It Out sidebar on page 38.)

BRIC by BRIC

Brazil, Russia, India, and China, the BRIC Union countries, are all highly populated, falling in the top ten world rankings. (China and

Fun Fact

Lists of imports and exports for a given country can often look very much the same. Weird? Not really. Categories are broad, so if a country imports motorcycles and exports cars, both items are listed as "motor vehicles." Also, countries often import an item, make some additions to it, and then re-export it.

Sorting It Out

According to financial investment publication *Money and Markets*, an emerging market is a foreign economy that is developing because of the spread of capitalism and that has created its own stock market. Using these criteria, more than 80 countries qualify for the designation "emerging market." However, only some of these countries can claim the status of Big Emerging Market (BEM).

Internet Securities Inc. (ISI) bases its classification on factors including population size, infrastructure, income levels, and expansion of the middle class. Its (alphabetical) list includes the following BEMs: Brazil, China, Egypt, India, Indonesia, Mexico, Philippines, Poland, Russia, South Africa, South Korea, and Turkey.

Financial Times Stock Exchange (FTSE, pronounced "footsie"), divides Emerging Markets into two classes: Advanced and Secondary. Advanced Emerging Markets (AEMs) have either upper middle incomes with advanced infrastructure or high incomes with less developed infrastructure. They designate the following (alphabetized) countries as Advanced Emerging Markets: Brazil, Hungary, Mexico, Poland, South Africa, and Taiwan.

FTSE's Secondary Emerging Markets (SEMs) have either upper middle/lower middle/low income with reasonable infrastructure or upper middle incomes with lesser developed infrastructure. The Secondary Emerging Markets are, also alphabetically, as follows: Argentina, Chile, China, Colombia, Czech Republic, Egypt, India, Indonesia, Malaysia, Morocco, Pakistan, Peru, Philippines, Romania, Russia, Thailand, Turkey, and United Arab Emirates.

Besides discussing each of the United State's top trading partners, we've included in our country-by-country discussion those nations that are designated either as BEMs or as Advanced Emerging Markets.

India—ranked first and second, respectively—each have over a billion people.) Furthermore, these nations have rapidly expanding middle classes, which means more people able to afford luxury items, from televisions, stereos, and cordless phones to designer clothes, family cars, and fine foods.

With the exception of Russia, BRIC countries have younger populations than the United States. Like the U.S., they have gross domestic products (GDPs, the measure of all goods and services produced by a nation) valued in the trillions of U.S. dollars. All four have economic growth rates at least twice the average rate among more highly developed countries, according to the U.S. Department of State.

Challenges facing BRIC Union nations, as well as those trading with them, include highly uneven distribution of wealth, government corruption, and lack of fully developed infrastructures—airports and seaports, roads, bridges, telecommunications networks, and power plants.

These infrastructure weaknesses mean that, as a trader, you'll have to pay extra attention to the nitty-gritty of production, distribution, and marketing in these countries. But they also mean that opportunities abound in infrastructure imports and also in consumer goods.

Leading world economists expect the BRIC countries to rebound from the global recession much quicker, and more robustly, than the United States and EU countries.

Brazil

Population: 198.7 million

Median Age: 28

GDP: $2.39 trillion

Annual growth in GDP: 9 percent

Per Capita GDP: $12,100

Total Annual Exports: $242.6 billion (iron, crude oil, soybeans, sugar, coffee)

Total Annual Imports: $223.2 billion (iron, refined petroleum, cars, crude oil, capital goods)

Brazil has the highest biological diversity of any country in the world. It also has 14 percent of the world's renewable fresh water. Half of the country is covered in forest. As if all this weren't enough, Brazil has the most currently unused-but-serviceable arable land in the world.

In recent years Brazil has enjoyed sustained growth, strong exports, moderate inflation, decreasing unemployment, and high economic development. These factors combine to make Brazil what *World Trade* magazine calls a "bright spot" in the export sector.

According to the U.S. Deptartment of State, Brazil was spared the worst of the global financial crisis because of careful fiscal policy. Traditionally, the United States has been Brazil's top foreign investor and also its top supplier. Brazil's recent annual exports to the United States totaled $26.9 billion. Its U.S. imports totaled $37.6 billion.

Fun Fact

The U.S. is currently the top agricultural producer in the world. France ranks second. And Brazil is the most dynamic rising agricultural producer. According to the Food and Agricultural Organization of the United Nations, it is the number-one world exporter of beef, chicken, soy, sugar, orange juice, and coffee.

Russia

Population: 143.5 million

Median Age: 39

GDP: $2.55 trillion

Annual growth in GDP: 3.4 percent

Per Capita GDP: $18,000

Total Annual Exports: $529.6 billion (petroleum, petroleum products, natural gas, wood, metals, chemicals)

Total Annual Imports: $334.7 billion (machinery and equipment, vehicles, chemicals, semi-finished metals, medicines, meat)

Russia has large oil reserves, timber, and the largest geographical area of any country. Its economic health is closely tied to the price of oil and the availability of finance credit. Its population is declining.

According to the U.S. Department of State, Russia was hit hard by the global financial crisis. This is partly because of generally high levels of poverty, but also because Russians, like Americans, use credit heavily. The 2008 flight of investment capital resulted in a crisis in the Russian stock market.

Although GDP increases at the end of 2009 caused the government to declare its recession over, unemployment has been rising. Leading economists suggest that Russia may be one of the last countries to recover from the global financial crisis. Russia is therefore a country to watch. It does have potential. How much, and how soon, will depend on when it emerges fully from the global recession.

> ## Stat Fact
> Gross domestic product (GDP) is the value of total goods and services produced within a country in a year. GDP data come in two types: nominal and Purchasing Power Parity (PPP). These figures differ widely. GDP (PPP) reflects differences in cost of living and is the type we use here. Achieving a PPP figure involves more estimation than using nominal data.

Recent Russian exports to the United States totaled $25.9 billion. Imports from the United States stood at $10.4 billion.

India

Population: 1.2 billion

Median Age: 25

GDP: $4.76 trillion

Annual growth in GDP: 6.5 percent

Per Capita GDP: $3,900

Total Annual Exports: $298.4 billion (petroleum products, precious stones, machinery, cotton, apparel)

Total Annual Imports: $500.4 billion (petroleum, precious stones, machinery, electronic goods, edible oils, fertilizers)

Beware!
As with any industry, import/export has its share of scam artists. Be wary of unsolicited interest, especially if it is accompanied by requests for payment, samples, or prototypes to be sent in advance of negotiations. Also be wary of requests for cash for an event to be held or for future travel expenses.

India has the fourth largest economy in the world and a rapidly growing middle class. According to the U.S. Department of State, India's middle class is forecasted to grow tenfold by 2025. The country also has a large number of well-educated speakers of English and a young population. Research and Development (R&D) facilities for approximately 100 Fortune 500 companies are located in India. The country launches its own satellites and makes its own supercomputers. Its Bombay Stock Exchange, located in the capitol city of Mumbai (formerly Bombay), is a major exchange.

India's problems include an inadequate infrastructure and high fiscal deficit. However, the World Bank has instituted a $3 billion annual aid package to India.

The country has emerged from the global financial crisis and, along with China, is expected to be a major driver for the world economy.

The United States is India's largest investor and its largest trading partner. India exported $41.5 billion to the United States. Recent imports from the United States totaled $16.9 billion.

China

Population: 1.4 billion

Median Age: 40

GDP: $12.61 trillion

Annual growth in GDP: 7.8 percent

Per Capita GDP: $9,300

Total Annual Exports: $2.1 trillion (electrical machinery and equipment, power generation equipment, furniture, toys, apparel)

Total Annual Imports: $1.7 trillion (electrical machinery and equipment, mineral fuel and oil, power generation equipment, ores, slag and ash)

China has the highest population in the world, but it lacks the natural resources to keep pace with its large amount of people. Although it has 22 percent of the world's population, China has only 8 percent of its arable land and 7 percent of its water. These facts mean that China relies heavily on imports.

China was the first nation to recover from the global financial recession. According to the U.S. State Department, this is due in large part to its government's quick adoption of stimulus packages, along with other government initiatives. China's economy has now surpassed its pre-recession peak, making the country the top driver for the world's economy.

China exports $438.1 billion to the United States and imports $114.3 billion.

Familiar Territory

As a newbie on the international scene, you should familiarize yourself with our biggest trading partners and see what they have to offer. Then take your best shot, either with them or with another country.

Canada

Population: 34.9 million

Median Age: 40

GDP: $1.51 trillion

Annual growth in GDP: 1.8 percent

Per Capita GDP: $43,400

Total Annual Exports: $462.9 billion (vehicles, aircraft, chemicals, lumber, oil, gas)

Total Annual Imports: $474 billion (machinery, electrical supplies, durable consumer goods)

Canada has the second largest land area in the world, behind Russia, but more than 90 percent of all Canadians live within 160 kilometers of the U.S. border. Canada's abundant natural resources—oil, natural gas, minerals and metals, forests, wildlife, fresh water—contribute to its trading economy. Canada is one of the world's major producers of minerals.

Although its population is about one-tenth the size of the United States, Canada is very much like the United States in terms of economy, environment, and marketplace. Pair this with the facts that Canada is a nearby travel destination and that most

Smart Tip

You can research possible trade countries on the U.S. Department of State website. Go to state.gov/r/pa/ei and select "Background Notes." Then select by country. Also, find out more about exporting on the U.S. Commercial Service's sites at export.gov and buyusa.gov.

of its citizens are native English speakers, and you have an ideal jumping-off point for the newbie exporter.

Canada was not entirely immune from the global financial crisis. However, its sound monetary policy, trading surplus, and policies that promote stable prices shielded it from most of the financial fall-out.

Trade with the United States accounts for about 75 percent of Canadian trade. Canada and the United States are each other's top trade partners. According to the U.S. Census Bureau, Canada exports over $332 billion in goods from its southern neighbor and imports over $251 billion.

Mexico

Population: 120.8 million

Median Age: 26

GDP: $1.79 trillion

Annual growth in GDP: 3.9 percent

Per Capita GDP: $15,600

Total Annual Exports: $370.9 billion (manufactured goods, petroleum, silver, fruits, vegetables, coffee)

Total Annual Imports: $370.8 billion (machinery, electrical equipment, motor vehicle parts, aircraft parts)

Mexico is another major trading partner for the United States. Its natural resources include oil, silver, copper, gold, natural gas, and timber.

When you think Mexico, think young. Thirty percent of its population is under 14. Mexico's infrastructure—seaports, airports, satellite systems, railroads, and power systems— is weak. According to the International Trade Administration, the leading edges for U.S. exporters are in electrical machinery, sound and TV equipment, nuclear parts and machinery, and plastics.

Beware!

Make sure your export goods have packaging information in the language (or at least in one official language) of the target country. And make sure this text is in the same font, size, and clarity as any other language on the box.

Mexico's export-dependent economy is firmly tied to the U.S. economy, so it has felt the effects of the global recession. Its recovery will therefore depend on the United States.

Mexican exports to the United States total $277.7 billion, and it imports $181.7 billion in goods and services from the United States.

Smart Tip

Tip...

Interested in importing products from Mexico? Your most lucrative bets are in the areas of electrical parts and products, automotive vehicles and parts, mineral fuels and oils, and nuclear products.

Japan

Population: 127.6 million

Median Age: 44

GDP: $4.70 trillion

Annual growth in GDP: 2 percent

Per Capita GDP: $36,900

Total Annual Exports: $773.9 billion (motor vehicles, semiconductors, iron and steel products, electrical machinery, plastics)

Total Annual Imports: $830.6 billion (petroleum, fuels, clothing, semiconductors, coal)

Japan has the second largest economy in the world (behind the United States). It is a country of islands and home to the world-famous Mt. Fuji. About 73 percent of Japan's land is mountainous. Its natural resources include fish, gold, magnesium, and silver.

Japan has a primarily urban society. It is one of the most energy-efficient developed countries in the world. It's also a major exporter. (Think Nissan, Toyota, Honda. Or Sony and Mitsubishi.) The Japanese also export large amounts of fish as well as other agricultural products.

The U.S. State Department notes that as one of the world's top exporters, Japan has suffered from the recession-related sharp decrease in world demand for its products. An aging population—only 14 percent of its population is under the age of 15—and large government debt are additional concerns. However, a well-educated, industrious population and high personal savings and investment will aid in its recovery.

Japanese exports to the United States total $138 billion. Imports from the United States total $60 billion.

Fun Fact

Japan developed a seclusionist policy in the early 17th century. The only point of international trade contact was the city of Nagasaki—and only with Chinese and Dutch traders. And although the Chinese were allowed quarters in town, the Dutch were based offshore on an island.

Germany

Population: 81.9 million

Median Age: 43

GDP: $3.25 trillion

Annual growth: .7 percent

Per Capita GDP: $39,700

Total Annual Exports: $1.5 trillion (motor vehicles, machinery, chemicals, electronics, electrical equipment, pharmaceuticals)

Total Annual Imports: $1.2 trillion (machinery, data processing equipment, vehicles, chemicals, oil and gas)

Germany's natural resources are iron, coal, and natural gas. According to the World Trade Organization (WTO), Germany is the world's top exporter. Another "car" country, it is famous for its exports of finely-engineered vehicles.

Its economy is heavily dependent on trade, and because of this and its chronic high levels of unemployment, Germany's recovery from the global recession is tightly linked to that of its trading partners.

Germans have a high standard of living. Consumers appreciate innovative, high-tech products with a modern flair. The newbie trader should consider multimedia merchandise, such as computers and software, electronic components, health-care and medical devices, synthetics, and automotive goodies. When you think Germany, keep in mind cutting-edge technology.

German exports to the United States total $112.2 billion while imports total $42.3 billion.

United Kingdom

Population: 63.4 million

Median Age: 40

GDP: $2.38 trillion

Annual growth: 2 percent

Per Capita GDP: $37,500

Total Annual Exports: $474.6 billion (manufactured goods, fuels, chemicals, food, beverages, tobacco)

Total Annual Imports: $642.6 billion (manufactured goods, machinery, fuels, foodstuffs)

The United Kingdom (England, Scotland, Wales, and Northern Ireland) has enjoyed economic growth since the early 1990s. It has many natural resources, including coal, oil, natural gas, tin, limestone, iron ore, salt, clay, chalk, gypsum, lead, and silica.

The U.S. Department of State notes that in response to the global financial crisis, the U.K.'s government put forth a variety of initiatives to facilitate stability and recovery. Fiscal stimulus packages, a bank recapitalization initiative, and a credit stimulus package have all helped the U.K. emerge from the recession.

Much of the United Kingdom's trade is with members of the European Union, but it's still a major American trading partner and one of our biggest European markets. Waterford crystal, Scotch whiskey, and Sheffield steel are all U.K. exports. These, and other goods, make export totals to the United States of $52.2 billion. According to the Department of State, imports from the United States total $41.2 billion. The U.K. provides a good jumping-off point for the European Union, which has more than 498 million consumers.

France

Population: 65.7 million

Median Age: 40

GDP: $2.29 trillion

Annual growth: 0 percent

Per Capita GDP: $36,100

Total Annual Exports: $561.7 billion (machinery and transportation equipment, aircraft, plastics, chemicals, iron and steel, beverages)

Total Annual Imports: $641.3 billion (machinery and equipment, vehicles, fuels, aircraft, plastics, chemicals)

France is the second largest trading nation in the EU, behind Germany. It has the fifth largest economy in the world. Extensive agricultural resources, a large industrial base, a dynamic service sector, and a highly skilled work force help make the economy flexible. The country typically enjoys low unemployment and low inflation rates.

The United States imports many French gourmet foodstuffs, and the French are a terrific market for our food exports. Fish, seafood, fruits, and vegetables are high on the take-out list, as are organic foods, candies, chocolates, and wild rice.

According to the Department of State, France was one of the first European countries to officially exit the global recession. It exports $44.7 billion in goods to the United States. In return, France imports $28.4 billion in goods from the U.S.

Republic of Korea (South Korea)

Population: 50.0 million

Median Age: 38

GDP: $1.64 trillion

Annual growth: 2.0 percent

Per Capita GDP: $32,800

Total Annual Exports: $552.6 billion (semiconductors, wireless telecomm equipment, vehicles, computers, steel, ships)

Total Annual Imports: $514.2 billion (machinery, electronics and electrical equipment, crude oil, chemicals, plastics)

South Korea's natural resources include coal, tungsten, graphite, lead, and hydropower potential. The country's gross domestic product is growing at a rapid pace, and its business environment is transforming into a market-driven, less regulated economy. This is good news for the international trader.

Foodstuffs, especially beef, pork, seafood, wine, fruits, and pet food, are a good bet. So are telecommunications—South Korea has more cell phones than land lines—and apparel. Don't forget infrastructure goods and energy products.

Government initiatives, including fiscal stimulus packages and low interest rates, have allowed South Korea to recover well from the global recession.

Unlike its neighbor to the north, South Korea maintains a friendly relationship with the United States. Its exports to the United States total $62.0 billion. South Korea imports $39.0 billion in U.S. goods.

Taiwan

Population: 23.3 million

Median Age: 38

GDP: $918.3 billion

Annual growth: 1.3 percent

Per Capita GDP: $39,400

Total Annual Exports: $299.8 billion (electronics, optical and precision instruments, base metals, textile products, plastic and rubber products)

Total Annual Imports: $268.8 billion (electronics, machinery, oil, optical equipment, chemicals, metals)

Over the last 50 years, Taiwan has transformed itself from an underdeveloped, agricultural island with a per-capita GDP of $100 into an economic power and one of the world's largest producers of high-technology goods, according to the Department of State.

With just 23 million people and few natural resources, Taiwan is a surprisingly significant U.S. trade partner. Because its natural resources are poor, it imports almost everything necessary for energy and industrial production as well as a tremendous number of agricultural products. Taiwanese consumers, both individual and business, like foreign imports and don't mind spending money on them. Taiwan is a major aid donor and foreign investor (especially in China). Taiwan has the world's fourth largest stock of foreign exchange reserves. This, coupled with sound fiscal policy, has helped it weather the global recession.

Smart Tip

Tip...

"Plan on visits to the market into which you are exporting," says industry expert Wendy Larson. "Also, cultural understanding is imperative. Though we live in a small world, honoring the differences between cultures is a must."

Give Us the Goods

Trade statistics list capital goods, consumer goods, and manufactured goods as import/export categories. So what exactly are these entities? To help us out, we consulted the Free Online Dictionary, Wikipedia, and the *Financial Times* Lexicon.

○ *Capital goods.* Items used to produce other goods. Machines are a good example.

○ *Consumer goods.* These, as the name implies, get used directly by consumers. They fall into two categories: durable and nondurable goods. The former are items like cars, appliances, and furniture. The latter include food, clothing, and gasoline.

○ *Manufactured goods.* Items made using machines. This is a very broad category. Any given capital good or consumer good could very well also be a manufactured good. For example, a sewing machine that is used to produce clothing is not only a capital good (because it's used to produce clothing goods) but also a manufactured good (because it is assembled from parts made by machines.)

While Mandarin Chinese is the official language of the country, English is the language of business. According to the U.S. Trade Representative, Taiwan exports $37.6 billion worth of goods to the United States and imports from the United States to the tune of $23.3 billion.

A Cultured Voice

To ensure you don't offend clients and jeopardize deals, be aware of the customs and culture of the nation(s) you deal with. The saying *Think global, act local* definitely applies! It's preferable to have a cultural native smooth the way for you. Also, check out kwintessential.co.uk and search by country for tips. Here are a few areas where cultures can differ significantly.

- *Business greetings.* Some countries do not shake hands (especially if any women are involved), while others regard a handshake as obligatory. And among handshakers, degree of firmness varies. Also, eye contact is not a universal plus. In some cultures, it indicates aggression.

- *Business meetings.* The amount of small talk before getting down to business varies by culture.

- *Negotiation strategies.* Expectations differ for how quickly terms should be reached. Aggressive negotiation is regarded as rude in India, but it's respected in Russia.

- *Conversational style.* Whether interruption is tolerated is a cultural factor. Willingness to say "no" also varies. (In India, "we'll see" or "possibly" often mean "no.")

- *Refreshments.* Turning down refreshments (or accepting but not tasting) can be a major breach of etiquette.

- *Punctuality.* This is optional in Russia and Brazil, among other countries, yet it's vital in India and China.

- *Gifts.* Type and monetary value of ideal gifts varies.

- *Color significance.* In western cultures, black is the usual color of mourning, while white is a bridal color. In Asia, white or purple signify mourning. Yellow is associated with mourning or bad luck in some countries.

- *Humor.* Even if jokes translate well (which they usually don't), they are risky cross-culturally.

▲

Venezuela

Population: 28.5 million

Median Age: 27

GDP: $408.5 billion

Annual growth: 5.5 percent

Per Capita GDP: $13,800

Total Annual Exports: $97.3 billion (petroleum, aluminum, minerals, chemicals, agricultural products)

Total Annual Imports: $59.3 billion (agricultural products, livestock, raw materials, machinery and transport equipment, construction materials)

Venezuela is a land of diverse landscape and a young population. Bordering the Caribbean Sea and the North Atlantic Ocean, between Colombia and Guyana, Venezuela is home to the Andes mountains, the Guiana highlands, and 2,800 kilometers of coastline. Its natural resources include petroleum, natural gas, coal, iron ore, gold, diamonds, minerals, and hydroelectric power. About 95 percent of Venezuela's export earnings come from oil revenue.

Government regulation is high, and there is considerable income inequality. Infrastructure is poor, largely because of inadequate maintenance. The country has one functioning rail line, and its ports—recently nationalized—are inadequate for their volume of trade. Importers and exporters have complained of delays and high costs.

According to the U.S. State Department, diplomatic relations with Venezuela have been tense in recent years. The United States has been dissatisfied with Venezuela's efforts at stopping the drug trade. The 2008 expulsion of the American ambassador by then President Chavez has not improved diplomatic relations.

Venezuela exports $27.0 billion in goods (mostly oil) to the U.S. and imports $12.4 billion.

Note that Venezuela appears on the top-ten list of U.S. trade partners. In fact, the United States is the country's main import and export partner, garnering about 60 percent of Venezuela's exports and just over 25 percent of imports. For these reasons, we include Venezuela in our discussion of potential trade markets. However, we do not recommend it, at least until diplomatic relations improve.

Netherlands

Population: 16.7 million

Median Age: 40

GDP: $718.6 billion

Annual growth: –.9 percent

Per Capita GDP: $42,900

Total Annual Exports: $538.5 billion (machinery, chemicals, mineral fuels, processed food and tobacco, agricultural products)

Total Annual Imports: $474.8 billion (machinery and transport equipment, chemicals, mineral fuels and crude petroleum, foodstuffs, clothing)

Sitting like a puzzle piece between Belgium and Germany, the Netherlands has natural resources of petroleum, natural gas, and fertile soil.

The Dutch have always been on the cutting edge of economic and social development. During the 17th century, when the country was known as the Dutch United Provinces, it was a major economic and seafaring power. The Netherlands was a founding member of NATO and the European Union, and played a role in the introduction of the euro at the turn of the century.

Trade is most definitely the key to the Netherlands' success, garnering it stable industrial relations, low unemployment, and a budget surplus. It has no significant trade or investment barriers. Its reputation as a strong trade and transportation hub for Europe is sealed by its past success and prime location.

Although the Netherlands was hit hard by the global recession, the U.S. Department of State notes that its government-sponsored stimulus packages have done much to get the economy moving again.

The United States has its largest trade surplus with the Netherlands. The United States has a trade surplus with the Netherlands. Dutch exports to the U.S. total $18.9 billion, while imports total $37.1 billion.

Singapore

Population: 5.4 million

Median Age: 40

GDP: $331.9 billion

Annual growth: 1.4 percent

Per Capita GDP: $52,700

Total Annual Exports: $435.8 billion (machinery and equipment, chemicals, refined petroleum)

Total Annual Imports: $374.9 billion (machinery and equipment, mineral fuels, chemicals, food, consumer goods)

Singapore consists of a main island—joined to the southern tip of Malaysia by a causeway and a bridge—and about 50 small surrounding islands. It was founded in

1819 as a British trading colony but has been an independent country since 1965. Finance and electronics manufacturing drive Singapore's thriving economy. Its financial center is the fourth largest in the world, and its high per-capita income ranks it as one of the world's most prosperous countries. Singapore's main natural resource is fish. The country is a major commercial hub, and its deep-water ports, allowing for the docking of extremely large vessels, are among the busiest in the world.

Foreign investments, as well as local company investments through Singapore's government, play a key role in an economy that is heavily dependent on trade. In at least six of the past recent years, the World Bank has ranked Singapore as the easiest country in which to do business. This top ranking is due to its business-friendly laws, flexible immigration policy, and simple tax filing. Singapore's government is conservative and exerts strict social controls. Recent initiatives include incentives to boost the birth rate.

Singapore rebounded well after the 2009 banking crisis and resultant global recession, showing a 14.8 percent growth in GDP in 2010. Although its growth has subsequently slowed during the second European recession, due to soft demand for its exports, the country remains an extremely attractive one in which to do business.

Singapore's recent exports to the United States totaled $17.7 billion. Its imports totaled $26.7 billion, making it one of the relatively few countries with which the U.S. has a trade surplus.

Saudi Arabia

Population: 28.3 million

Median Age: 21

GDP: $921.7 billion

Annual growth: 6.8 percent

Per Capita GDP: $31,800

Total Annual Exports: $395 billion (petroleum and petroleum products, fertilizer, gems, plastics)

Total Annual Imports: $136.8 billion (machinery and equipment, foodstuffs, chemicals, motor vehicles, textiles)

Saudi Arabia has the largest oil reserves in the world, amounting to one-fourth of the world's known reserves. Other natural resources include gold, uranium, bauxite, coal, and minerals.

The Saudi Arabian population is very young, and its growth prospects good. Although the United States has trade-related issues with Saudia Arabia from time to time, its relations are generally positive, according to the U.S. Department of State. Uneven distribution of wealth and gender discrimination are disadvantages for the country.

Just prior to the global financial crisis, five years of high oil prices resulted in considerable Saudi financial reserves. These reserves shielded Saudi Arabia from the worst of the global crisis. However, tight international credit and falling oil prices have reduced growth.

Saudi Arabia is a major exporter of oil to the United States, and its exports in our direction total $46.6 billion. Its United States imports total $17.7 billion.

Breaking Out

Stat Fact

According to the Unesco Institute for Statistics, most countries discussed here have 90 percent or higher rates of literacy (population over age 15 able to read and write). Which countries are the exceptions? India, Egypt, Turkey, Saudi Arabia, and South Africa. Several of these countries' literacy rates vary significantly by gender.

Although the remaining countries covered in this chapter are not currently among the United States's top trading nations, all have been identified as either Big Emerging Markets (BEMs) or Advanced Emerging Markets (AEMs). Our sidebar ("Sorting It Out," on page 38) explains these designations.

Many of these countries have young populations and economies that are growing much faster than the economies of more developed nations. Most have rapidly growing middle classes that are ready and willing to buy foreign goods.

South Africa

Population: 48.6 million

Median Age: 26

GDP: $592 billion

Annual growth: 2.5 percent

Per Capita GDP: $11,600

Total Annual Exports: $100.7 billion (gold, diamonds, platinum, minerals and metals, machinery and equipment)

Total Annual Imports: $105.8 billion (machinery, transportation equipment , chemicals, petroleum products, scientific equipment, foodstuffs)

South Africa's natural resources are many. In fact, it has everything required to run the country except petroleum products and bauxite. It is the only country that manufactures fuel from coal.

As a result of its apartheid past, South Africa has a two-tiered economy, according to the U.S. Department of State. One part is a productive and industrial economy. The other part, mainly rural-based, has many of the characteristics one finds in developing countries—namely poor infrastructure and low income levels. South Africa is working to solve its major social problems of uneven distribution of wealth and income, and uneven education.

The country typically has high unemployment. However, its lack of dependence on foreign trade kept it from suffering badly in the global recession.

South Africa is the top exporter of platinum, but it has a relatively small trading relationship with the United States. South African exports to the United States total $8.4 billion. Its imports total $6.7 billion.

South Africa has eliminated most import permit requirements. In addition, U.S. goods qualify for Most Favored Nation tariff rates. South African goods enter U.S. markets duty free as a result of the African Growth and Opportunity Act.

Poland

Population: 38.5 million

Median Age: 38

GDP: $814.1 billion

Annual growth: 2 percent

Per Capita GDP: $20,900

Total Annual Exports: $188.5 billion (machinery and transport equipment, manufactured goods, food, live animals)

Total Annual Imports: $195.4 billion (machinery and transportation equipment, manufactured goods, chemicals, minerals, fuel)

Poland's natural resources include coal, copper, sulfur, natural gas, silver, lead, and salt. The nation supplies potatoes, apples, and other agricultural products to its fellow Europeans.

According to the U.S. Department of State, a growing middle class has produced consumers who want more variety and year-round availability in their food supply. This fact, along with the country's strong economic growth potential and political stability, make it a good bet for exports.

However, key infrastructure components, especially roads and railways, remain underdeveloped.

> **Beware!**
> Like small, high-growth companies, Emerging markets are characterized by high potential—and high risk. The Pacific Rim markets, for example, grew rapidly and then collapsed in 1997 and 1998.

Poland had few assets tied to real estate, so the country has weathered the global crisis as well as any country in Europe and better than many. In addition, it is less dependent on trade than its Central European neighbors.

More than 80 percent of Poland's trade is with European Union countries, but its trade with the United States totals $4.8 billion in exports, with an added $3.7 billion in imports from the United States.

Hungary

Population: 9.94 million

Median Age: 41

GDP: $198.8 billion

Annual growth: −1.7 percent

Per Capita GDP: $20,000

Total Annual Exports: $90.2 billion (machinery, manufactured goods, food, raw materials, fuels and electric energy)

Total Annual Imports: $87.4 billion (machinery and transportation equipment, manufactured goods, fuels and electric energy, food products, raw meat)

Hungary's natural resources include bauxite, coal, natural gas, and arable land. Its central European location is a trading advantage. Also, its recent status as a popular country for foreign investment has resulted in slightly higher incomes and a more solid infrastructure than many other of the less wealthy European countries.

Because of its prior high budget deficits and high external debt, Hungary was hit hard by the global crisis, according to the U.S. Department of State. Although a $25 billion financial stabilization package from the International Monetary Fund (IMF), the EU, and the World Bank should help considerably, Hungary may still take longer than average (for Europe) to recover.

Hungary exports $3.7 billion in products to the United States and imports from us to the tune of $1.5 billion.

Egypt

Population: 80.7 million

Median Age: 25

GDP: $548.8 billion

Annual growth: 2.2 percent

Per Capita GDP: $6,700

Total Annual Exports: $26.8 billion (petroleum, cotton, clothing and tex-tiles, metal products, chemicals)

Total Annual Imports: $59.7 billion (machinery and transportation equip-ment, food and beverages, chemicals, paper and wood products, fuels)

Egypt's natural resources include petroleum and natural gas, iron ore, phosphorus, manganese, limestone, lead, and other minerals. Although much of its land is inhos-pitable desert, the Nile Valley and the Delta areas produce cotton, rice, wheat, corn, sugarcane, sugar beets, onions, and beans.

The Egyptian GDP relies on tourism, revenue from the Suez Canal, private trans-fer funds, and exports of oil and gas.

In recent years, rapid urbanization, as well as a high level of tourism, has led to crowding and smog. However, Egypt's capitol, Cairo, is an important crossroads of Arab commerce and culture.

The global recession left Egypt much less affected than other countries, according to the Internation Monetary Fund (IMF). Because of its rigid state regulation and scant contact with global finance, the Egyptian banking system remained solid. Even tourism, which was a concern, was less affected than expected because many Europeans substituted a vacation in nearby Egypt for a more expensive one in the Far East.

The United States allows tariff-free imports from Egypt as long as they've been produced in Qualified Industrial Zones, with a certain small percentage contributed by Israel. What are Qualified Industrial Zones, you may ask? Put simply, they're free trade zones—industrial parks that house manufacturing facilities. Some are located between Israel and Egypt, while others are between Israel and Jordan.

Egypt is traditionally the United States largest export market for wheat. It is one of the few countries with which the United States has a trade surplus. Egyptian exports to the U.S. total $1.6 billion; imports total $5.1 billion.

Turkey

Population: 74.0 million

Median Age: 28

GDP: $1.14 trillion

Annual growth: 2.6 percent

Per Capita GDP: $15,200

Total Annual Exports: $163.4 billion (apparel, foodstuffs, textiles, iron and steel, transportation equipment)

Total Annual Imports: $228.9 billion (machinery, chemicals, semi-finished goods, fuels, transportation equipment)

Turkey is increasingly a land of urban dwellers. Its natural resources include coal, chromium, mercury, copper, boron, oil, and gold. However, it has relatively small deposits of these natural resources, and the country relies substantially on trade.

The Turkish economy is making the transition from a mainly agricultural and industrial economy to one that is more balanced, with a stronger services sector.

The global crisis affected Turkey considerably, but according to the *Global Times*, the country is on track to shed its recession-induced problems and achieve high growth.

Turkey is another country with which the United States has a trade surplus. Turkey's exports to the United States total $6.6 billion. Its imports total $11.7 billion.

Indonesia

Population: 246.9 million

Median Age: 28

GDP: $1.24 trillion

Annual growth: 6.2 percent

Per Capita GDP: $5,100

Total Annual Exports: $187 billion (oil, natural gas, electrical appliances, plywood, textiles, rubber)

Total Annual Imports: $178.5 billion (machinery and equipment, chemicals, oil and fuel, food)

Indonesia has the greatest marine biodiversity on earth. Its natural resources include oil and gas, bauxite, silver, tin, copper, gold, and coal. Agricultural resources of timber, rubber, rice, palm oil, and coffee are important additional sources of export revenue.

Indonesia is the fourth most populated country in the world (right behind the United States). Its population is still expanding rapidly, as is its middle class.

Quick government action has helped Indonesia recover from the global recession, according to the U.S. Department of State. To stabilize the financial markets and improve liquidity, the government increased deposit insurance guarantees 20-fold. In addition, Indonesia has played an active role in the G20 coordinated response to the global crisis.

English is the most widely spoken foreign language.

Indonesia trades with the United States to the tune of $18.8 billion in exports and $8.9 billion in imports.

The Philippines

Population: 96.71 million

Median Age: 23

GDP: $431.3 billion

Annual growth: 6.6 percent

Per Capita GDP: $4,500

Total Annual Exports: $46.3 billion (semiconductors, transportation equipment, textiles and apparel, copper products, petroleum products, coconut oil, fruits)

Total Annual Imports: $61.5 billion (electronics, mineral fuels, machinery and transportation equipment, iron and steel, textile fabrics, grain)

The Philippines is a string of islands. Its land is 65 percent mountainous, with narrow coastal lowlands. It sits astride a typhoon belt.

One of the world's most highly mineralized countries, the Philippines holds untapped mineral wealth estimated at over $840 billion. Natural resources include copper, nickel, iron, cobalt, silver, and gold. In fact, the Philippines' deposits of copper and gold are among the largest in the world.

Many Filipinos work overseas as migrant workers. The money they earn and send back home in the form of overseas workers remittances is an important part of the Philippine economy.

According to the U.S. Department of State, a high level of poverty and lack of infrastructure are significant problems for the Philippines, but the population is young and growing. English is the language of government and of educational instruction. The literacy rate of 93 percent is one of the highest in the developing countries. The nation plans to increase spending on social services and infrastructure.

Because of its limited exposure to global financial markets and its recent sound fiscal policy, the Philippines was comparatively well equipped to weather the global crisis. The Philippines exports $9.2 billion to the United States and imports $7.9 billion.

Moving On

Now that you've got a good start deciding which international market(s) to work in, it's time to think about setting up your business. In the next chapter we'll discuss startup issues for import/export businesses.

4

Tricks of the Trade
Startup Basics

The gestation period for any business can be trying. Why? Because aside from money, you're investing a great deal of time, energy, and emotional intensity. You're pushing to get people interested in your service, from persuading manufacturers or artisans to work with you to finding foreign contacts to securing financing. Going over all the details—especially the financial ones—with a magnifying lens and a critical eye is crucial to your success.

That old refrain "The best things in life are free" does not quite apply when you are starting a business. Fortunately, an import/export company is typically not at the expensive end of the startup costs spectrum.

In this chapter we help you figure out what you'll need in your office and what you can expect to pay for it. The second part of the chapter gives you a preview of the tasks you'll need to accomplish to legally set up your business.

Filling Your Trunk

One of the many advantages of an import/export business is that its startup costs can be comparatively low. You have the advantage of operating from home, if you want to. This strategy cuts office lease expenses down to nothing. Unless you're starting as a distributor, you can get away without purchasing inventory, which means no outlay of funds for pretty doodads to grace display spaces (you have no display spaces!). Your major financial outlay will go toward office equipment and market research expenses, and if you are like many people, you already have the most crucial piece of office equipment: a computer system.

But let's take it from the top. The following is a breakdown of everything, from heavy investment pieces to flyweight items, you'll need to get up and running:

- Computer/monitor/keyboard
- Fax machine/printer/copier
- Internet/email service
- Website (optional)
- Software
- Market research and/or trade leads
- Phone/cell phone
- Voice mail or answering machine
- Stationery and office supplies
- Postage
- Travel expenses for conducting market research on foreign turf

You can add many goodies (of varying degrees of necessity) to this list, and we'll cover them all in Chapter 10, which features a sort of shopping bonanza. For example, a copier is a plus. It's also nice to have bona fide office furniture: a tweedy upholstered chair with lumbar support that swivels and rolls, gleaming file cabinets that lock, and real oak bookshelves.

But let's consider that you are starting from absolute scratch. You can always set up your computer on your kitchen table or on a card table in a corner of the bedroom. You can stash files in cardboard boxes. It's not glamorous, but it'll suffice until you get your business steaming ahead.

Computing Computer Costs

The computer system is at the top of the list. It will allow you to access the myriad trade leads and market research materials available online, communicate with potential and established customers via email (the quickest and cheapest method available), and generate stationery, invoices, certificates, and forms quickly, easily, and inexpensively.

It used to be possible to start off without a computer system. However, doing so is much tougher now for many reasons, including the recent regulation changes that require electronic interface with government agencies. (The new Importers Security Filing, discussed in Chapter 6, is one example.) Even if you have other professionals to file paperwork for you, you'll still find it difficult to do much without a computer.

For a basic computer system that can have you surfing the internet within two hours after you buy it, you should allocate funds in the $500 to $800 range. We will go over the various permutations in Chapter 10, but this will give you a figure to pencil in for starters.

Fax Facts

Although you technically don't have to have a fax machine, your life as an international trader will run much more smoothly with one. You can shoot off and receive hard copy materials to and from clients, representatives, and distributors instead of waiting on both U.S. and foreign postal services. Sending a pro forma invoice, for example, has a lot more impact on a potential customer when it directly follows a request for information. You can purchase a basic plain-paper fax machine for as little as $60 to $120. If you spend a little more ($150 to $250), you can get a combined fax/printer/copier.

Nosing Around the Net

A good internet and email service is a must for the international trader. With the power of the web at your command, you can go anywhere on the globe instantaneously—access trade leads as soon as they're posted, communicate with clients and client wanna-bes in a keystroke, and garner market information from worldwide sources while seated at your desk. And it's cheap! Most Internet Service Providers (ISPs) run about $20 to $25 per month and give you unlimited access to the web and email.

The Skinny on Software

Software prices can vary radically, depending on which programs you buy and from whom. You won't need any special import/export programs, but you'll want a good, strong word processing program, a desktop publishing program, and an accounting program. Again, this is a subject we'll discuss in depth in Chapter 10. For startup purposes, let's say that you'll want to allocate anywhere from $200 to $400.

> **Smart Tip**
> *Tip...*
> You can find free downloadable office software at openoffice.org. You may still want to buy some software, but first check out what's offered free of charge.

Lead Me On

Like just about everything else in the international trader's world, the amount you'll pay for market research and trade leads is a variable, almost entirely dependent on you and your personal style. If you choose to go with the Commercial Service's trade leads and other market research information, you can pencil in about $75 per month or $200 per year.

Back to the noncommercial Commercial Service, the Gold Key Matching Service program pencils in at $250 to $1,000—or more, if you really want a lot of help. It's hard to pin a price tag on the Matchmaker program because costs vary with the countries involved, but as a thumbnail, you can figure between $1,500 and $3,000.

As you travel the internet, you'll find other trade lead services and sources of market research that may cost more or less, or nothing at all.

> **Dollar Stretcher**
> The International Trade Data Network offers leads and market information for the best price of all—it's free. Just set your mouse on export.gov.

Phone Fun

If you're using a land line at home, you already know that your cost depends at least partly on the different features you choose. If you don't have a land line, you should install at least one dedicated line for your business. In fact, you'll probably need two business lines, one for phone calls (unless you plan to use only a cell phone for business) and another for your fax machine. For the purpose of startup budgeting, let's allocate about $25 per line. You'll also need to add the phone company's installation fee, which should be in the range of $40.

A cell phone will prove invaluable if you're out and about much, or even if you'd like to take a lunch without worrying about missing a call. Get a good one that won't run out of charge every five hours. (OK, maybe that's an exaggeration, but still . . .) Chances are, you'll want one that's better than the standard free-with-plan offer. We'll budget $100. Whether you use a calling plan or a calling card, rates for cell phone minutes, especially to foreign countries, vary tremendously. So shop around. We'll assume an average monthly cost of $60 for cell phone use, at least for starters.

The Mechanical Receptionist

You won't always be available to answer your phone. Often you will be traveling abroad, out interfacing with local suppliers, or running errands. During these times, you will need somebody or something to answer your phone. A Murphy's Law of business life is that people most often call when: 1) you are not in your office, 2) you are sitting down to a meal, or 3) you're in the bathroom. Another business life law is that an unanswered phone is extremely unprofessional.

So you have two ways to go: the trusty answering machine or the phone company's exciting voice mail feature. For estimating startup costs, let's figure a basic answering machine at about $40 and voice mail at about $6 per month.

Stationery Style

Business stationery is as important to a savvy international image as a well-answered phone. To create that cosmopolitan identity that will help sell your product or service, you'll need letterhead, envelopes, and business cards. There are lots of routes to take with all this stuff.

Let's say, however, that to create the basics you can purchase blank stationery, including business cards, and print them up yourself with a word processing or desktop publishing program. Or you can have a set of stationery and business cards inexpensively printed for you at a quick-print house such as FedEx Kinko's or through Office Depot's in-house service. Either way, you should allocate $75 to $100.

> **Tip...**
>
> ## Smart Tip
> When you travel abroad on trading trips, bilingual business cards are a much-appreciated gesture in some countries—and an absolute necessity in others. So do your homework!

Office supplies—pens, pencils, paper clips, mailing envelopes, reams of blank paper for designing brochures or catalogs, stapler, staples, letter opener, tape, printer cartridges—can be penciled in at about $120 to $160. This, of course, is if you start from absolute scratch, buying everything brand new for your business.

Stamps Around the World

Your startup postage costs will be fairly low, but you will need to tally them. How much you spend depends a great deal on how much material you are mailing out and where on the globe you are sending it. Clearly, snail-mailing price sheets or brochures will be much pricier than sending fax or email price quotes or listing your prices on your website.

Given current initiatives to reduce paper usage, not to mention recent hikes in postal rates, you will probably want to concentrate your promotional efforts online. This is even more true if you are positioning your company as an environmentally responsible one.

Traveling Trader

This category, too, will vary tremendously according to how you choose to tailor your market research, your startup costs, and, ultimately, your business life. Some traders are on the road more often than not, while others are basically armchair travelers. And, of course, when you do travel, your costs will vary depending on where you go, for how long, and whether you choose to spend your nights at the Ritz or the local youth hostel.

You may find that you can conduct all your market research from your desktop, or you may discover that for your particular product and style you need to study the market up close and personal.

All That Jazz

Other expenses you'll need to plug into your startup expense chart are business licenses, business insurance, legal advice, utility deposits, and all that jazz, the costs intrinsic to any company's invocation. Use the worksheet on page 67 to pencil in and then tally up these costs and all the others we've discussed in this section. If you photocopy a couple extra sheets, you can work up several options, compare them all, and decide which will work best for you so you can arrive at your official startup figure.

Cranking It Up

Check out the startup costs (the ones necessary to officially throw open your doors) on page 66 for two hypothetical international trade companies, Cargo Bay Traders and Clipper Trading Service Co.

Cargo Bay is a homebased company (office in the spare bedroom) run by an owner who's retired and decided to start out small with a minimum outlay. The Cargo Bay owner invested in a new (basic) computer, a printer/copier/fax machine, a cell phone, a desk, and a chair. He also bought some advertising and office supplies. The company has internet service and a simple website produced and maintained by the owner.

Clipper Trading Service, on the other hand, has rented a 900-square-foot office near the airport, purchased top-of-the-line equipment, hired a website designer, and employed an administrative assistant.

Both companies are acting as representatives of the manufacturer and will receive compensation based on commissions. Cargo Bay is projecting an annual gross income of $75,400, while Clipper Trading Service is projecting $254,360. Neither owner will draw a salary; instead, they'll take a percentage of their net profits as income.

The Trader's Trunk

This part of the chapter explores the bottom of the trader's trunk, those features that form the basics of the business, from company name, to legal structure, to permits.

Name That Business

Every business, like every child, has to have a name, and you should devote (almost) as much thought to choosing an appellation for your company as you would for your offspring. After all, you plan to have your business baby around for a long time. You want a name you can be proud of, one that identifies it—and by extension, you—as worthy of your clients' confidence.

Because import/export is a more serious business than, say, pizza delivery or greeting card design, you should probably rule out names like Thyme to Trade (even if you specialize in herbs and spices). Instead, your name should call attention to your expertise and efficiency. The terminally creative, however, can take heart. Noncutesy doesn't mean dull. Your name can—and should—deliver a snappy punch.

One trader attacked the name problem from the standpoint of his vision of his company. "With Global Partners," says Wahib Wahba, "we wanted to say that we're all partners, me and my clients and manufacturers. We all have to be partners to make it work."

Sample Startup Costs

Costs	Cargo Bay Traders	Clipper Trading Service Co.
Rent		$2,200.00
Office equipment & furniture	$2,308.00	6,365.00
Market research/trade leads	175.00	3,000.00
Software	200.00	400.00
Phone	90.00	265.00
Utility deposits		150.00
Employee payroll		2,000.00
Grand opening advertising	100.00	500.00
Legal services	375.00	525.00
Postage	100.00	155.00
Internet service	25.00	25.00
Website design		900.00
Stationery/office supplies	50.00	175.00
Insurance	600.00	800.00
Travel		5,500.00
Miscellaneous expenses (add roughly 10% of total)	400.00	2,200.00
Total Startup Costs	**$4,523.00**	**$25,160.00**

Startup Costs Worksheet

Costs	Your Company
Rent	$
Office equipment & furniture	
Market research/trade leads	
Software	
Phone (add $150 for a cell phone)	
Utility deposits	
Employee payroll	
Grand opening advertising	
Legal services	
Postage	
Internet service	
Website design	
Stationery/office supplies	
Insurance	
Travel	
Miscellaneous expenses (add roughly 10% of total)	
Total Startup Costs	$

When brainstorming your company name, keep in mind that, with a few exceptions, the people you'll target won't be using English as a native language. So take care with the expressions you choose. Colloquialisms and slang words sometimes aren't clear even to people in different parts of the United States; don't make things more difficult by pressing them on non-Americans. Everyone in the industry, on the other hand, easily understands international trade buzzwords like "global" and "overseas."

Many importers and exporters incorporate the name of the region with which they trade into their business moniker, for example, Far East Imports or Amazon Traders. Or you might want to incorporate a geographic feature of your own region, such as Desert Traders if you live in Palm Springs or Sea-to-Sea Exports if your office is near a seaport.

You might even decide on a variation of your own name. Lloyd Davidson, owner of LND Export Management, used his initials as the basis for his company name. Sam Nelson, owner of Nelisco Inc. in North Carolina, also used part of his name.

Whatever you go with, remember that you will be repeating your business name every time you answer the phone. Sound out the title before you settle on it. Some names look great in print but are difficult if not impossible to understand over the

Beware!

When brainstorming a business name, be careful not to fence yourself in with a moniker that may limit you later. If you're starting out importing Mexican pottery, for example, you may not want to call your company Mexican Pottery Imports—unless you're certain that's the country and product category you'll stick with.

Talking Trade

Where to start naming your business? How about with a lexicon of trader's lingo sure to set that international image in the mind of any potential client or customer?

Abroad	Global	Pacific
Atlantic	Inter-Continental	Passport
Caravan	International	Seven Seas
Cargo	Hemisphere	Trader
Compass	Mediterranean	Tropical
Earth	Overseas	Worldwide

Business Name Brainstorming

List three ideas based on the geographic area you plan to trade with (i.e., Into Africa, European, Down Under):

1. _____

2. _____

3. _____

List three ideas based on the types of products you plan to trade, remembering not to limit yourself to one product alone (i.e., Arts and Antiques, Gourmet Goods, Image Imports):

1. _____

2. _____

3. _____

List three ideas based on a local feature (i.e., mountain, seaside, or historical reference like Alamo, or even a botanical feature, if that's what your area is known for or you like, such as magnolia, rose, or chaparral):

1. _____

2. _____

3. _____

After you've decided which name you like the best, do the following:

❑ Say it aloud to make sure it's easily understood and pronounced. (Has it passed muster with your family? Have you had a friend call to see how it sounds over the phone?)

❑ Check your local Yellow Pages and online listings to make sure the same or a similar name is not already listed.

❑ Check with your local business name authority to make sure it's available.

❑ Verify that it's available as a domain name. (Register.com is a good place to check.)

phone. M&A Associates, for example, may seem like a perfectly reasonable name for partners Marty and Andrea, but when spoken, it sounds like MNA.

Most callers rate about a C-minus in listening comprehension. No matter how clearly you enunciate, they aren't going to understand M&A. So save yourself hours of telephone frustration and choose something simple.

For a list of some words that might help get your creative gears cranking, check out the international lexicon in our sidebar, "Talking Trade" (page 68).

Newly Registered

After you've decided on a name, you'll need to register it. Basically, registering your name means that you notify the proper authorities that you're doing business under a name other than your own. This is to let the public know that Tropical Trading Partners is owned by you, professional exporter.

The process varies in different regions of the country. In Florida, for example, you access the state government website and click around until you finally call up the page about fictitious business names. You fill out a series of forms, swear you are who you say you are, and enter your credit card number. Eventually, you'll receive a letter confirming that you registered your name with the state. If you want a nice little certificate to frame and hang on your wall, you need to shell out extra bucks.

In California on the other hand, you file an application with the county clerk, then advertise your name in a "general circulation" newspaper in that county for four weeks. Once that's all said and done and you've paid the fee, you receive your statement of registration. Check with your city, county, and state government to find out what the story is in your state.

Structurally Sound

To appease those picky IRS people, your business must have a structure. You can operate it as a sole proprietorship, a partnership, or a corporation, with variations thereof. Many international traders go with the simplest version, the sole proprietorship. You'll probably be starting out on your own, so there's no need to get complicated or expensive. You can always switch to another format later on if and when you take on partners and/or employees.

Beyond the basic structure for your company—the ones we've just discussed—various

> ## Smart Tip
> Tip...
>
> Delve into Entrepreneur's online resource for franchises at entrepreneur.com/franchise-zone. You'll find lots of information on the benefits and drawbacks of franchising as well as a directory of franchise opportunities.

other international trade configurations exist. There's the joint venture, which is a sort of marriage or partnership between two distinct and separate companies, for example, yours and one in a foreign country. And there's the strategic alliance, an agreement between your company and another one to work toward a common goal.

Why would you want to form a venture with an overseas company? One reason is to get around trade barriers. If your company is part domestic in whatever country you're working with, you can skim around prohibitive tariffs and quotas. Another reason? You can form a team or network with an in-country company that already has effective trade channels in operation. And a third reason is to get into government-controlled infrastructure-type projects, like power plants or telecommunications.

Then there's the wholly owned subsidiary or branch, in which your company or your client's company becomes owner of a firm. You can encounter a spider's web of entanglements in international arrangements of this type because the host country often sets up all sorts of special rules, such as how long a "foreign" company (that's you) can own property or how much profit you can collect.

So why would anybody want to open a subsidiary or branch abroad? In a word: "Profit." In order to vitalize their own economies by creating jobs and cash flow for their people, emerging nations often offer hefty incentives to businesses from more developed countries. If you do your homework and check out every permutation of foreign business ownership laws, you're less likely to get stung by unpleasant surprises.

There's also the licensing or franchising type of business. With licensing, you give a foreign company or licensee permission to sell your, or your client's, trademarked product and in return, they pay royalties on their sales. Everybody recognizes the world's preeminent licensing products: anything stamped with the likeness of Mickey, Minnie, or their Disney cohorts. You might develop a gold mine in licensing characters developed by a client with loveable little chaps just waiting to be discovered.

With a franchise, you give your or your client's foreign buyer permission to sell your licensed products with your special sales or service techniques.

The ultimate franchisor is, of course, that other Mickey: McDonald's. American food franchises traditionally do very well abroad, but

Smart Tip

Tip...

Do not fear the behemoth that is the IRS website. Yes, it's big, but surprisingly user-friendly. Find everything you need to know about small business tax issues at irs.gov/Businesses/Small-Businesses. From deductible business expenses to applying for EINs (employer ID numbers), the IRS has you covered.

Bright Idea

The Commercial Service people and their compatriots at your local Export Assistance Center can help you set up a joint venture program.

there are many other franchises available or that you can put together yourself. All you need is your imagination and some attention to detail.

Trading Places

Where should you locate your business? You have a lot of choices. Because most of your business will be conducted long-distance via mail, phone, and the internet, you won't need to be available at set hours as you would if you were running a retail establishment or restaurant. Because you will rarely have clients dropping in, except via a long-distance phone call, you will not need a receptionist, a lobby, or even meeting rooms. You also won't need signage or substantial client parking.

For these reasons, many of the traditional (and more expensive) options aren't the best choice. Instead of paying for retail or office park space, consider a warehouse location or even a home office.

If you plan to work from home, you should check into zoning regulations. A small international trading company is not likely to attract much attention from local authorities, but you should still play it safe. Find out from your local city or county government whether any permits are necessary. While you're at it, check to see if you'll need a business license, which is usually an official-looking piece of paper you get in exchange for a nominal annual fee.

We will have more to say about a home office in Chapter 10.

Attorney with ELAN

Attorneys are like plumbers; you don't want to think about them until you need one. But as a business owner, you should have a good attorney on call, one who knows international trade. You'll want her to look over any contracts you write with manufacturers, representatives, or distributors, and to advise you on the fine points of foreign trade law. You won't need to call her every week, or even every month. But there's no point in waiting until you have a problem to try to establish a relationship and get help.

To get you off on the right foot and to answer any startup questions, the Small Business Administration (SBA) and the Federal Bar Association have developed The Export Legal Assistance Network, otherwise known as ELAN. As an enticement to the red-tape-phobic would-be trader, the ELAN folks will sit you down with a volunteer trade attorney who'll answer all your questions—for free! After the initial consultation, you can either sign on with the volunteer as your permanent trade attorney or take your newfound knowledge and hit the road without a backward glance.

You can also find a reliable import/export attorney by asking for referrals from associates in the field or your international banker, but with the ELAN program, what

Hello? Is Anybody Out There?

The Export Legal Assistance Network (ELAN) is a jumping-off point for traders with legal questions. National Coordinator Judd Kessler spoke to us from his Washington, DC, office about the group's behind-the-scenes work.

According to Kessler, fear is one of the greatest obstacles for people interested in becoming a professional importer or exporter. One cause for this fear is lack of familiarity with legal issues. However, says Kessler, that is what ELAN is there for— to allay those fears. A service of the Department of Commerce, ELAN has legal counselors in 70 cities who provide import/export legal service in addition to their daily legal pursuits. Since 1984, the group has performed free initial legal counseling sessions for both new and established traders.

You only get one call, so do your homework first. Know your product(s), your target market(s), and your representatives, as well as how you'll be paid. Above all else, says Kessler, "Have a business plan in place."

The ELAN lawyers hear many kinds of issues on the phone, from questions about foreign trade agreements to how to avoid risks, customs concerns, trademark registration, and more. Kessler advises traders to be conscious of export regulations and terrorism concerns. Make sure you check that your product(s) and target market are not on the United States's forbidden list. (For further discussion, see Chapter 2.)

Kessler says ELAN has advised exporters of products ranging from liquid-dispensing and bottle-filling equipment (how did you think your Heinz 57 got in the bottle?) to scrap metals.

have you got to lose? Contact the network at exportlegal.org or through the SBA's Small Business Answer Desk at (800) U-ASK-SBA.

Details, Details

We've given you a peek at what's involved in starting up an import/export business, and we've investigated the basic underpinnings of the business. Remember, however, that expenses, licenses, and fees can crop up, depending on what you're importing and exporting, to where and from whom. Do your homework, and look before you leap into that cargo hold. The more you know about running an import/export business, the better a trader you'll be. With that in mind, check out the next chapter.

Trade Routes
Daily Operations

Now that you're versed in the ins and outs and whys and wherefores of import and export in general, let's take a look at operations. In this chapter, we explore what an international trader's daily work life is really like, what sorts of tasks you can expect to perform on a routine basis, and how they're completed.

▲

Trading Particulars

Let's face it. Most beginning traders do not have it in their budgets to sail off to Africa in search of the latest handcrafted items or jet to France each November to sample the fresh bottles of Beaujolais Nouveau. Most traders starting out do their footwork on the information superhighway, not the autobahn. So chances are good you'll spend much of your time online.

What, exactly, you'll be doing online during your peak hours and beyond will depend upon how you have structured your services. Some traders act only as sales representatives, finding buyers and taking commissions, and choose to steer clear of the shipping, documentation, and financing aspects of the deal. Others are happier offering a full line of services, buying directly from the manufacturer and taking on all the responsibilities of the transaction from shipping to marketing. These traders often specialize in either import or export and stick to the merchandise industry they know best.

The Exporter at Work

No matter how exotic you want to get, your most basic tasks will be obtaining merchandise, selling it, transporting it, and getting paid for it. Because exporting is usually considered to be easier than importing (less red tape), we'll start with an exporter's project. But even if you have your heart set on importing, pay close attention. Exporting and importing are two sides of the same coin, so what you learn here will stand you in good stead whether you're shipping into or out of the country.

The Export Path

Let's discuss what the export process is for products in general. Say you've found a buyer for your merchandise. So now what do you do? Follow the export path:

1. Generate the pro forma invoice. Give the importer a quote on your merchandise; negotiate if necessary. (See the next section.)

2. Properly classify merchandise with correct Harmonized Tariff Schedule (HTS) code. (See Chapter 6.)

> **Smart Tip**
>
> Exporting American products can not only help your company grow but also strengthen the U.S. economy. As the U.S. Trade Representative noted at the height of the global recession, "American companies of all sizes must export their goods and services to get our economy going again."

3. Determine if your merchandise has an Export Control Classification Number (ECCN). (See Export Control 101, page 84.)

4. Screen merchandise against U.S. Export Administration Regulations (EAR) to determine if it requires an export license. (See Export Control 101.)

5. Screen all parties in your export transactions against the various governmental Restricted or Denied Parties lists to ensure you're not shipping to someone you shouldn't be. (Once again, see Export Control 101 on page 84.)

Beware!
Make sure to check that your proposed goods to export don't require an export license. And remember that exports to the following countries are prohibited: Cuba, Iran, N. Korea, Sudan, and Syria.

6. Receive the letter of credit (L/C) from your bank.

7. Fulfill terms of the L/C.

   a. Have the merchandise manufactured if necessary.

   b. Make shipping and insurance arrangements.

   c. Pack the merchandise.

   d. Have the merchandise transported.

   e. Collect shipping documents.

8. Present shipping documents to your bank.

9. Pass Go. Collect your payment and give yourself a pat on the back!

Now keep reading for a discussion of each of these procedures.

The Pro's Pro Forma

Let's say you've noticed on your trips through Italy that while the Italians are the original experts on gourmet coffee drinks, nobody takes their beverages "to go." After doing some culture research (Remember Chapter 3?) to make sure Italians don't hate everything to do with drinking on the run, you've decided that "go cups," those ubiquitous insulated mugs, would go over well in Italy. You've contacted a Miami manufacturer and gotten his OK to represent his product (which we'll now call "yours"). Then you've contacted an Italian company and sent them your brochure and price list and, when they asked for it, a sample. They love it! And they email you with a request for a pro forma invoice.

The pro forma invoice is a quotation—an invoice that the buyer gets to approve before it becomes fact. Keep in mind, however, that once your buyer accepts it, you're stuck with it, too, so think it through carefully. It contains a lot of information, including the following:

- Price
- Shipping date and terms
- Letter of credit information, including bank to be used and expiration date
- Necessary documents
- Packing or labeling requirements

Check out the sample pro forma invoice on page 80. The From, To, and Date sections should be self-explanatory. (If they're not, we've got some real problems.) Below the date is your quote for the number of cups you understand the importer wants and the amount you're charging per cup. USD is international code for U.S. dollars. (For other currency codes, see Chapter 12.) Because Canada, Australia, New Zealand, and Singapore also use dollars, quoted with the $ sign, the use of USD makes a clear reference to U.S. currency.

The term EXW on the next line means Ex Works, or at your works—your (or your customer's, the manufacturer's) shop, warehouse, or factory. This tells the Cappuccino

Beware!

Get quotes from your freight forwarder before you send out your pro forma invoice. If you guesstimate, without checking, that it will cost you $200 to ship the cups to Rome, and in reality the cost is $2,000, you'll lose profit—and give yourself a headache.

Pro Forma Invoice Particulars

Here's a rapid-fire review of a pro forma invoice's main ingredients. For your first few efforts, you might make copies of this list and check off the items as you go.

❏ Product description
❏ Price
❏ Terms of sale (How is your merchandise going to be picked up or shipped? When will ownership—or title—change hands?)
❏ Terms of payment (How are you going to be paid? L/C, prepayment, 90-day time?)
❏ Length of time prices are valid
❏ Length of time necessary for shipping

Remember to check shipping dates and prices and special documentation questions with your freight forwarder *before* you issue the pro forma invoice.

Imports people the price for 5,000 go-cups if they arrange to pick up the shipment at your place. The term CIF on the next line is import/export shorthand for cost, insurance, and freight. This is your price—after adding in freight costs—if you pay for shipping the 5,000 go-cups, insured, to Rome, which, of course, will make it much easier for the Cappuccino Imports people to pick them up.

You won't see the little numerals in the Terms & Conditions section on most pro forma invoices. We've put them in to make it easier to explain each point. So are you ready? Follow along on the sample on page 80:

1. A sight letter of credit means a letter of credit, a sort of bank draft, paid as soon as you've fulfilled the conditions spelled out in it. This is in contrast to a time or term letter of credit, which gets paid after a period of time.

2. The 2 percent discount is an incentive for the Cappuccino Imports people to prepay, but it's not something they have to do. And, of course, you can make the discount, assuming you want to offer it, any amount you like.

3. This item is a hint: Italians, it would be nice if you opened the letter of credit at The Bank of Berry. As the exporter, you can specify that it must be opened at your own bank, but here we're giving them an option.

4. This is another little courtesy. It will save the Cappuccino Imports people some money and, in this case, won't cost you a whole lot more. Again, though, make sure you've figured your packing costs properly before offering the quote. When you're shipping items like fine china or crystal, packaging and packing is going to be a much bigger issue than it would be for plastic cups. And when you're shipping steak or seafood, it's also going to be a big issue, so get in the habit of checking this stuff out before you open your pro forma mouth and insert foot.

5. This protects you from the buyers hemming and hawing until sometime next year or the year after when it might cost you more to obtain the go-cups.

6. This item gives you time to have the cups manufactured, packed, and shipped before the letter of credit runs out. You don't have to stipulate this amount of time; pick what's comfortable for you and your supplier. Keep in mind that you may need to have the cups specially labeled or include some kind of user information, such as whether they are dishwasher safe or contain hot beverages that may burn, and that this will have to be translated into Italian. All this can take extra time. Also be sure to allow for plenty of shipping time. There's nothing worse than finding out that the ship your cups are booked on sails one week before they're ready to go.

And at the bottom of your invoice, don't forget the Thank You! People the world over appreciate courtesy. It will often take you further than you'd imagine.

Sample Pro Forma Invoice

From: Coffee Holic Exports
          123 Cafe Street
          Berry, FL 30000, USA

To: Cappuccino Imports
          456 Via Espresso
          Ostia Antica, Italy

Date: June 4, 20xx

For: 5,000 (five thousand) Coffee Go-Cups, Style A
          @ USD 3.00

Shipping Terms: EXW Miami, Florida, USA   USD 15,000.00
                       CIF Rome   USD 16,000.00

Other Terms and Conditions:

1. Sight letter of credit in U.S. dollars on a U.S. bank
2. 2% additional discount from EXW cost ($300.00) for advance payment in U.S. dollars (check payable at a U.S. bank)
3. Our bankers: The Bank of Berry, Berry, Florida, USA
4. Export packing included
5. Prices good for 90 days
6. Shipment: within 60 days after receipt of check or letter of credit; please open letter of credit for 90 days total

Thank You!

Pro Forma Invoice

From: _____

_____

_____

To: _____

_____

_____

Date: _____

For: _____

_____

Shipping Terms: _____

_____

Other Terms and Conditions: _____

_____

_____

_____

_____

_____

_____

_____

_____

_____

_____

_____

_____

Thank You!

Documentation

There's one other item to think about on a pro forma invoice: special documents. Some countries require certification for certain items—for example, food and pharmaceutical goods. Other countries, particularly those in Latin America, the Middle East, and some Sub-Saharan countries, tend to require legalization or consularization of documents, which is another way of saying they like to have a special fee paid for the privilege of stamping the document "legal." Many countries have abolished this requirement, as the process makes it extremely difficult (if not impossible) to document via electronic methods.

Frequently, your customer will inform you of this requirement when she asks for your pro forma invoice. But don't assume. Do your homework. Check with your freight forwarder. If he thinks special documentation will be required and your customer hasn't asked for it, make sure your invoice says "Price does not include legalization" or whatever the documentation may be. Bring the issue up again in the cover letter you send with the pro forma invoice. Make sure you've covered all the angles.

Take a Letter

Now, about that cover letter. This is another "courtesy stamp" that can set you apart as the kind of company potential importers will want to work with (see page 83). The first paragraph speaks for itself: It thanks your customer for his order, reiterates what he's purchasing, and indicates that you plan to work with him over the long haul—you're not just a fly-by-night operator. He's now got a friend in the business: you.

Paragraph two offers two important points. It asks whether the order will be prepaid by check or whether the customer plans to pay by letter of credit, otherwise known as an L/C. The opening bank is the customer's bank. This bank cannot issue a letter of credit number until the letter of credit itself has been issued. So what you're saying here is "Tell me the L/C is on its way."

The last paragraph is a typewritten, faxable smile and handshake, the same treatment you'd give your Italian customer if you were dealing with him in person. Don't hesitate to use it!

Now, how are you going to get this terrific cover letter and the pro forma invoice to your customer? Not necessarily by mail. Anyone who's had the experience of sending a "wish you were here" postcard from a foreign land knows you usually arrive home long before the postcard does. Mailing documents to other lands is not a speedy process. And in Third World countries with shaky infrastructures, it can be downright miraculous if your mail arrives at all.

Sample Pro Forma Invoice Cover Letter

COFFEE HOLIC EXPORTS

123 Cafe Street • Berry, FL 30000 • USA
(305) 000-0000 • (305) 000-0000
email: CoffeeHol@Holiday.com

June 4, 20xx

Sr. Antonio Franco

Cappuccino Imports

456 Via Espresso

Ostia Antica, Italy

Dear Signore Franco:

Thank you for your order of our Coffee Go-Cups! Please find herewith our pro forma invoice. We believe your customers will love the cups, and we look forward to a long and mutually prosperous relationship with you and your firm.

Please advise either when payment is to be sent or the name of the opening bank and letter of credit number.

Again, we thank you for your order and look forward to hearing from you soon.

Very best,

Charlie Holic

Charlie Holic

Coffee Holic Exports

CH/ta

Many international traders still rely on the good old fax machine. It's quick, it's reliable, and it's relatively inexpensive. You'll probably do a lot of your preliminary negotiations by email, which is even faster and less expensive, but a faxed pro forma invoice, a sheet of paper your customer can hold in his hand, lends a more formal note. Even better, consider emailing your documents with a request for receipt as well as faxing them so you have all bases covered and have proof that contact has been made with your client.

> **Tip...**
>
> ### Smart Tip
>
> Include a descriptive headline on all emails, particularly if some action is required. Be specific. If you wish to know the price of a specific Grecian urn and you need to know ASAP, don't just write "Grecian Urn" in the header. Instead, write "Action Requested: Need Grecian Urn Quote by Tomorrow."

Export Control 101

All items exported from the U.S. must have an Export Control Classification Number (ECCN). This is a five-character code. Take, for example, 4B994. The first digit refers to one of ten different broad classifications for items. In this case, the 4 indicates a computer-related item. We won't go into all the additional characters, as this classification system is complicated.

How do you come up with the ECCN number for your product? There are three ways:

1. *Determine it yourself.* You can look at the alphabetized index to the Commerce Control List (CCL) on the U.S. Export Administration Regulations (EAR) website. Go to access.gpo.gov/bis/index.html. Select "EAR data."
2. *Go to the source: the manufacturer.* Often manufacturers know the ECCN. They may also know what countries require a license for that product.
3. *Submit a classification request online through Simplified Network Application Process Redesign (SNAP-R).* Go there via bis.doc.gov and select "SNAP-R."

The BIS and EAR websites will also provide you with information about whether your items need an export license. In addition, you can find the Restricted or Denied Parties lists.

Let's Talk Shipping

Now that you've gotten a feel for the pro forma invoice, let's talk shipping terms. Remember that your price quote will vary depending on how you or your customer decide to send the merchandise. In the coffee go-cup order, for example, there's a $1,000 difference between the price if the customer arranges for the order to be picked up or if you send it off to Rome for him. Your freight forwarder can make all these actual arrangements for you and carry them out, but you need to understand them to quote your prices profitably.

International shipping terms are sometimes referred to as "Incoterms," referring to the International Chamber of Commerce. Incoterms are a worldwide standardization of definitions, used in shipping documents. Most shipping terms can be used interchangeably for air, sea, and ground transportation. Here are the most common terms:

Ex Works (EXW)

This one you already know! This is where the merchandise is picked up at your "works"—your shop or warehouse, or your supplier's warehouse or factory. The unstated agreement here is that you'll have the product ready to go, properly packaged for shipping, stacked on a shipping pallet if necessary, and properly banded and labeled. You'll also, of course, have the merchandise ready and waiting at the time the customer has specified for pickup.

In an EXW transaction, your responsibility for the merchandise ends when the customer or his representative picks up the goods. He's taken legal possession or title. If the go-cups are lost at sea in a freak storm or are blasted out of the sky by the aliens, you're off the hook and you still get paid under the terms of the letter of credit.

Free Carrier (FCA)

This is the same thing as EXW, except that it means you'll load the truck or mini-van or whatever carrier the customer sends to pick up the goods. Because this is basically a courtesy, you should plan on charging the same price for FCA as you would for EXW. You won't see this term used for ground transportation—when you're shipping by truck or rail—because in this case it's basically the same thing as FOB, which is described later.

Free Alongside Ship (FAS)

This means that you as the exporter will have the merchandise delivered, just as it sounds, right alongside the ship (or air carrier). In other words, instead of just having the goods ready for pickup, you'll deliver them to the ship or plane to be loaded. "Ship" can also mean a warehouse in the port area where the steamship line will later pick up the go-cups and whatever other goodies are waiting for pickup and take them to the ship. The point is that you pay for transportation to the ship or ship's warehouse, whichever your customer has specified, and you have responsibility for the cups until the shipping line representative signs for them and takes over the title. If the coffee cups meet with a nasty accident on the freeway in this instance, they're your responsibility and your problem. You'll have to replace them if you want to get paid.

How much do you charge for FAS delivery? That's up to you. If you live near the point of delivery and the load is light, say, 50 Styrofoam statuettes, you'll probably hop into your station wagon and deliver them yourself. Or you might call UPS or Joe's Cheap Delivery Service.

But chances are you'll rely on a common carrier, one of those fleets of semis you see rumbling down every interstate in the land—especially if you live someplace like Pocatello, Idaho, which is not exactly next door to a major seaport.

Free on Board Vessel (FOB)

This term means that you not only have the merchandise delivered to the port, but you also see that it's loaded on board the ship, or vessel. Here you're taking on several additional charges. For starters, there's the transportation fee to the port. Then there are the terminal receiving charges (TRC), or wharfage, which the shipping line charges to load your go-cups onto the ship. And then there's the freight forwarder's fee.

In this instance, your responsibility does not end until the merchandise is safely loaded onto the ship and signed for by the captain or his representative. So, again, you can charge what you like for the added anxiety.

Be sure you check with your freight forwarder before committing yourself to an FOB price quote. Steamship line prices can vary among ports. And trucking or common carrier prices will vary among cities and can even change with fluctuations in fuel prices. You'll also want to double-check the matter of legalization or consularization fees, because if they're necessary, you'll have to supply your importer with a certificate of origin, packing slip, and invoice stamped by somebody in the importing country's local American embassy. What's a certificate of origin? A form signed by your local chamber of commerce verifying that the product was manufactured in the United States.

FOB prices are usually requested and quoted with the port of departure listed, as in FOB airport, Seattle, or FOB vessel, Panama City, Florida, or just FOB Panama City, Florida, without the words "vessel" or "airport."

Cost and Freight (CFR)

Here you're taking on even more responsibility. This means you'll not only transport the packaged go-cups to the port or airport and have them loaded onto the ship, but you'll also pay the shipping charges. You might see CFR written as C+F or C&F, but these are elderly forms that have mostly been retired from service.

Cost, Insurance, and Freight (CIF)

You might recognize this one from the pro forma invoice. It means that you're paying to ship the coffee cups to Rome and you're also paying the insurance to cover their safe arrival. Marine insurance usually includes transportation to the port as well as on board the ship, so if something hideous happens anywhere en route, you're responsible, but you're also insured. Again, as in every example above, you can tack on whatever fee you like. CIF prices and quotes are written with the destination listed, as in CIF Rome.

Cost, Insurance, and Freight Paid To (CIP)

This one tacks on one more stipulation. You'll arrange and pay for having the coffee cups insured, trucked to the port or airport, shipped or flown to Rome, and then delivered directly to your customer's door (or other specified location) by local ground transportation. Of all the shipping terms we've just reviewed, this is the only one you won't see applied to air freight as well as ocean. Why? Because CIF and CFR will cover your shipment. You also won't see this term used for ground transportation.

Delivered Duty Paid (DDP)

Not to be confused with DDT, DDP is like CIF, except that besides having the coffee cups insured and shipped to Rome, then delivered to your customer's door, you also pay all customs duties. This is not so hot for you as the exporter (although you'll do your homework before you agree so you know how much money to tack onto your invoice, right?). But if you're the importer, especially a newbie, it's a nice way to have someone who knows the ropes take over the tough stuff. You should be aware, though, that DDP is not the most common way for the exporter to ship, so don't expect to have it handed to you without some negotiation.

Beware!

If a particular shipping port or airport is mentioned, make sure to use it. If the letter of credit specifies Los Angeles International Airport and you ship out from nearby Burbank, you could end up not getting paid because you didn't follow directions. Avoid this by simply stating California Airport or West Coast Airport.

Delivered at Frontier (DAF)

This term applies to ground transportation only and means the merchandise gets dropped off at the border, or frontier. You pay the freight costs to the drop-off point and take responsibility for getting the shipment to that location.

Carrying the Day

While you might book yourself on any one of a plethora of ritzy cruise lines with six pools, three movie theaters, and ten restaurants, there are only three types of ocean carriers on which to place your merchandise:

▲

1. *Conference lines.* This is an association of carriers that join together in Ocean Freight Conferences to establish common shipping rates and conditions. They offer two fee schedules—the regular one and the lower one they'll give you if you sign a contract to use only their ships during the contract period.

2. *Independent lines.* These lines operate on their own and usually offer rates about 10 percent lower than their conference competition. So why wouldn't you just go with them and forget the conferences? Because the independents' space is based on availability, and there isn't always room for your goods.

Shipping Terms on Parade

Terms of Sale	Exporter's Job and Responsibilities	Buyer Takes Title At
EXW—Ex Works	Pack and label merchandise; have it ready for loading	Exporter's facility
FCA—Free Carrier	Pack and label merchandise; have it ready for loading; load truck	Exporter's facility
FAS—Free Alongside Ship	Ship to port or airport; pay truck freight	Ship or plane, departure city
FOB—Free on Board	Ship to port or airport; have loaded; pay freight forwarder	Ship or plane, departure city
CFR—Cost and Freight	Ship to destination port or airport	Destination port or airport
CIF—Cost, Insurance Freight	Ship, insured, to destination port or airport	Destination and port or airport
CIP—Cost, Insurance Paid To	Ship, insured, to destination port or airport; then have delivered by ground transport	Importer's facility
DDU—Delivered Duty Unpaid	Ship, insured, to destination port or airport; then have delivered by ground transport; pay customs duties	Importer's facility
DAF—Delivered at Frontier	Ship to border; pay truck freight	Specified border point

3. *Tramp vessels.* This is the kind of ship Indiana Jones sailed back to the States with the Lost Ark on board. They can be conference or independent, but they're called tramps because instead of operating on a fixed schedule, they tramp around the world, seeking out whatever bulk cargoes might be available at the last minute.

> ## ⚠ Beware!
> The insurance granted by an airline's waybill is not the same as the insurance certificate that may be required on your letter of credit. Make sure you've got the real thing or you may not be in compliance with the L/C, which means you may not get paid.

Just Say No

Listen up, importer! It's not always in your best interest to let the exporter ship her merchandise CIF (cost, insurance, and freight). Having her pay the freight and insurance and handle all the paperwork may sound wonderfully simple (and it is), but the money will come out of your pocket anyway. Possibly more than is necessary. Why? She might tack on a tidy little sum for her trouble. Or she might not have gotten the best price.

So do your homework. Ask for the weight and dimensions of the shipping containers and how many containers there will be. Then get on the horn with your customs broker and get your own price quotes. If you discover that you can do better than what the exporter has quoted, renegotiate. Say you want your goods shipped EXW (ex works), FCA (free carrier), or FOB (free on board). Then make sure the letter of credit specifies your preferred carrier.

On the other hand, if you're a newbie importer and you decide that the difference in price between the exporter's quote and the ones you've received is minimal, it might just be worth it to let her carry the ball—at least for your first few forays until you learn the shipping ropes.

The Import/Export Referee

Now that you know how to get your merchandise shipped, let's talk about getting paid. Over the centuries, international traders have devised the letter of credit (L/C) as an honorable, safe method of insuring that the importer gets the goods he's paid for in the manner he wants them shipped from an exporter who could be halfway around the world. At the same time, the letter of credit assures the exporter that he will get paid for his merchandise once he's sent it across international borders to someone he may never have seen up close and personal.

The letter of credit does this by acting, with the help of the bank, as a sort of import/export referee, making sure that the exporter has carried out the importer's

▲

instructions down to the last dotted "i" and crossed "t" before it hands over payment to him. For the exporter's peace of mind, the letter of credit guarantees that his payment is already in the bank and that once he's carried out the instructions embedded in the L/C, he'll receive the money.

A letter of credit, sometimes also called a documentary credit, is often abbreviated as L/C. Let's run through a letter of credit transaction and show you exactly how the whole thing works. Letters of credit can take on various "looks," from the flowery formal business letter to the snappy let's-get-to-the-point list to the unimaginative-but-works fill-in-the-blanks form, depending on the issuing bank's modus operandi. But whatever the style, each L/C will contain the same information and will be used the same way. Check out the samples on pages 93 and 94 to get an idea of what typical L/Cs can look like.

Exporter's Letter of Credit Checklist

As the exporter, there are a number of items you'll need to know or negotiate before the importer sends you the letter of credit. Here's a handy checklist to help you make sure you've covered all your bases. You might want to make copies of this list and check things off as you go.

❑ Which will be the advising bank (i.e., your bank)? _____

_____

❑ How much time will you have to ship your merchandise after you receive the L/C? _____

❑ How much time will you have to get your documents to your bank? ____

_____

❑ Will the letter of credit be irrevocable? The answer should be yes. _____

❑ Is the L/C payable at sight (when you present the done-deed documents, not after another 30, 60, or 90 days)? The answer should be yes. _____

❑ Will you pay your bank charges, and will the importer pay his? _____

❑ What will your bank charges be? _____

❑ Are there any special requirements? If so, what are they? _____

_____

❑ Remember: When the L/C is opened, get the name of the opening bank and the L/C number.

Importer's Letter of Credit Checklist

When you're the importer, you'll need to ascertain a number of points before issuing your letter of credit. Here's a handy checklist to help you make sure you have everything present and accounted for. Why not make copies so you have it on hand for each transaction?

❑ Will the letter of credit be confirmed? _____

❑ What will your bank charges be? _____

❑ Is the L/C payable in the exporter's desired currency? What is that currency (U.S. dollars, Mexican pesos, etc.)? _____

❑ How much time do you want to allow for shipment? _____

❑ How much time do you want to give the exporter to get his documents to the bank? _____

❑ What documents will you need? _____

❑ Is everything in the letter of credit on the pro forma invoice? _____

❑ What are your shipping requirements? _____

❑ What about insurance? _____

❑ Remember: Notify the exporter of your bank and letter of credit number.

❑ Also remember: Get the loading date and other information so you can file your ISF form on time (see Chapter 6).

Tale of an Importer

Signore Franco of Cappuccino Imports zips down to his bank, the Banco della Roma, and applies for a letter of credit in the amount of USD 16,000, the amount he needs to have the exporter, Coffee Holic, send him the 5,000 coffee go-cups CIF Rome. (CIF, remember, is cost, insurance, and freight paid to Rome.) The bank checks Sr. Franco's account to make sure he has USD 16,000 available. The bank may (or may not) freeze this sum until the letter of credit becomes payable.

As the importer, Signore Franco could be called either the applicant or the opener, since he's the person applying for or opening the L/C. The exporter (in this case, Charlie) is called the beneficiary because he ultimately receives the deposit into his account.

You should note that the Banco della Roma is an international bank and is used to dealing with L/Cs. If Sr. Franco had gone to a dinky bank without an international department, then either he'd have been bundled out the door to find another bank to work with or his bank would have found an international affiliate to help it through the ropes. But in this instance, it's not a problem.

Sr. Franco tells his bank exactly which documents he'll want from the Coffee Holic people. In this case (see page 98), he's asked for the following:

- Full set of clean, on board air bills of lading, issued "to order"
- Commercial invoice, original and five copies
- Packing slip, original and five copies
- Insurance certificates

Sr. Franco's bank neatly condenses all this into L/C format and sends the letter of credit to the Coffee Holic people's bank in Berry. When The Bank of Berry receives the L/C, it sends it on to Charlie Holic, the exporter. Again, if Charlie's bank is the dinky-town type and doesn't know how to deal with L/Cs, it will either send him packing or find an international bank to help with the transaction. But, as in Rome, this bank is used to dealing with letters of credit.

The importer's bank is called the opening, originating, or issuing bank, while the exporter's bank is known as the advising bank because it advises the exporter of the L/C.

So now the ball is in Charlie's court. It's up to him to carry out every detail of the letter of credit exactly as it's spelled out. This includes using a particular ocean carrier or sending the go-cups from a particular port, if that's what's specified. Here, Charlie has it pretty easy. He can ship from any East Coast port on any carrier, so long as the cups end up in one piece in Rome on or before September 1, 20XX.

Once the coffee cups have made it to Rome, Charlie takes a trip to the bank with all the documents—including the bills of lading, the commercial invoice with all its copies, the packing slip with all its copies, and insurance certificates—proving that he's done his job as set out in the letter of credit. The bank people, in their capacity as "import/export referee," check over all these documents and assure themselves that everything is fine. Then they have Charlie's payment, which has been waiting patiently all this time in Sr. Franco's account at the Banco della Roma, transferred to Charlie's account.

Beware!

Unless otherwise stated, a letter of credit is irrevocable. This means that once it's been opened, neither the importer nor the exporter can change his mind about anything in it without a tremendous amount of hassle. So whether you're acting as importer or exporter, make sure you know, understand, and can carry out what you're committing to.

Sample Letter of Credit #1

The Bank of Berry
Specialists in Small-Town & International Banking
Berry, Florida 30000, USA

July 2, 20xx

Coffee Holic Exports
123 Cafe Street
Berry, FL 30000, USA

Dear Sirs:

Our correspondents, Banco della Roma, request us to inform you that they have opened with us their irrevocable letter of credit in your favor in the amount of Maximum Sixteen Thousand and 00/100 ($16,000.00) United States Dollars by order of Cappuccino Imports, 456 Via Espresso, Ostia Antica, Italy.

We are authorized to accept your 90 days sight draft, drawn on us when accompanied by the following documents, which must represent and cover full invoice value of the merchandise described below:

1. Signed commercial invoice in original and five (5) copies
2. Full set of clean ocean bills of lading, dated on board, plus one (1) non-negotiable copy, if available, issued to the order of Banco della Roma, notify: Cappuccino Imports, 456 Via Espresso, Ostia Antica, Italy, indicating Credit No. 0123
3. Insurance certificates in duplicate, in negotiable form, covering all risks, including war risks, strikes, and mines, for the value of the merchandise plus 10%

> Covering: Coffee Go-Cups, Style A
> As per pro forma invoice dated June 4, 20xx
> CIF Rome

> Merchandise to be forwarded from Miami to Rome
> Partial shipments prohibited
> Transshipments prohibited

The above-mentioned correspondent engages with you that all drafts drawn under and in compliance with the terms of this credit will be duly honored on delivery of documents as specified, if presented at this office on or before October 1, 20xx. We confirm the credit and thereby undertake that all drafts drawn and presented above will be duly honored.

Jennifer Schneider Jordan

for The Bank of Berry

The Bank of Berry

Berry, Florida, USA

Opening Bank L/C No.: 0123   Our Reference No.: 0456D

July 2, 20xx

1. By order of Cappuccino Imports, Ostia Antica, Italy, we advise this irrevocable Documentary Credit No. 0123 in favor of Coffee Holic Exports, Berry, Florida, USA, in the amount of USD 16,000.00 (Sixteen Thousand and 00/100 United States Dollars) available at sight, against your drafts, accompanied by the following documents:

2. Full set of clean on board bills of lading issued to order of shipper, marked notify applicant, freight prepaid

3. Beneficiary's signed commercial invoices in original and five copies

4. Packing slip in original and five copies

5. Insurance policy in negotiable form issued to our order and showing claims payable at destination for the full invoice amount plus 10% covering all risks, SRCC, and war clause

6. For: 5,000 Coffee Go-Cups per pro forma invoice dated June 4, 20xx

7. Shipment from: East Coast port

8. Shipment to: Rome, Italy

9. Shipment not later than: September 1, 20xx

10. Date of Expiry: October 1, 20xx

11. Part Shipments: Prohibited

12. Transshipments: Prohibited

13. Documents must be presented within ten days after shipment

14. Banking charges in the United States for the account of beneficiary

15. Applicant's bank: Banco della Roma

16. We hereby confirm this letter of credit.

Jennifer Schneider Jordan

for The Bank of Berry

Meanwhile, back at the FedEx counter, all the documents Charlie (or his freight forwarder) assembled in the course of shipping the coffee cups are sent to the bank in Rome to be handed over to Sr. Franco.

End of transaction. Pretty simple, really!

Something Smelly in Denmark

All letters of credit are generated through banks. Usually, the importer will arrange for your bank to be the advising bank, but occasionally he'll use another American bank. If this is OK with you, go for it. If not, you can ask that your bank be included in the loop. You'll have to pay its fees on top of whatever other bank charges you're committed to, but you'll have the security of knowing that the folks you're familiar with are on the job.

If you ever receive an L/C directly from an importer, be on guard! Letters of credit can only come from banks, so an L/C generated by any other entity is a dead giveaway that something is smelly. Turn the letter of credit over to your international banker and let him or her take it from there.

The L/C Revue

Now that you understand why and how a letter of credit works, let's go over each item in the L/C in a sort of choreography, one step at a time. Follow along on the Sample Letter of Credit #2 on page 94 as we review (or is that revue?).

1. This gives the basic information—who the L/C is from, who it's written to, how much money it's for, and in which currency, and—important!—states that this is an irrevocable letter of credit. This is standard operating procedure, but worth repeating. Never accept a revocable letter of credit, because that would mean the importer could back out of the deal any time she felt like it. This section also gives the information that this L/C is available at sight. As you already know, this means the money will be paid as soon as the terms of the L/C are met; it's not a time draft to be paid out over a designated period.

2. This section spells out that the merchandise is to be sent CIF (cost, insurance, and freight) by sea. How do you know this? Because it calls for a full set of clean on board bills of lading, for starters. Bills of lading are forms issued by the sea, land, or air carrier to verify the merchandise they're transporting. The term on board is used by steamship lines to indicate that, yes, the merchandise is on board the ship as opposed to sitting on the dock. This way, the exporter knows his product is actually underway and not baking in the sun waiting for the next available ship to come along. Full set is another term used exclusively by steamship lines and refers to the three original bills of lading traditionally

▲

issued and signed by the captain or one of his subordinates, so that's how you know the order is to be sent by sea. The steamship line people, who enjoy getting repeat business, will provide you with as many copies marked non-negotiable as you need. To order of shipper means that the merchandise is consigned to the steamship line and not to the importer, although the shipper will turn the goods over to the importer when they reach their destination. The applicant, to be notified when the merchandise reaches its destination, is the buyer (in this case Cappuccino Imports). Last but not least, the section clearly says freight prepaid—and that's how you know that the coffee cups are being sent CIF. Got it? Good!

3. This sentence says that the beneficiary (the exporter, remember?) must provide not a pro forma invoice, but the familiar, ordinary one he uses for routine transactions, signed in his own hand, along with five copies.

4. The packing slip called for here is, like its compatriot, the invoice, not some exotic hybrid but the ordinary, everyday packing slip with copies that Charlie Holic uses all the time.

5. An insurance policy for your merchandise is a must—and not difficult to obtain. Your freight forwarder can make all the arrangements. The acronym SRCC means strikes, riots, and civil commotion. The importer wants the coffee cups covered for risks, such as storms at sea, running up on reefs, or run-ins with icebergs (yes, he's seen *Titanic*). And he also wants the shipment covered for possible torpedo or other war damage and any other violent act of man that can be thought up.

6. This one's simple: These are the 5,000 go-cups precisely as spelled out in the pro forma invoice. Type in this same phrase describing your merchandise per pro forma invoice dated (whatever) on every document you ultimately hand over to the bank.

7. This one's simple, too! For review, remember that "East Coast port" gives Charlie Holic the freedom to choose any East Coast port he wants to ship from.

8. Another obvious one—the destination port.

9. This is the absolute latest date for the carrier to leave port with the merchan-

> ⚠️ **Beware!**
>
> Customs doesn't inform importers of shipment arrivals. This is the responsibility of the shipper or some other designated party. If you're the importer of merchandise arriving at an American port, find out in advance the scheduled loading date at the foreign port and also the scheduled arrival date. Then follow up. If the paperwork isn't presented to Customs within 15 days of arrival, the goods will be transferred to a warehouse, and you'll pay for storage.

dise on board—the last possible date Charlie Holic can send his coffee cups off to Rome. One day later and he runs a serious risk of not getting paid because he's violated the stipulations in the letter of credit.

10. The date of expiry is the date the letter of credit expires. Like time and tide, the L/C waits for no one. If you aren't at the bank by the date of expiry with all your documentation in hand and correct, you don't get paid.

Beware!

Be sure your insurance covers your merchandise from your driveway to the importer's door. Don't leave gaps in the coverage area; strange things can happen on piers or in air cargo bays.

11. Part or partial shipments are those sent in batches rather than as a complete set. Cappuccino Imports might want Coffee Holic to send a part shipment if it planned to sell only, say, 1,000 go-cups at a time and didn't want to warehouse the entire 5,000-cup order. In this case, though, the importer is eager to get all the merchandise at once. And he doesn't want to pay the extra expense of multiple shipments.

I, Applicant

As the importer, you get to apply for the letter of credit. Your bank will provide you with a form on which to submit all the necessary information. You can check out the sample on page 98 to see what the finished product will resemble.

Now, about those bank charges. If you don't already have an account with an international bank, you will be required to place all the funds guaranteed by the L/C into the institution's coffers. If you're already a customer with a gold star next to your name, the bank will set you up with a line of credit against your account. Either way, the bank sets the L/C funds into a sort of escrow account and holds them for you until the close of the transaction.

Aside from the money you need to pay the exporter, of course, there are various bank fees for letter of credit transactions. These include advising, assignment, payment, and transfer fees. The exact charges will depend on the bank, but you can expect to pay between $1,000 and $1,500 for a $50,000 transaction. Talk to your banker before you embark on a project.

Sample Request to Open L/C

Request to Open Documentary Credit
(Commercial Letter of Credit and Security Agreement)

To: Banco della Roma   From: Cappuccino Imports

Please open for our account a letter of credit in accordance with the undermentioned particulars. We agree that, except so far as otherwise expressly stated, this credit will be subject to the Uniform Customs and Practice for Documentary Credits, ICC Publication #500. We undertake to execute the bank's usual form of indemnity.

Type of Credit:	Irrevocable
Method of Advice:	Fax, full details
Beneficiary's Bank:	The Bank of Berry
In Favor of Beneficiary:	Coffee Holic Exports
	123 Cafe Street
	Berry, Florida 30000, USA
Amount or Sum of:	USD 16,000.00
Availability:	Valid until October 1, 20xx

This credit is available by drafts drawn at sight, accompanied by the required documents.

Required Documents:

1. Invoice in original and five copies
2. Full set of clean, on board bills of lading to order of shipper, marked notify applicant, freight prepaid
3. Packing slip in original and five copies
4. Insurance policy in negotiable form showing claims payable at destination for full amount plus 10% covering all risks, SRCC, and war clause

Quantity & Description of Goods:	5,000 Coffee Go-Cups, Style A, per pro forma invoice dated June 4, 20xx
Price Per Unit:	USD 3.00
Terms & Port:	CIF Rome
Ship From:	East Coast port
Special Instructions:	Part shipments prohibited
	Transshipments prohibited
	Documents must be presented within 10 days after shipment
	Banking charges in the U.S. for the account of beneficiary

12. Transshipment is the cargo opposite of nonstop. In other words, it means that the merchandise is off-loaded somewhere en route to the final destination, new bills of lading are issued, and the whole process starts over again. Not nonstop and not fun to keep track of.

Smart Tip

Some exporters who deal with importers in volatile areas, like parts of Africa or the Middle East, arrange for a bank in a stable country to confirm the L/C so that they're guaranteed payment.

13. This section spells out how long the exporter has to get the shipping documents (bills of lading, invoices, and packing slips) to the importer so that he has them ready to show his home-turf customs people when the merchandise arrives. It's not cool to make him wait for the documents because, if the goods arrive before the documentation, he'll have to leave all those eagerly awaited coffee cups sitting in a warehouse and pay storage fees. Sending documents ASAP will ensure you have a customer for life. And ensure that you get paid ASAP! Note: If the L/C doesn't specify how much time you have to send your documents, then you have 21 days.

14. This means that the beneficiary, or exporter, will pay his own bank's L/C charges and the importer will pay the fees charged by his bank. Occasionally, either exporter or importer will pay all fees. When do you pay? Not to worry—your bank usually deducts the charges from your L/C payment before it turns the funds over to you.

15. This, remember, is the importer's bank.

16. When your bank confirms the letter of credit, it is saying that, so long as you conform to the terms of the L/C, it will pay you, come hell or high water.

The Negotiator

A negotiable bill of lading is like a signed check with nobody's name on the "pay to the order of" line. The shipper can give it—and thus the merchandise it describes—to anyone you choose. So if something goes wrong with the letter of credit after your shipment has already arrived on foreign shores and your customer won't accept the merchandise, you can hustle and find someone else to buy it.

A non-negotiable bill of lading, on the other hand, is like a check made out to a specific person. Only that person (or company) can take receipt of the merchandise; if something goes wrong after it arrives on foreign shores and you want to sell the goods to someone else, you'll have to start the whole shipping document process over again.

Bright Idea

Think before you react. If things are not going your way, hold off before you fire off a nasty phone call or email. Even a one-minute delay can help.

▲

A Day in the Life

What does a trader's day really look like? What does he do in between preparing pro forma invoices, requests for letters of credit, and shipping documents? Here's a behind-the-scenes peek, courtesy of Michael R., the international trade consultant in Germany:

○ First hour. Read statistics printed overnight by the computer to see if each representative/agent has fulfilled his plans and initiate changes if necessary.

○ Work on the internet for one or two hours to see what inquiries have come in, then answer them personally or forward them to past or present clients who may be interested.

○ Have short meeting with colleagues to see if assistance is needed, then support them or troubleshoot.

○ Look at the day's newspapers to see whether there's any movement within my industry where I should act fast.

○ Take a coffee break.

○ Look at the mail and handle or forward items.

○ After lunch, take time to reflect on what has and what should have happened.

○ Discuss problems and/or chances for the future with prospects and/or business partners.

○ Look again at email and the internet for any news or try to find new situations.

○ At the end of the day, there should be about an hour to discuss again with colleagues how the day went and/or problems that came up.

○ One or two evenings a week, attend business events or meetings with partners for discussion.

Which should you use? It all depends on your preferences and the specifics of each transaction. As a newbie, ask for advice from your customs broker.

Oops!

This is all terrific, you say, but what happens if somebody goofs? Surely, since life is full of surprises, someday something will go wrong with the letter of credit transaction. Well, you are right. So what do you do?

Panic! No, no—just kidding . . .

Smart Tip

Tip...

Ask your international banker for a copy of UPC 600, otherwise known as *ICC Uniform Customs and Practice for Documentary Credits*. Or order it from store.internationaltradebooks.org. Published by the International Chamber of Commerce, this must-read document sets forth the guidelines for all letter of credit transactions.

Keep your wits and call your bank. Your bank then contacts the importer and explains the problem, euphemistically called a discrepancy, such as, "The air carrier screwed up and delivered the merchandise 30 miles from where it should have landed." Or "Because of calving icebergs, the ship is still in the North Atlantic, 500 miles (and two days) from where it's supposed to be." The importer can then forgive these little transgressions and agree to pay you anyway. Or she can decide not to accept the whole shebang, and the letter of credit is immediately rendered null and void. Then all your carefully gathered documents get returned to you.

So what happens to your merchandise, the stuff that's sitting in the North Atlantic or on an airstrip in East Nowhere? If you can't come to an agreement and save the deal, you can have the merchandise put into a warehouse while you find a new buyer. You'll have to start all over again with a new letter of credit and new shipping documents, but you can still sell those goods to somebody else.

Is That All There Is?

So you're probably thinking, Is that it? One mistake and kaboom! All my work goes down the tube? Well, not necessarily. You can always ask the importer for an amendment to the letter of credit. After your bank contacts her bank, which then contacts her, she may agree to extend your deadline, which is great! Or she may agree to extend the deadline but penalize you by lowering the price, which is not so great. So keep in mind that you don't have to accept the amended L/C that comes down the pike to you.

Here's what you do if you don't like the amended letter of credit: Pop on down to your bank, hand over the darn L/C along with a letter stating that you are rejecting the thing, and have them give you a receipt. Then, send a letter to the importer telling her why you've rejected her amended L/C. Hopefully, she'll generate another amendment and you can get your deal back on track.

Tip...

Smart Tip

The best and brightest way to avoid the whole L/C discrepancy mess is to give yourself a little more time than you actually think you'll need when you quote time periods in your pro forma invoice. Build in a margin of safety.

Cash Is King

Although the letter of credit is the safest way to ensure payment (especially for newbies) and is a common method of payment, there are other ways to negotiate an international trade transaction. Here's a rapid-fire list of other ways and means:

- Cash in advance
- Open account
- On consignment
- Collection draft

Cash is always good, so you might think (and rightly so) that the first of this lot is the best. But the other methods have their good points, too. Let's go over each transaction in more detail.

Cash in Advance

The importer pays for the merchandise before it's even shipped. With this method, the buyer must implicitly trust the exporter to follow through on the deal. You might see it used in a strong seller's market when demand for a product is sky-high or for small deals where both parties agree that the cost in time and money isn't worth investing in a method such as a letter of credit.

As a variation on a theme, sometimes when a manufacturer needs a lot of upfront money, he may demand partial cash in advance, such as 25 percent, to offset his costs.

Open Account

The buyer has an account with the exporter. When she receives the merchandise, she sends payment to the seller. In essence, the exporter is offering credit to the buyer, and this can be risky. As with the cash in advance transaction, this type of account is used when the exporter feels comfortable with his buyer. However, where cash in advance puts all the risk on the importer, open account puts all the risk on the exporter's shoulders.

Another tack that's gaining popularity is to use an open account and buy credit insurance in case the deal sours. This payment method is cheaper than an L/C: $250 or so vs. the $1,000 to $1,500 for a letter of credit. To find out more about credit insurers, check out the website for the International Union of Credit and Investment Insurers at berneunion.org.uk. It is the leading international organization and community for the export credit and investment insurance industry with over 70 member companies spanning the globe.

On Consignment

The seller ships his merchandise without any sort of payment and doesn't get paid until the importer sells the goods in her own country. This system is by far the riskiest

On the Road

A trader isn't always at home behind his desk. What does he do when he's out on the road? Here's another behind-the-scenes peek, courtesy of Jan H., the Belgian tire trader:

Note that Jan's day, in typical European fashion, evolves through a 24-hour clock, or what we think of as military time. In this system, the hours of 1 in the morning to noon are expressed as 1:00 to 12:00. For every hour after noon, you add onto 12, so that 13:00 is 1 o'clock (12 + 1) and midnight is 24:00 (12 + 12).

Day in Belgium

07:00–09:00: Office work, email, fax offers, mail, etc.

09:00–12:00: Drive to airport, meet customer from Finland; back to warehouse, customer chooses products

12:00–13:00: Lunch with customer, general discussions

13:00–18:00: Visit with a customer from Nigeria; long discussion, haggling over prices, payment terms, etc.; supervise loading of containers bound for the United States; phone calls, fax, email; arrival of a customer from France, discussions

18:00: Quick trip home to change and shower

19:00–??: Pick up French customer at hotel, have cocktails, dinner, and more negotiations

Day on the Road in Germany

05:00: Leave home for 400-km drive

08:00: Arrive at first supplier; discussions and purchase of goods

10:00: Leave for next supplier

11:00: Next supplier; discussions without any result

12:00: Visit customer, make a sale

13:30: Visit another supplier; more discussions

15:00: Leave for another 300-odd km drive

18:00: Arrive at hotel; check email on laptop, phone calls

19:30: Sauna and swim at hotel pool

20:30: Dinner with supplier, then to bed!

Day in Miami

07:00: Swim in hotel pool; breakfast, phone calls, and faxes

08:30: A good friend, customer, and supplier, picks me up; go to his office, business discussions

13:00: Free afternoon; go to shopping mall and hotel pool; check email, make a few phone calls

19:00: Dinner and a show with friend

23:00: Bed

▲

Smart Tip

Tip...

Air waybills (bills of lading (bills of lading from air carriers) are never negotiable. (Think FedEx. Would it accept a package with nobody's name and no street address on it? Of course not.)

and is not advisable for any deal, because if the buyer can't liquidate the product, she'll return it without payment, thus sticking the exporter with both an Excedrin headache and unnecessary shipping costs.

Collection Draft

This transaction, also sometimes called a cash against documents transaction, is similar to the letter of credit in that the bank acts as the go-between for buyer and seller. In a collection draft transaction, the exporter ships the merchandise. His bank then sends the bill of lading and other specified shipping documents (which are necessary to collect the goods down at the dock) to the importer's bank, which keeps a tight grip on the documents until the importer coughs up the exporter's payment. Once this has been extracted, the bank releases the documents to the importer, sends the funds to the exporter, and everybody's happy. Bank charges for collection drafts run between $250 and $500.

A Date with a Draft

Now, lest you thought you were done with all this, there's more: To complete the collection draft, the exporter has to draw up the draft part of the deal, which is basically the buyer's order to pay. There are three types of drafts:

1. *Sight draft*. This requires payment before the importer can get her hands on the goods. The exporter retains title until they've reached their destination and are paid for. It's called a sight draft because as soon as the merchandise has arrived and is theoretically "in sight" of the dock, the draft is payable. The risk here is that the buyer may change her mind while the merchandise is somewhere out at sea and decide to forget the whole deal. Then it's the exporter's responsibility to pay return passage for his stuff.

2. *Time draft*. The exporter extends credit to the importer. She has a certain amount of time, say, 30, 60, or 90 days from the moment she picks up the merchandise and accepts the draft, to make payment.

Fun Fact

Lots of international banks have accounts at American banks. You can be paid your dollars that way or by wire transfer. Working in reverse, if you're the importer, you can have the exporter paid in his native currency, whether it's Mexican pesos or Polish zloty.

With some time drafts, payment is due within a specified number of days after "sight," or arrival of the goods. In this case, the draft is called a date draft.

3. *Clean draft.* The shipping documents are sent to the importer at the same time as the merchandise. This is basically the same as sending the goods on open account and is extremely rare. Again, it's used only when the exporter has extreme confidence in his customer.

Signing Off

Now that you've had a look at some of the forms and letters needed to satisfy clients, it's time to check into the demands of government entities. These are the topics of the next chapter.

6

Rituals and Red Tape

We've figured out how to ship your merchandise and how to get you paid once the goods arrive. Sort of. But what about all those documents we've been discussing? The ones you need to get signed off on the letter of credit or collection draft? Yeah, those! In this chapter we'll tackle the documentation needed to get the merchandise the rest of the way into the importer's hands. We'll also discuss what the importer, or the importer's representative, does with these documents to get the merchandise through Customs.

In Great Form

Before we dive too deeply into the topic of the various forms you'll need, let's talk briefly about where to get them. We have provided you with an arsenal of example forms in this book. But say you really don't want to deal with setting up and filling out your own forms for every single transaction. Hop online and check out the wealth of forms designed specifically for the import/export industry. A simple Google search for "Export

Smart Tip

Tip...

Try a shareware service, such as EZ Forms at ez-forms.com. About $200 will get you most of the necessary forms you need to keep rolling. Updates are available, and output comes in PDF form so you can scan, fax, email, etc. For an extra fee, EZ Forms will customize your forms and site license the shareware for use on multiple machines.

Standard Operating Procedure

As a trader, you should become familiar with the ISO 9000. It's quickly becoming a fact of life among international companies, as are the QS 9000 and the ISO 14000. So what are these entities?

They're quality management systems devised by the International Organization for Standardization (yes, we realize the acronym should be IOS!) in Geneva, Switzerland, and they're rapidly becoming a common product requirement, especially in European Union countries but also in the United States and other nations.

If the product you're representing has an ISO 9000 certification, it can hold its head up among its competitors. It's been manufactured with quality, customer service, and the well-being of its own work force well in hand.

A QS 9000 certification is the next step up (the "more mature version," according to The ISO 9000 Network, a commercial certification group) and relates specifically to the automotive industry, while the ISO 14000 focuses on management of the environment.

For more information, you can contact the ISO Central Secretariat at iso.org or check with the National Institute of Standards and Technology at nist.gov.

Forms" will spit out hundreds of options, everything from government agency example forms to shareware that you can purchase and manage yourself.

What's Up, Doc?

Most shipping records are known as collection documents and in some ways are exactly the same as cash. Why? Because once you present the documents to the bank, demonstrating that you've fulfilled the conditions of the L/C, the bank issues payment. Now, you can have your freight forwarder handle all the paperwork so that all you have to do is trot down to the bank with the completed documents in hand. However, as the exporter, you need to know how each link in the chain functions. You need to understand these documents when you're the importer, too, because either you or your customs broker will use them to claim your cargo once it arrives at the harbor, loading dock, or airport.

So here they are for your review, like big-name stars in a Hollywood movie, listed in alphabetical order:

- *Bill of Lading.* "Lading" means freight or cargo, so a bill of lading is basically a receipt from the cargo handler—the steamship, air, or truck line—showing that it's got your goods. To make things official, the document is signed by the captain (on a ship) or other agent of the transporter as binding evidence that the merchandise has been shipped. There are various permutations of the bill of lading, including:
  - *Clean or Clean on Board.* This does not mean clean as in sprayed-with-Lysol, but clean as in the transport company hasn't noted any irregularities in the packing or the condition of the goods. This is the standard bill of lading.
  - *Foul.* Not to be confused with the baseball term, a foul bill of lading is the opposite of the clean one. It indicates that the transport company has discovered, for example, something sticky leaking from those boxes marked "blood byproducts." If your bill of lading gets marked "foul," you'll want to exchange the bum container for a "clean" one and have the shipment relabeled before it's presented to the importer.
  - *On Board.* This one confirms only that the cargo has been placed on board the vessel and carries no other guidelines or stipulations. It's an elderly shipping term and isn't used much these days.
  - *On Deck.* This is relevant only if the goods, such as livestock, must be transported on the deck of the ship.
  - *Order.* A negotiable bill of lading that must be endorsed by the shipper before it's handed over to the bank for collection. An order bill of lading is

usually made out to the bank or customs broker, or it can be left blank—again, like a blank check.

- *Order Notify*. This is like the order bill, except that the consignee (the buyer) and sometimes the customs broker must be notified when the ship reaches port. This is particularly nice if you're the importer because the shipper will notify you in advance when the vessel will arrive.

- *Straight*. This one is non-negotiable, like a check with the name of the payee filled in. It spells out to whom the merchandise is consigned. Because it prohibits release of the goods to anyone but the person specified on the documents and thus offers the most protection, the straight bill of lading is usually preferred by newbie importers.

- *Through Bill of Lading*. This is the "pass it on down" bill used when several carriers are involved if, for example, the merchandise needs to go by rail or truck to the port and then by ocean, or vice versa.

- *Certificate of Manufacture*. Used when the buyer pays for the goods before shipment, this document verifies that the merchandise has really been manufactured and really does fulfill the general product requirements (see page 112). In other words, it's proof that the goods are on hand and ready for shipment.

- *Certificate of Origin*. Some countries require a separate certificate of origin (see pages 114–115), even though this information is provided on the commercial invoice. The certificate is especially important when you're importing goods that require regulatory approval, such as medical equipment or food. Our own Food and Drug Administration, for example, requires a certificate of origin for every imported product. Some countries will count a piece of paper with your signature below the statement "I certify that these goods were manufactured in the United States of America" as acceptable. Others want the statement notarized, on a form from your local chamber of commerce or on a special form for that particular nation.

- *Commercial Invoice*. The commercial invoice is the same as any invoice used by a domestic company and is essentially a finished version of the pro forma invoice. You can make up your own commercial invoice on your trusty desktop computer or buy preprinted blank forms with carbon copies at an office supply store. When you fill in those blanks, you'll want to be sure you've added the same particulars you have on your pro forma invoice and the L/C number, if you're using an L/C. Plus, you'll need to add the terms of the

Smart Tip

You can purchase a number of these forms through Unz & Co. at unzco.com.

sale (i.e., FOB or DDP) and—important!—a statement certifying the goods were manufactured in the United States, followed by your signature. This will help skate the merchandise through customs. Check out the sample commercial invoice on page 116 to get an idea of what yours should look like.

Beware!
Some countries require more information on shipping documents than others. Be sure to check with your customs broker to make sure the form you're using covers everything.

- *Consular Invoice.* Not every country will demand one of these—the ranks are mostly filled by emerging nation types. Basically, a consular invoice is one for which you fill out a form available from the local consulate office here in the States, pay a nominal sum, and go on your merry way. The presumed idea behind the invoice is to ensure that overpriced or underpriced goods don't enter the country, but in actuality it's a sort of collection plate for the national economy.

- *Dock Receipts.* This receipt is used if the importer is responsible for shipment from a U.S. port. It verifies that the merchandise has indeed made it as far as the dock.

- *Inspection Certificate.* The importer may request one of these to certify the quantity, quality, and/or conformity of the product. Say, for example, that you are bringing in cookie-making equipment from whatever country the Keebler elves live in. You may want to have an inspector check the machines to make sure

Build a Better Bomb

Although you don't need a license to export most merchandise, you'll need a validated export license to ship goods that the U.S. government wants to control, such as articles of war, advanced technology, and products in short supply. Obtaining a validated license can be time-consuming, costly, and, in some cases, impossible. If you're an export novice, you should probably leave exporting sensitive materials to somebody else, but if you simply must send sensitive materials, be sure to contact the Department of Commerce first. It can tell you if your potential export is on the Commerce Control List (CCL), which means it needs a validated license.

they're in good working order before you take title. You can elect a standard export inspection, which is done by a (surprise!) standard inspector nominated by the exporter or shipping line, or you can hire a specialized private company to do the job.

- *Insurance Certificate.* This confirms that marine insurance has been provided for the cargo and indicates the type and coverage. We'll cover insurance in greater detail in Chapter 9.

- *Packing List.* The packing list or packing slip is a sort of shopping list of the merchandise in the shipment, along with

Beware!

Do you need to submit an SED, or shipper's export declaration, for shipments to and from U.S. territories and possessions? The answer depends on where you're shipping to and from. Check with your freight forwarder or customs broker, or call the Foreign Trade Division Regulations people at the Census Bureau at (800) 923-8282.

information on how it was packed, how the various items are numbered, and the serial numbers, if applicable, and weight and dimensions of each item. The packing list is an important ingredient in the letter of credit because it (again) verifies the shipped goods and shows to whom they're consigned.

Sample Certificate of Manufacture

From: Coffee Holic Exports
123 Cafe Street
Berry, FL 30000, USA

To: Cappuccino Imports
456 Via Espresso
Ostia Antica, Italy

Date: July 15, 20xx

Opening Bank: Banco della Roma

L/C or Other Reference No.: 0123

Merchandise: 5,000 Coffee Go-Cups, Style A

We hereby certify that the above-described merchandise has been manufactured as of <u>July 30, 20xx,</u> and is available for shipment as of <u>August 1, 20xx</u>.

By: *Charlie Holic, Owner*

              (signature and title)

Certificate of Manufacture

From: _____

_____

_____

To: _____

_____

_____

Date: _____

Opening Bank: _____

L/C or Other Reference No.: _____

Merchandise: _____

We hereby certify that the above-described merchandise has been manufactured as of _____, and is available for shipment as of _____.

By: _____

(signature and title)

- *Shipper's Export Declaration (SED).* This one is required by the U.S. government on all exports in excess of $2,500 or ones that require an export license. The reason behind it is to give the folks down at the Census Bureau fodder for their statistics (which you, for one, will probably want to take advantage of during your market research phase), and it gives all the usual information, including product descriptions, value, net and gross weight, and license information.

The Importer at Work

OK, importer. You've found the merchandise you want to buy and then resell. So now what?

Here is the typical import path:

1. Receive pro forma invoice, the exporter's quote on the merchandise; negotiate if necessary.
2. Open a letter of credit at your bank.

Sample Certificate of Origin

I, __Charlie Holic__ , __Owner__ of __Coffee Holic Exports__ , declare that the
 (name of person)   (title)   (name of company)

goods described herein are the product of the United States of America.

Marks & Numbers	No. Containers	Gross Weight or Quantity	Description
As Addressed 1 thru 50	50	5,000 pieces	Coffee Go-Cups

Certified by: ___*Charlie Holic*___ Date: *July 10, 20xx*
        (signature of person named above)

This space for notary, if required:

The __Berry__ Chamber of Commerce, a recognized chamber of commerce under the laws of the state of __Florida__ , has examined the manufacturer's invoice or shipper's affidavit on the above-described goods and, to its best belief, certifies that the merchandise originated in the United States of America.

By: ___*Shelby Anne Bean, President*___
        (signature and title)

Certificate of Origin

I, _____ , _____ of _____ , declare that the
  (name of person)   (title)   (name of company)
goods described herein are the product of the United States of America.

Marks & Numbers	No. Containers	Gross Weight or Quantity	Description

Certified by: _____ Date: _____
                  (signature of person named above)

This space for notary, if required:

The _____ Chamber of Commerce, a recognized chamber of commerce under the laws of the state of _____ , has examined the manufacturer's invoice or shipper's affidavit on the above-described goods and, to its best belief, certifies that the merchandise originated in the United States of America.

By: _____
              (signature and title)

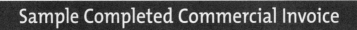

Sample Completed Commercial Invoice

Date: July 15, 20xx

From: Coffee Holic Exports
                   123 Cafe Street
                   Berry, FL 30000, USA

To: Cappuccino Imports
                   456 Via Espresso
                   Ostia Antica, Italy

Merchandise Ordered: 5,000 Coffee Go-Cups, Style A

On Order or L/C No.: L/C 0123

Shipping Terms: CIF Rome

Price: USD 16,000

We hereby certify that these goods were manufactured in the United States of America and that this is a valid, true and correct invoice.

By: *Charlie Holic*   Owner
              (signature)   (title)

Commercial Invoice

Date: _____

From: _____

_____

_____

To: _____

_____

_____

Merchandise Ordered: _____

On Order or L/C No.: _____

Shipping Terms: _____

Price: _____

We hereby certify that these goods were manufactured in the United States of America and that this is a valid, true and correct invoice.

By: _____
       (signature)   (title)

Sample Packing List

From: Coffee Holic Exports
             123 Cafe Street
             Berry, FL 30000, USA

To: Cappuccino Imports
             456 Via Espresso
             Ostia Antica, Italy

Date: July 15, 20xx

Per your order No. ___L/C 0123___ , the following merchandise has been shipped to __Rome__ , departing _August 3, 20xx_ , by _ship_ .

Item No.	Quantity Ordered	Quantity Shipped	Description
Style A	5,000	5,000	Insulated Plastic Coffee Go-Cups

No. containers & type: _____50 cardboard boxes_____
Weight per container: _____4 kilos_____
Dimensions of each container: _3.5 x 3.5 x 3.5 meters_
Containers numbered: _1/50_
Marks: _Cappuccino Imports_
      Ostia Antica, Italy
      Boxes 1/50

Packing List

From: _____
_____
_____

To: _____
_____
_____

Date: _____

Per your order No. _____ , the following merchandise has been shipped to _____ , departing _____ , by _____ .

Item No.	Quantity Ordered	Quantity Shipped	Description

No. containers & type: _____
Weight per container: _____
Dimensions of each container: _____
Containers numbered: _____
Marks: _____
_____
_____

3. Receive confirmation of the deal and also a schedule for loading and arrival of the goods.

4. File an electronic Importers Security Filing (ISF) form *by 24 hours prior to merchandise loading at the point of origin.*

5. Verify that the merchandise has indeed been shipped.

6. Receive documents from the exporter.

7. See merchandise through customs.

8. Pass Go. Collect your merchandise and give yourself a pat on the back!

We've already covered the pro forma invoice, the request to open a letter of credit (L/C), and the L/C itself in Chapter 5. Now let's tackle the rest.

Adding 10+2

On January 26, 2010, full enforcement of the new maritime shipping regulations from Customs and Border Protection (CBP) took effect. Before going into the details, let us first say that these regulations affect only *nonbulk* goods arriving *by sea to a U.S. port.* If your merchandise is flown into the U.S. or shipped to Mexico or Canada and then trucked or railed into the U.S., it (and you) are exempt from these requirements. Bulk cargo (grain, coal, oil) is also exempt.

The official name of the new procedure is Importers Security Filing and Additional Carrier Requirements (ISF). The American Association of Exporters and Importers (AAEI) calls the measure "one of the biggest regulatory changes to occur since 9/11."

Customs instituted the ISF for security purposes, to keep ocean containers safe. The goal of the measure is to ensure supply chain security back to the point of stuffing (i.e., packing) of the shipping container. The information provided on the ISF form is used only for security purposes. It is not a substitute for the entry documents.

The Importers Security Filing and Additional Carrier Requirements is familiarly known as "ISF 10+2," because importers are required to electronically file 10 (actually, 11, but we'll get to that later) data points about the contents of shipping containers, and carriers (i.e., shipping companies) are required to file an additional two pieces of data. Even though you're not responsible for these last two, we'll cover them in the next section.

So what are these data points? They include the following:

1. *Seller's name and address.* This refers to the exporter, as listed on the commercial invoice.

2. *Buyer's name and address.* This is the importer from the commercial invoice.

3. *Importer of record number/foreign trade zone applicant identification number.* This is the importer's IRS, EIN, Social security, or importer's ID number. If you're

having the goods stashed in a foreign trade zone (FTZ), you also must provide an appropriate number.

4. *Consignee number(s).* The IRS (or other, see above) number of the individual in the United States on whose account the cargo is shipped. This number will often be the same as #3.

5. *Manufacturer (supplier) name and address.* This one's self-explanatory.

6. *Ship-to name and address.* This is the information for the person who will physically receive the goods.

7. *Country of Origin code.* This is the code for the country of manufacture, growth, etc., of the goods, as used by U.S. Customs.

8. *Commodity Harmonized Tariff Schedule (HTS) number—first six digits.* This is the classification number of the goods. Because of the ISF requirement, goods must now be pre-classified instead of simply being classified upon arrival at Customs. Because classification is still part of the entry process, however, we'll discuss it later in the Entry section of this chapter.

All eight of these data points must be electronically submitted via the Automated Manifest System (AMS) or the Automated Broker Interface (ABI) no later than 24 hours prior to loading of the goods at the foreign port. This means that the importer must stay "up to speed" on when the goods are to be loaded and when they are scheduled to arrive in the United States.

Two additional data points that make up the "10" must be submitted in the same way by no later than 24 hours before the goods arrive in the United States. These are the following points:

9. *Container stuffing location.* This is the location where the goods were put into the containers. Since this can sometimes change at the last minute, Customs gives importers more time to file this information.

10. *Consolidator's name and address.* This is the information about the individual who stuffs the container. It, too, can often not be determined much in advance, hence the extra time.

One last data point (Remember we said there are actually 11?) is not a new data point. It's also not as crucial as the rest. Therefore, it's not usually discussed as part of the "10+2" regulation. Nevertheless, if you don't have this data point, its absence will delay the processing of your INS form and probably the release of your goods. So here it is:

11. *Master bill of lading (B/L) number.* We discussed the bill of lading at the beginning of the chapter.

Let us point out one more time that you must file these data points well in advance of the goods' arrival in the United States. In fact, the first eight must be filed no later than 24 hours before loading of the goods. (Yes, we've said this several times now, but it's really important.) Cargo shipments lacking filed ISF information will not be loaded. (See why it's important?)

Sometimes changes to the data occur in transit. For example, if the ship-to party changes or the cargo containers ended up being stuffed somewhere other than where you indicated, you must update your filing with these changes before the goods arrive in the United States.

Beware!
If you fail to submit an ISF and your cargo is inadvertently loaded anyway, it's likely to be off-loaded at another port of call before reaching the United States. This will create a logistical problem—and considerable expense—for you.

Besides completing the ISF filing, importers (or their representatives) are required to post bond. This bond assures Customs that the ISF will prove to be timely, accurate, and complete—in other words, not a headache or time-sink for Customs.

Note that noncompliance with the ISF filing requirement results in fines, usually 20 percent of the dutiable value of the goods.

And just for clarity's sake, we'll say one more time that the ISF 10+2 electronic filing requirement applies only to nonbulk goods arriving by sea to a U.S. port.

If your head's spinning right about now, or you're worried about completing your ISF filing successfully, take heart. You can have a representative do it for you. Also, a quick Google of "ISF 10+2" will produce links for any number of logistics and regulatory compliance companies who will handle the filing for you.

We also note here that the ISF 10+2 regulation actually took effect in January 2009, but was not put into full enforcement until January 26, 2010. During that year, Customs gave importers and carriers some flexibility while everyone adjusted to the new regulations. Customs has indicated that it will monitor the first year of full enforcement and perhaps make further adjustments.

Open Seas

While the goods are in transit, the shipping company is responsible for completing the "+2" part of the equation, a.k.a. the Additional Carrier Requirements. These two submitted data points are the following:

1. *Vessel stow plan*. This indicates how the container is stowed on board.
2. *Container status*. This is a confirmation that the container remains secure.

Both data points must be submitted no later than 48 hours after departure.

You've Arrived

When the goods arrive, the importer takes over. The first task is to shepherd the new arrivals through customs.

So how is this done? Usually through a customs broker. In fact, unless you have an import license (for which you have to take a government-administered test), you typically can't take your own merchandise through customs.

Still, it's important for you to know how your merchandise gets imported. The more you know, the better you'll be able to help your customs broker—and yourself. There are four basic steps to taking your goods through customs:

1. *Entry.* Deciding where and how you'll enter your merchandise
2. *Examination and valuation.* Determining the legality and tariff or duty value of your goods
3. *Classification.* Determining the percentage of tax that will be charged on the value of your merchandise
4. *Payment and liquidation.* Coughing up the cash to pay the tariff or duties

But let's take this one item at a time.

Entry

There are eight main types of import entry into the United States. They are the following:

1. *Consumption entry.* Merchandise to be offered for sale
2. *Formal entry.* Goods worth more than $2,000
3. *Informal entry.* Goods worth $2,000 or less
4. *In-transit entry.* Goods moving from the port of unloading to the port of destination
5. *Mail entry.* Items sent by another country's mail system
6. *Personal baggage entry.* Goods arriving in a passenger's suitcase
7. *Transportation and exportation entry.* Goods arriving at a nondestination country's port and passing through to the destination country
8. *Warehouse entry.* Goods sent to a bonded warehouse or a foreign trade zone

While it's good to know about these entry types, the most common distinction made is between informal and formal entry, involving the value of the goods. Some informal entries can be made without use of a customs broker, if the merchandise is imported by an individual for personal use or sale in the individual's shop, *and* if said merchandise is worth $2,000 or less. Merchandise imported by a trader, no matter how small its value, must be handled by a customs broker.

Because this book is all about the business of being an international trader, we're going to go with the formal entry version of the customs game. This means you'll need a customs broker to handle the entry for you.

> **Tip...**
>
> ## Smart Tip
>
> In the event of a change in the party receiving the goods, a negotiable bill of lading or document can be used to claim title to the merchandise; a non-negotiable one cannot.

Special Operations

There are a few circumstances that don't fit the usual import scenarios. For example, what do you do if you want to travel abroad with your sales samples so you can show them to prospective buyers?

You could go through the whole complicated import process in each country. Or you can take your samples on the Grand Tour duty-free with an ATA carnet. ATA is an acronym for the combined French and English "Admission Temporaire/ Temporary Admission." It means exactly what it says, in whichever language you choose. The carnet, a sort of passport for merchandise, is an international customs document that gets the goods into certain countries without any duties paid until they're returned to home port.

A carnet is

- valid for one year,
- good for as many international stops as you care to make with it during that year, and
- used not only for commercial samples but advertising materials and professional equipment as well.

Currently over 69 countries and territories recognize the ATA carnet, including most European countries, Canada, India, China, Korea, Taiwan, Singapore, and South Africa. Visit atacarnet.com for a complete list.

Another possible scenario involves bringing items into the United States temporarily for purposes including (but not limited to) sample, display, emergency use, competition, breeding (e.g., animals), or exhibition. So if you need to import vehicles for a race, animals for competition or breeding, fine art or theatrical materials for show, merchandise samples for pre-selling, or a host of other possibilities, you can bring them into the country duty-free with a Temporary Importation Under Bond (TIB). With a TIB, you post a bond for double the estimated duty amount, thus assuring the customs people that you'll cover the import fees should you fail to return the samples to their country of origin within one year. This period may, with the grace of the district or port director, be extended for up to three years.

Customs Limbo

According to U.S. Customs, goods brought into the country are in a sort of import limbo—not considered legally entered—until after the following actions have been taken:

- Shipment has arrived within the port of entry.
- Delivery of merchandise has been authorized.
- Customs duty has been paid.

When your merchandise arrives at the U.S. port of entry (the dock, airport, or border), the carrier submits the bill of lading or air waybill to the on-site customs office. This document is now known as evidence of right to make entry.

The shipper notifies your customs broker—and the clock starts ticking. Your broker has 15 days to provide the necessary documents to get your goods out of hock. You and your broker will probably already have a fair idea of when your merchandise is due to arrive because the exporter will have notified you of its ETA and the vessel it's coming in on.

Released from Custody

Next up is entering your merchandise. The most common type of entry is called entry for consumption. This, of course, is consumption as in "to be consumed" (i.e., used or sold), and the customs people have handily broken down this stage of the process into two parts:

1. filing the documents necessary to determine whether merchandise may be released from customs custody; and

2. filing the documents that contain information for assessing duty and for statistical purposes.

Beware!

If you don't file for entry of your merchandise within 15 days, Customs considers it abandoned and puts it into a bonded warehouse of its own under general order, otherwise known as G.O. After a six-month holding period, G.O. goods are sold at public auction unless they're perishable or explosive, in which case they get dealt with a lot sooner.

Here's a list of the entry documents your customs broker will need:

- Entry manifest (also known as Customs Form 7533) or Application and Special Permit for Immediate Delivery (aka Customs Form 3461)
- Bill of lading or air waybill (also known as the evidence of right to make entry)
- Commercial invoice or pro forma invoice if the commercial one can't be produced
- Packing lists
- Certificate of origin, if necessary
- Customs bond (which is posted by your broker and assures customs that it will get the duties, taxes, and any penalties out of you one way or another)

You can see why it's so important to do your homework and make sure the exporter sends you copies of all documents ASAP.

Out on Bail

After customs has gone through all these documents, accepted the bond, and decided that everything's legal and up to snuff, the merchandise is released. Sort of. You could say it's out on bail, pending the last two phases of the customs game.

The first of these is the entry summary documentation. Now your broker has ten days to deposit the estimated duties and file the necessary documentation, namely:

- Entry summary (also known as Customs Form 7501)
- Any other invoices and documents necessary for the assessment of duties, collection of statistics, or other determination that you've met import requirements

Stat Fact
According to its website, the U.S. Customs and Border Protection (CBP) collects over $30 billion in import tariffs annually, making it the second highest revenue generator for the U.S. government. The Internal Revenue Service (IRS) ranks first.

Hold on to Your Hats

Now, let's back up a little. Just because your merchandise has arrived at the port of entry, you don't have to rush home with it right away. In fact, you don't even have to enter it immediately. You can choose instead to stash it in a bonded warehouse or transport it to a foreign trade zone.

A bonded warehouse is a yard, shed, storage area, or (surprise!) warehouse within customs territory where you can store your imported merchandise for up to five years without paying duty. While your goodies are in the bonded warehouse, you can clean, sort, and repack them, but that's it. You can't assemble them or attach them to something else and create a new product in the process. It's called a bonded facility because the owner has to post a bond with customs.

A foreign trade zone, or FTZ, is a sort of customs limbo in which you can store and also process your imported goods without having to pay duties or jump through the usual customs hoops. Although it sounds like it might be a chunk of foreign land floating somewhere above the surface of American soil, an FTZ is much more prosaic. It's usually a large warehouse located near a port of entry, say in an industrial park or on the docks, with rental

> **Tip...**
>
> **Smart Tip**
>
> In special cases, such as with perishable items, Customs will issue a permit for immediate release of goods. (Customs isn't stupid; it doesn't particularly want 500 kilos of fish sitting on its dock for five days or more.) You can't make up your mind at the last minute, however; you must apply for the permit before your merchandise has arrived.

spaces available for importers. And unlike the bonded warehouse, the FTZ allows you the freedom to assemble or manufacture your goodies into any other product you choose. So what's the catch? Believe it or not, there isn't one. Local governments set up FTZs to promote international trade, which, in turn, stimulates economic growth. As mentioned in Chapter 3, Qualified Industrial Zones, such as the one between Israel and Egypt and another between Israel and Jordan, are one type of foreign trade zone.

What the FTZ means to you is savings. If you plan to export the merchandise immediately and you're only holding it in the United States for a short time, you get away with not having to pay customs duties. If you're going to enter the products into the country, you can alter or modify them to lower the import costs. For example, you might bring in fancy sequined fabric squares from Thailand and sew them onto American-made cushions to create decorator throw pillows. When you're ready to bring them out of the foreign trade zone, you pay duties on the throw pillows. If duties on throw pillows are cheaper than those on the sequined fabric squares, the FTZ saves you money.

Another FTZ bonus is that you can duck around the import quota issue. If U.S. Customs allows only so many straw hats, for example, per year and that quota has already been filled, you might hold onto your hats in your FTZ space until the next quota period rolls around.

You would probably use the bonded warehouse when planning a quick in-and-out entry for your merchandise, while you'd use the FTZ when you need to manipulate your products as we've explored. As always, the best way to choose which to use is to consult your customs broker or freight forwarder.

We are not the only country with foreign trade zones. Every country uses a different term, but the idea is the same. As an exporter, you can use these zones to receive goods that will be reshipped in smaller lots to customers in the region.

Earlier in this chapter we mentioned eight main types of Customs entry. It's worth saying a little more here about the three you're most likely to deal with. These are:

1. *Consumption entry.* You already know this one, used when the merchandise is intended for immediate resale. This type is the most common.

2. *In-transit entry.* This is used when you want the goods whisked to another location within the United States for customs clearance. For instance, you may have arranged to have them brought in by ship to New York, but you want to store—and assemble—them in an FTZ in Ohio.

> **Fun Fact**
> Customs' Canine Enforcement Program routinely sniffs out narcotics tucked into legitimate cargo shipments. You can see the dog of the month, among others, at cbp.gov. The dogs are also featured on collectible cards. Each lists the port of entry worked, age, breed, weight, year started in customs, and largest or most notable seizure.

3. *Warehouse entry.* This is sort of a layaway plan. You leave your imported goods in a customs-bonded warehouse and withdraw them in portions. Each time you make a withdrawal, you pay duty on that part.

Examination and Valuation

After you've decided to enter your merchandise, customs personnel will inspect your shipment to make sure it can legally enter the country and to determine its tariff or duty value. Why do they want to dip into your goods? They're checking to verify the following:

- The merchandise is marked with the country of origin.
- Any required markings or labelings are clearly displayed.
- The merchandise is correctly invoiced.
- The merchandise quantity matches the quantity on the invoice.
- The shipment contains no prohibited articles.
- The shipment contains no illegal drugs.

They're also checking the dutiable status and value of your goods. The value is the price you've actually paid for the merchandise, plus any added amounts, if not included in the price. These added amounts include the following:

▲

Last Person in America

U.S. Customs insists that each item imported into the country be marked or labeled with the country of origin. This marking must be done so that it's readily visible to the ultimate end user, "the last person in the United States," as the customs people word it, "who will receive the article in the form in which it was imported."

In other words, if you're importing ceramic pigs from the Emerald Isle, each little porker must be stamped or labeled "Made in Ireland" on its underside, so that the last person in the United States can tip over the little chap and read where he came from. You can't settle for a "Made in Ireland" marking on the box in which a dozen pigs are shipped, because the ultimate consumer will probably only be buying one piglet at a time.

There are, of course, exceptions to this rule, and they're rather eclectic, ranging from playing cards to rags to wood shingles (except red cedar ones) to hairnets to certain types of fishhooks to cut flowers to Christmas trees. Because you can't know and probably could never guess the extent of all these exceptions, it's best to check with your customs broker while you're still in the final negotiations stage with the exporter. You don't want someone shipping you 1,000 bales of barbed wire you can't use because it's unmarked; nor do you want to pay extra for the marking of 5,000 ceramic bricks from Mexico when it's unnecessary.

- Packing costs incurred by the importer
- The value of any assists (An assist can be a tool, die, mold, engineering drawing, or artwork, that is, something that assists in the assembly and sale of the product.)
- Any selling commission incurred by the importer
- A royalty or license fee required from the importer as part of the sale
- The proceeds accruing to the exporter of any subsequent resale, disposal, or use of the imported goods

You can see why it's important to make sure everything is listed on the commercial invoice!

Bright Idea

You can find Harmonized Tariff Schedule (HTS) numbers online via the only free HTS lookup tool. Check it out at findhts.com.

Classification

The Customs Service classifies goods according to tariff schedules. Different types of goods are assigned different percentages on which they're taxed. The amount of duty varies dramatically depending on exactly what the products are and what specifically they're made of. Cotton knit shirts, for example, may be taxed at 17 percent, while woven (nonknit) cotton shirts might be taxed at only 8 percent. During the classification step, the customs people will decide exactly which category your merchandise falls into.

Their decision is based on an extremely complicated set of rules called the Harmonized Tariff Schedule of the United States. The word "harmonized" refers to the fact that it harmonizes with, or matches, the tariff schedules of the rest of the industrialized world. The harmonized schedule comes in a book big enough to serve as a booster chair for a hefty three-year-old and is jam-packed with enough classifications, subclassifications, and sub-subclassifications to satisfy even the most nit-picking person on earth.

Cotton fabric, for example, is classified by whether it's bleached or unbleached, printed, composed of yarns of different color or dyed, whether it's pure cotton or a mix of fibers, the number of single threads per square centimeter, yarn sizes in the warp, whether the fabric is or is not napped, etc. Even fish livers must be classified by how much oil, fat, or grease they contain. Now you see why you need a customs broker!

As mentioned in the "Adding 10+2" section of this chapter, if your goods are nonbulk items and are arriving in the United States by sea, new regulations now demand the preclassification of the goods before they're even loaded onto the ocean carrier. Any classification disagreement that might arise is handled at entry.

If, however, your goods are not arriving by sea or if they are bulk items like grain or oil, classification will be handled at entry. Note that the broker, while versed in the harmonized system and armed with the basic HTS number for your merchandise, is not the one who hands down the final classification decision. This falls

Beware!

Don't wait for a last-minute shocker when you learn the import tariff. Make sure you've checked with your customs broker for an idea of what the HTS number for your products will be before you bring them into the country. Also, don't leave it to Customs to decide this number; there's a fee for that!

to the customs officer. Teams of customs inspectors rove each port of entry, with various inspectors specializing in different types of goods.

Payment and Liquidation

Now that your merchandise has been classified, it's on to the exciting phase of paying the piper, or in this case, the customs person. As with many assignments under government aegis, this is not always a simple, cut-and-dried operation.

It can be, of course. Your entry summary and documentation can be accepted as submitted without any changes. In this case, you simply hand over a check for the amount of duty, or tariff, owed, and your merchandise or entry is entered as liquidated. This means, in essence, done, over, finished, complete. You and customs have figuratively shaken hands and closed the books.

In other cases, however, customs may send you notification that the classification is not correct and cannot be liquidated as entered after all. If the revised classification results in a tariff change in your favor, they'll send you a refund. Like their compatriot, the IRS, however, they can also decide on a change in their own favor, in which case you need to send them money.

If you don't agree with the change, you have 90 days to file a protest, which then goes on to review or, in some cases, to court. The entry is not considered liquidated until the final ruling.

A Happy Ending

Nothing makes customs inspectors happier than a shipment they can go through easily. (And trust us: When Customs is happy, you're happy . . .) So suggest that your exporter follow these Customs tips:

- Invoice merchandise in a systematic manner.
- Show the exact quantity of goods in each box, bale, case, or other package.
- Number each package (e.g., box three of four).
- Put these numbers on the invoice next to the itemized goods in each package.

Once you have your happy ending, with your goods safely in your possession, you can get to the fun part: selling! Provided, of course, you know who you're selling to. The next chapter covers this topic, among others.

Charting Your Trade Route
Market Research

In order to live long and prosper, as the Vulcans so eloquently put it, every business needs consumers for its products and services. Now that you know what running an import/export business entails, you need to plan, or target, your market and determine who your potential clients will be, which

▲

Bright Idea

Trade shows, art festivals, crafts shows, and even small shops are all good venues for spotting the perfect international trade product.

geographic areas you'll draw from, and what specific products or services you'll offer to draw them in.

This is a very important phase in the mega-trader building project. The proper market research can help boost your trading company into a true profit center, and the more research you do and the better prepared you are before you officially open your doors, the less floundering you're likely to do.

This chapter, therefore, hones in on market research tips and techniques for the newbie importer/exporter. Here's a rapid-fire overview of your market research tasks. You'll want to do some in-depth investigation into each of the following areas:

- The product or service you'll sell
- The end user you'll aim for (mass-market consumer, heavy industry, light industry, medical or hospital use, government, business, or professional)
- The country or countries you'll export to or import from
- The trade channel you'll use (direct sales, representative, distributor, or commission representative)

Manufacturer or Artisan?

Your target market, the customers you are aiming for, can encompass any product or service you can think up. Any manufacturer, supplier, importer, exporter, artisan, crafter, or retailer is fair game. You can go after companies that deal in heavy construction equipment or delicate jewelry, gourmet goodies or pet food, telecommunications or toys. The only essential requirement is that they want to sell their merchandise or buy someone else's.

Targeting by definition means homing in on a specific group.

If you have previous experience in a particular field, for example, you should seriously consider targeting that market first. You'll feel comfortable with the jargon and procedures, so your sales pitch—and your initial sales—will go more smoothly and easily. As an added bonus, you may already have contacts in the

Trader's View

Follow the lead of John Laurino in Brazil. Skip areas you just don't know. "We are able to provide good assistance in several fields except machinery and commodities of high volume, such as soy, oil, and sugar," John explains. "Both fields require very special knowledge and a big infrastructure."

field who can either become your first clients or steer you toward colleagues in that area.

Wahib Wahba began in a field he knew well: runway and navigational lights. Then he went on to other international construction projects. His company exports railroad and telephone pole materials and construction services, as well as other heavy equipment materials.

Smart Tip

Tip...

Need information about a specific country? Get connected with every national embassy in Washington, DC, through The Electronic Embassy at embassy.org. You can also get country-by-country statistics and and other information through The World Bank at data.worldbank.org.

Where In the World?

Besides deciding what products you'll specialize in, you want to think about what countries you'll work with. Some traders start off with a part of the world they already know; others let their products be their guide to far corners of the globe.

Wahib Wahba, raised in Egypt, found exporting to Egypt a natural. North Carolina exporter Sam Nelson began his trade with Africa, where he has contacts. He now also exports to the Middle East and Europe, among other places. In Brazil, John Laurino works mostly with Brazilian companies locating and developing international business opportunities. Searching for leads for these clients takes him around the globe. "I have business relations with the entire world," John explains, "except . . . places very poor in foreign trade."

In Germany, Michael R. counts only one area of the world where he hasn't done business. "[I have dealt] with all internationally interesting markets worldwide," he says, "except South America, as I don't speak Spanish."

What's My Niche?

OK. You've narrowed the list of products you'll target. Now you'll want to find your niche, the unique angle that will set your business apart from—and above—the competition. This is where you can really let your creativity shine through.

Sources for finding import/export customers are abundant, says Wahib Wahba. But as an international trader, the trick lies not merely in what information you can find but in what you do with it. "Where do you want to be?" Wahib asks. "Which country do you want to go with? This is what you're targeting."

"I have to start from me," the construction projects exporter continues, "from what I can offer, what I can sell, or what I can do to make a profit. That's my niche."

As examples, Wahib offers slices of his own company's life: "I act sometimes as a buyer for a government, like a purchasing agent. Some companies want us to go and solicit projects for their product. So now we know there's a certain product we want to go and sell. Or we have a government in Egypt that wants telephone poles. I have the specifications, and I have to go solicit the manufacturer to make them for me. In that case, I can act as a prime or general contractor, and the American company will be the subcontractor. They sell to me, and I sell to the foreign government."

You may decide to start as an export management company (EMC, remember?), seeking out buyers for domestic manufacturing firms, or as an export trading company (ETC), finding domestic sources willing to export. Or you might want to stick with the original, more typical formula, importing and exporting on your own as an import/export merchant.

In Florida, Lloyd Davidson positioned his company as both an EMC and ETC, depending on his clients' needs. "[As an EMC, we] work directly for a manufacturer, or his exclusive distributor/manager for international sales, as a marketing and screening provider," Lloyd explains, "and will search for and locate overseas buyers-for-resale and/or qualified distributors/sales representatives. [Our] objective is to function as an extension of [our] principal's in-house export sales efforts."

Under its ETC hat, Lloyd says, "[my company] performs in a fashion similar to that previously described, except for a diminished principal relationship, and business is typically conducted on a case-by-case or ad hoc basis. It is more a sourcing function for the buyer and the seller."

John Laurino in Brazil also has structured his business from the viewpoint of assisting clients rather than selling products. "My company," John explains, "is an international business services provider. We assist companies in locating and developing worldwide business opportunities."

In Germany, Michael Richter describes his company's role this way: "[We are] a worldwide consultancy to SMEs [small- and medium-sized enterprises] that wish to increase their sales and profits by using the available world markets more successfully."

In France, Bruno Carlier works with a broad range of merchandise. "We export a wide range of products, from protection and security products to computing products," Bruno says. "We also export products such as plastic films and bags and some ferrous and aluminum products."

Sam Nelson in North Carolina sells medical equipment manufactured in either the United States or China to companies in both developing nations and highly industrialized countries. "We trade all over," he says.

These strategies are all excellent examples of finding a unique angle, that special niche. You might want to formulate your business as an EMC for a particular type of merchandise or for a particular country.

Another good strategy might be to consider worldwide social movements that appear to be gaining momentum and could provide good trading opportunities. Any number of such movements could occur in the future. At present, we identify two: sustainable growth and fair trade. We discuss these in the next few sections.

"Secondhand Rose"

"Reduce, Reuse, Recycle" is a popular slogan. It's not a bad idea for trading, either, especially if you want to export to countries less wealthy than the typical highly industrialized nations.

In Belgium, Jan Herremans has focused his company on specific products, specializing in the worldwide import and export of new and used tires, secondhand vehicles and machinery, and—as in the Barbara Streisand hit "Secondhand Rose"—secondhand clothing.

Secondhand items are a good example of the "reuse" philosophy. If you're considering exporting secondhand items, give the emerging market countries discussed in Chapter 3 a closer look. Many of these are good candidates for the following secondhand items:

- *Clothing*. According to numerous online sites for used clothing exporters (bestusedclothing.com is one), Africa is already a significant export destination for used clothing. The Middle East, Asia, and parts of Europe are also good markets.

- *Designer clothing and accessories*. (For example, hats, purses, belts, etc.) Eastern European countries, with their increasing exposure to western fashion but lack of corresponding wealth, may be good markets for these items.

- *Jewelry*. Eastern European countries as well as developing nations in Asia and Africa are good possibilities.

- *Household goods*. All the countries listed for items above are good candidates.

One way to recycle is to create something new with discarded material. Recently, handbags and coin purses made out of recycled Capri Sun juice boxes have made their appearance in the United States. "Generally, I think new products made from recycled materials is a

> **Tip...**
>
> **Smart Tip**
> Used clothing is graded from AAA (highest quality) down to B (lowest quality), with AA, A, and A-B in between. Sold wholesale in 1,000-pound or 100-pound bales with typical minimum orders of 20,000 pounds and prices ranging from $.15 per pound to $2.25 per pound, used clothing comprises everything from suits to swimwear. Check out online information and videos at sites like used clothingwholesale.com.

wide open field," says industry expert Wendy Larson. "Consumers all over the world could respond to that message."

Organically Yours

Another aspect of the environmentally conscious sustainability movement is organic products. Wendy Larson, member of the Organic Trade Association (OTA) and Manager/CEO of a marketing cooperative, notes double-digit growth in the past and predicts a strong future for the organics industry. "The newest generation of consumers is eager to do better in caring for our environment (reduce, reuse, recycle)." She further notes that consumers "realize that the choices they make with their buying dollars have longer impact than just today's comforts."

> **Bright Idea**
> According to the International Centre for Trade and Sustainable Development, sustainable practices can lower costs and make U.S. exports more competitive. Check out this organization at ictsd.org.

Your choices in organic exports are enormous. Nuts, grains, dairy products, meat, fruits, vegetables, and frozen foods are among these choices. Other possibilities, especially for emerging markets, include agricultural goods like organic seeds and fertilizers.

Fair and Square

You could also decide to specialize in Fair Trade goods. The World Fair Trade Organization (WFTO) has a directory where you can find supplier sources for giftware, household goods, furniture, and clothing. Find them online at wfto.com.

The Fair Trade movement is an organized social movement to help producers in developing countries get higher payments for their goods. A recent global consumer survey conducted by GlobeScan in 15 countries on behalf of the Fairtrade Labelling Organizations International (FLO) indicated an increased consumer awareness and belief that companies should be held accountable for their trading practices with developing countries.

Recent Fair Trade certified sales of $4.08 billion worldwide represent only a tiny fraction of world trade. However, some Fair Trade products account for 20 to 50 percent of all sales in their categories.

Proponents of the Fair Trade movement include organizations like SERRV International, Oxfam, and Amnesty International. Typical additional products involved in the movement include: handicrafts, coffee, cocoa, sugar, tea, bananas, honey, cotton, wine, fresh fruit, chocolate, and flowers.

Support Services EMC

As your special niche, you might specialize in smaller manufacturers who haven't even considered exporting or maybe providers of services—everything from bridge building to telecommunications—who have no idea how to go about it. For these people, you might promote yourself as a sort of Support Services EMC, a full-service company offering everything for the international product wanna-be. Consider doing any—or some combination of—the following:

❍ Finding, evaluating, and appointing dealers, distributors, and commission representatives in foreign markets

❍ Providing all promotional support: advertising, marketing, and trade show exhibitions

❍ Translating documents and correspondence

❍ Preparing all foreign distributor agreements

❍ Preparing all acceptances and approvals

❍ Arranging financing

❍ Overseeing all order-processing correspondence

❍ Managing all shipping and documentation

❍ Providing all after-market assistance

My Mission: Trade

As an import/export newbie, you may start out by simply selling your clients' products in foreign markets. Acting as their representative, you'll transact business in their name for a commission, salary, or retainer and commission. But again, you need to research your market, find out what sorts of buyers are available, and know the types of goods they're buying. This is an extremely important step in setting up your international trade business and one that you cannot afford to overlook.

So how do you accomplish this task? Well, as long as you're hoping to export goods out of the United States, a mind-boggling array of resources is available at your fingertips. Because exports give the economy a big charge, our friendly government agents are happy to help you sell just about anything to foreign markets.

Arguably the largest clearinghouse of information for finding foreign buyers is the International Trade Administration (ITA), a division of the U.S. Department of Commerce. And the ITA's Commercial Service is on permanent standby, alert and

▲

willing to help you. Its only mission is to help you develop and flex your export wings, which it does by providing some phenomenal services—everything from country-specific market analyses to trade leads to setting up and chaperoning personal meetings between you and interested foreign businesspeople. The Commercial Service is one place you can actually see your tax dollars at work, seemingly just for you.

According to the Commercial Service website (trade.gov/cs) the organization's mission is "to create prosperity by strengthening the competitiveness of U.S. industry, promoting trade and investment, and ensuring fair trade and compliance with trade laws and agreements."

The group employs trade specialists in 107 cities and more than 80 countries to help you meet your importing/exporting goals. Services include, according to the website, "world-class" market research, trade events that will help you promote your product, introductions to buyers and distributors, and counseling and advocacy services.

While you're studying this section (you're not just giving it a glance and a promise, are you?), keep these resources in mind. You'll want to go back to them as your career moves along. They're terrific wellsprings not only for market research but for advertising, marketing, and promotional purposes as well.

Unfortunately, if you're hoping to sell foreign-made doodads in the United States, you'll have to find this information without help from the government. Don't despair. There are still plenty of resources for market research. See the "Up Close and Personal" section on page 146.

Unlocking Mysteries

USA Trade Online, at usatrade.sensus.gov is a terrific source for export market research. Provided by the Foreign Trade Division of the Census Bureau, it offers current and cumulative U.S. import and export data, with over 9,000 export commodities and 17,000 import commodities. Videos demonstrate how to tackle the following tasks, among others:

- Identify top and emerging markets
- Monitor foreign competition
- Obtain values and growth rates

Subscription rates are $25 weekly, $75 monthly and $300 annually.

Intelligence Agency

How about a sort of (not) for-your-eyes-only intelligence report on the countries of your choice? Check out Country Commercial Guides, which furnish every piece of

Product Market Research Worksheet

Don't be befuddled by market research tasks. Use this handy worksheet. Make copies and use one for each product or service you're considering. Then give each one a grade: Fantastic, Has Potential, or Not Such a Hot Idea. When you've completed several sheets, compare them, weed out the NSAHIs, start working on the Fantastics, and keep the Potentials on file for future reference.

1. Name or description of product _____

    _____

2. What are the product's selling features? _____

    _____

3. Are there competitive products? If so, list them: _____

    _____

4. What are their selling features? _____

    _____

5. What is the sales potential of the product or service in my target market?

    _____

6. What are comparably priced goods going for in my target market? __

    _____

7. Who will be the end user of the product? _____

    _____

8. Is the population of potential end users large enough to have substantial sales? _____

    _____

9. Can I expand the market, or will I be taking a share of the existing market?

    _____

10. Is the existing market large enough to share? _____

    _____

11. Which elements have the most influence on potential customers or clients? Price, quality, brand name, "imported" cachet, service, credit terms, delivery terms, advertising, or marketing assistance? _____

    _____

    _____

Product Market Research Worksheet, continued

12. Where can I buy this product? _____
    _____

13. Will I need to have it manufactured? _____
    _____

14. If so, what is the turnaround time for manufacturing, and will this influ-
    ence sales? _____
    _____

15. What will be my cost for the product? _____
    _____

16. What variables will affect pricing (special packaging or marking require-
    ments, special shipping requirements as for perishables, other variables)?
    _____
    _____

17. What are the potential problems that will contribute to my price, such
    as end-user unfamiliarity with the product or service? _____
    _____
    _____

18. What are the potential benefits that can contribute to my price, such as
    high demand for the product or service? _____
    _____
    _____

19. What is the potential for licensing? _____
    _____

Final grade
❏ Fantastic
❏ Has Potential
❏ Not Such a Hot Idea

information you could ever want to know, including political, economic, and market analyses. The complete set of guides are free for the viewing. Type in export.gov/Germany (or whatever other country you're interested in). Select "Country Commercial Guides" or "Doing Business In . . . ."

Country Market Research Worksheet

Once you've done your product market research (or at the same time, if your market is intrinsic to product sales), move on to this worksheet. Again, use this handy checklist. Make copies and use one for each country you're considering. Then give each one a grade: Fantastic, Has Potential, or Not Such a Hot Idea. When you've completed several sheets, compare them, weed out the NSAHIs, start working on the Fantastics, and keep the Potentials on file for future reference.

1. Why does this country have potential for my product or service? _____

    _____

    _____

2. How can I gain exposure in this country? _____

    _____

    _____

3. Will I need to travel abroad to find markets, conduct research, and find distributors, or can I do this at home via phone and the internet? ____

    _____

    _____

4. Will I encounter language barriers or difficulties? _____

    _____

    _____

5. What cultural differences will I need to account for? _____

    _____

6. How will I handle them? _____

    _____

    _____

7. What is the economic climate (on a national level—unemployment rates, inflation, or depression; on a personal level—disposable incomes, spending patterns)?

    _____

    _____

▲

Country Market Research Worksheet, continued

8. What is the sociological climate (urban and rural populations, literacy and educational levels, any special religious considerations)? _____

_____

_____

9. What is the political climate? _____

_____

_____

10. Will I experience any special shipping or handling problems because of geography or local customs? If so, what? _____

_____

_____

11. What trade channel will I use (direct sales, representative, distributor, or commission representative)? _____

_____

_____

12. How will I locate my trade channel people? _____

_____

_____

13. What are the country-specific problems that will contribute to my price, such as quotas, duties, or country regulations? _____

_____

_____

14. What are the country-specific benefits that can contribute to my price, such as duty-free or low trade barriers? _____

_____

_____

Final grade

❑ Fantastic

❑ Has Potential

❑ Not Such a Hot Idea

I'm ITA!

The U.S. government's International Trade Administration (ITA) is on a mission: Help American businesses compete in the world marketplace by

○ Promoting and assisting American exports (and exporters)

○ Assuring American businesses equal access to foreign markets

○ Empowering American businesses to compete against unfairly traded imports

The ITA has created four units to carry out this mission:

1. The U.S. Commercial Service, which provides business counseling to U.S. exporters

2. Manufacturing and Services, which provides information for U.S. exporters, policy makers, and trade negotiators through industry sector specialists

3. Market Access and Compliance, in which country experts provide market analysis to American businesses

4. Import Administration, which guards our U.S. economy from unfairly priced imports

Remember those international intrigue movies where the hero works at an "intelligence desk" in a foreign country? Well, the Commercial Service has the same sort of people toiling at U.S. embassies and consulates abroad, compiling in-depth reports on industries around the world. These Country Commercial Guides detail everything you could possibly want to know, including:

• Market potential and demand trends

• Market size and import statistics

• Competition

• Market access

• Regulations and standards

• Best sales prospects

• End users

• Key industry contacts

Smart Tip

Tip...

Set up your internet account online by going to STAT-USA at stat-usa.gov or call (800) STAT-USA.

Again, this agency is pushing exports, not imports, so you're not going to find much useful information if you're looking to bring goods into the country. But if you have U.S.-made widgets you think the rest of the world will jump on, these guides are your friends.

Custom Tailored

Country Commercial Guides are not all the Commercial Service has to offer. Experts at its Export Assistance Centers will write up a Customized Market Analysis specially tailored to your product or service. This is a market research tool to make start-up entrepreneurs in other industries start salivating with envy. You choose your target country; specialists then conduct interviews with in-the-know local sources—importers, distributors, consumers or end users, and manufacturers of comparable products. In about 60 days, bingo! Your custom analysis is sent to your door. The cost for this service ranges from $1,000 to $3,000, depending on the country.

If you just have a few specific questions about your market, you can also pay for Flexible Market Research, which runs you anywhere from $200 to $3,000.

You can order a Customized Market Analysis and determine cost specifics for your area of interest through your nearest Export Assistance Center. How do you find a center? Go to export.gov/tradeleads or call (800) USA-TRADE.

Smart Tip

Tip...

Set up your internet account online at usatrade.census.gov or call (800) 549-0595.

Up Close and Personal

The Commercial Service is not the only place to turn for market research information. You can find out a lot on your own by reading local, national, and international newspapers and trade publications, by surfing international trade sites on the internet (see Appendix for lists), and through the personal interview, that is, talking to traders already at work in the field. These people can give you an insider's look at what works, what doesn't, and why.

Importers and exporters are not quite as accessible as professionals in some other industries. They're often abroad on business, and when they're back in the office, they're on overload with catch-up work. But if you present yourself in a pleasant and courteous manner, they'll probably share their expertise with you.

You'll find international traders in your local Yellow Pages, in various industry associations (check out our Appendix for a list), and, of course, on the internet.

If you plan to conduct a phone or in-person interview, be sure you call first to schedule a short meeting at a time convenient to your interviewee. If you're approaching your subject via email, write a short note explaining that you'd like to conduct a "mini-interview online" and would like the opportunity to submit some questions. It's professional courtesy to presume (correctly) that other people have busy schedules. Let your subject know the reason for the interview, about how much of his or her time you expect to take, and possibly even divulge a few of the questions you'll be asking. This will put them at ease about the interview and also get them thinking ahead.

Smart Tip

For your Agent/ Distributor Service "dating profile," contact your nearest Export Assistance Center. You'll find a complete directory of regional and state centers at trade.gov/cs.dom fld.html.

Most people, once you get them going, are only too happy to talk about themselves and their businesses. Take advantage of this fact to learn what you need to know, but don't take unfair advantage of a trader's time or personal space. Courtesy will get you further than you might imagine!

Now, with all these caveats firmly in mind, check out the International Trader's Interview on page 149. Make copies and use it for phone or personal interviews or use the questions for your email interview.

Up Closer and More Personal

If you prefer to get even closer and more personal, you'll want to check out the Commercial Service's Matchmaker Trade Delegation program, the ultimate in dating services for the export-ready trader. For this one, you'll need to have your merchandise market research already complete and be ready to implement sales. Then you simply contact the Matchmaker people and they do everything (and we mean everything) necessary to introduce you to the right business contacts at trade delegations that target two or three countries with strong sales potential for American products.

"The U.S. Department of Commerce staff will have completed all the legwork by the time you arrive in country," the Matchmaker people explain. "The hotel reservations, meeting facilities, interpreters, and appointment schedules are all arranged for you. All you have to do is arrive in country ready to interview your potential business prospects."

As a Matchmaker delegate, here is what you get:

What's In a Lead?

So what does a trade lead look like? A text advertisement or invitation. Check out these samples.

Company:	Car Hop Ltd.
Contact:	Ms. Daphne Denton
Position:	Head of Export
Business:	Car pennants and other designer car accessories
Address:	No. 1 The Groves, Greater Chestershire Industrial Estate, Chestershire
Country:	Great Britain
Phone:	011-44-181-000000
Fax:	011-44-181-000001
Email:	carhop@holiday.com

Car pennants from CAR HOP LTD. are the latest in auto accessories. Find your vehicle fast in a crowded car park with these colorful plastic banners that extend from the radio aerial. Pennants can be had in a variety of sport team logos, with city names, or personalized with your name, your girlfriend's or your dog's names. Any color, text, and graphics. Gift shops, clubs, service stations, and auto parts centres sell our products. Dealer inquiries welcome. Ask for our detailed catalog or inquire about your own designs. Also ask about your range of related CAR HOP accessories.

Date:	17 July 20xx
From:	Spencer Avalon
Company:	Avalon Traders Ltd.
Phone:	(000) 000-0000
Fax:	(000) 000-0001
Email:	avalon@holiday.com
Subject:	Pine Furniture
No. Units:	2 x 40 containers
When:	Immediate

Buyer's Location: Asia
Seeks Products From: USA and/or Canada
Transaction Range: $50,000+
Business Activity: Resell to dedicated distributors
Frequency: 4x per year
Acceptable Terms of Sale: FCA/FOB/FAS
Acceptable Payment Terms: Letter of credit, at sight
Comments: Seller must ship within seven days of receiving letter of credit. Contact Spencer Avalon for full details.

International Trader's Interview

Company name: _____

Name and title of contact person: _____

1. What does your company do? Import, export, or both? _____
   _____

2. What types of products do you deal with? _____
   _____

3. Which products have you had the most success with and why? _____
   _____

4. Which products have you had the least success with and why? _____
   _____

5. What type of competition do you face? _____
   _____

6. What countries do you work with? _____
   _____

7. Where and how do you find most of your customers? _____
   _____
   _____

8. What is your trade channel? Do you use direct sales, sales representatives,
   distributors, or commission representatives? _____
   _____
   _____

9. Could you explain why? _____
   _____
   _____

Don't forget the thank you!

- Market analysis of your merchandise or service
- Two days of prescreened business appointments in each country
- In-depth market and trade finance briefings by both American government and local experts
- "Logistical support," including hotel reservations, interpreters, and meeting rooms

Smart Tip

You will find trade missions on export.gov, as well as listings for trade opportunities and seminars. Simply access the homepage and choose the appropriate tab.

- Embassy receptions and site visits (with selected Matchmakers)
- Counseling and follow-up from your local Export Assistance Center

The sites and topics of Matchmaker Trade Delegations are set up about two years in advance, so you have plenty of time to get your product or service research done before you make your "date." Here's a sampling of the sorts of topics and countries you'll find on the Matchmaker schedule:

- Health-care technologies in the United Kingdom, Italy, Spain, and Greece
- Architecture, construction, and engineering in India
- Sporting goods in Brazil and Chile
- Franchising in Italy, Spain, Portugal, and Greece

Star Treatment

As the ultimate in export dating services, the Commercial Service offers its Gold Key program for exporters who want more personalized service. While the Matchmaker service sends you globe-trotting with 10 to 20 other company representatives and sets you all up with a booth and display, the Gold Key option finds potential partners for you and you alone—in the country you want. (With the Matchmaker program, you must choose from pre-set country formats.)

The basic charge for an agent distributor search will set you back $250. If you want star treatment—a car, an office, a driver, and interpreter—the bills grow from there. All you need to bring is your product or service literature. "Gold Key," says an Export Assistance Center spokesperson in Florida, "is our best program."

Compass Points

Amazing as the Commercial Service's programs are, they're not the only points on the compass. You can find lots of other sources for market research and trade leads simply by traveling the internet. You will find many services out there with helpful information for newbie traders. Check out the following organizations:

- *The World Bank* (data.worldbank.org). This organization is a United Nations financial institution. It provides loans to developing countries, and it also provides an enormous quantity of data useful to, among others, importers and exporters. This data, which can be viewed on a country-by-country basis, can provide good ideas for trade leads.
- *World Trade Point Federation* (tradepoint.org). A division of the United Nations. On this site you can post a notice saying what sort of widgets you're hoping to import or export. You may also be able to find trade partners in the countries you've targeted.
- *Organization of Women in International Trade* (owit.org). This not-for-women-only site provides networking and educational opportunities.
- *International Chamber of Commerce* (iccwbo.org). This site offers information about conferences, an online bookstore, and lots of lofty discussion about international trade.

You can—and should—find lots more trade lead services just by searching the internet. Try conducting a search on the country you're interested in trading with as well as "chamber of commerce," and you should get a good start on finding market leads.

Because some of these sites are freebies while others, like Trade Compass, are not, check out several before committing yourself to a fee-based service. If you decide to try a service that has a fee attached, it's a good idea to first make sure your company's piggy bank can handle the expense. This is among the topics of the next chapter.

Trade Dollars
What a Haul!

In Chapter 4 you determined how much it's going to cost you to get your business up and running. Now let's turn to the fun part—figuring out how much you can expect to make. The size of your cut will largely depend on two factors: How much you charge clients and how much you pay in expenses. This chapter covers both of those topics.

Pricing Your Products and Services

As an international trader, you are an intermediary in the buying and selling, or importing and exporting, transaction. Therefore, you have to determine not just the price of the product, but the price of your services as well. These two figures are separate yet interactive. Because you are a swimmer in the trade channel, the price of your services has to be added on to the product price, and that can affect its competitiveness in the marketplace.

Because the fee for your services impacts the success of the product, you may ultimately decide to change your pricing structure. You don't want to undercharge your client so that you can't cover your expenses and make a profit, but you don't want to overcharge and reduce the competitiveness of your company and the merchandise you represent.

Import/export management companies use two basic methods to price their services: commission and retainer. Normally, you choose one method or the other based on how salable you feel the product is. If you think it's an easy sell, you'll want to work on the commission method. If you feel it's going to be an upstream swim, difficult to sell, and require a lot of market research, you'll ask for a retainer.

A third method is to purchase the product outright and sell it abroad. This is a common scenario when you're dealing with manufacturers who would rather use you as a distributor than as a representative. You'll still market the product under the manufacturer's name, but your income will come from the profit generated by sales rather than by commission.

Commissioned Officer

OK, so we're not really talking military here. However, import/export management companies usually operate on a commission basis of about 10 percent. These fees are based on the product cost from the manufacturer.

With all these variables, estimating your commission might seem like a task fit for a professor of Boolean mathematics, but it's really not difficult. In fact, it's fun! (Adding up numbers is always more fun when it pertains to money in your pocket.)

Let's say you're working with English lawn chairs, which cost you $110 each. Here's what you do: First, take the price the manufacturer is charging for the product: $110. Now multiply $110 by 10 percent, which gives you a commission of $11 per chair.

So your product price at this point is $121 per chair ($110 + $11). To come up with the final price, you'll need to add other costs to this figure: any special marking or packaging, shipping, insurance, and any representative or distributor commissions that you'll pay to others in the trade channel, which we'll go over a little later. Once you've arrived at a final price, you'll check it against your competitors' prices. (You did do your market research, right?) If your product's price is comparatively low, you can bump up your commission percentage.

For now, however, you can see that for every chair you or your trade channelers sell, you'll get $11. If you sell a thousand chairs, that's $11,000 for you!

> ## Trader's View
>
> "I work based on a commission agreement," says John Laurino. "Most of my clients, however, pay me a monthly fixed amount to cover some current expenses, such as phone, fax, internet, and travel. When the project requires any detailed market survey, I charge the client for my working hours at a rate of USD 100 per hour."

Retaining Your Cool

If the manufacturer can't discount an item's price sufficiently or if you feel that the product will be a tough sell, you'll want to ask for a flat retainer. You'll pass all the costs of market research along to the manufacturer. By taking a retainer, you guarantee yourself a set income rather than one tied by commission to a "problem" product. And you save yourself some sweat.

Michael Richter, the German international trade consultant, makes a rule of working on a fee basis instead of on commission. Sometimes this is a retainer, sometimes a flat fee, depending on the kind of job—short term or long term—with a specific goal or offering of general support. "I bill my fees, even if relatively small," Michael says. "I do not work on a commission basis, as I would then have to concentrate on the products and not on [the client].

"I cannot, and do not want to, do everything because of the cost aspects," he tells potential customers. "But what I do I can arrange [to do with great flexibility]."

To determine what your retainer should be, you'll need to consider three variables associated with the performance of your services:

1. *Labor and materials or supplies.* This usually includes your salary or estimated salary on an hourly basis plus the wages and benefits you pay any employees involved in the performance of the job. To determine labor costs, estimate the amount of time it will take to finish a job, and multiply it by the hourly rate of your salary and that of any employees you might use. You can compute materials as a percentage of labor, but until you have past records to use as a guide, you should use 2 percent to 6 percent.

2. *Overhead*. This variable comprises all the (nonlabor) indirect expenses required to operate your business. To determine your overhead rate, add up all your expenses for one year, except for labor and materials. Divide this figure by your total cost of labor and materials to determine your overhead rate. Or use a rate of 35 percent to 42 percent of your labor and materials.

3. *Profit*. After all labor, materials, and overhead expenses are combined, profit can be determined by applying a percentage profit factor to those combined costs.

After profit is determined, adding it to the total operating costs produces the amount of the retainer.

> ### Trader's View
>
> "Don't work for free," advises Brazilian John Laurino. "Charge your clients for each step you do. In this way, prospective clients will respect you and see that you are a professional and not an IHEG (internet hunting everything guy)."

The Great Sock Caper

Sound like a job for that professor of Boolean mathematics? Nope! Let's say, for example, that you're working with a manufacturer who wants to export self-laundering socks (walk in them and they begin to exude detergent). Because you're not certain the world is ready for this breakthrough, you decide to take it on a retainer basis. You figure it will take you a week to complete the deal: to arrange for the export of 530 dozen socks priced at $24 per dozen. To calculate your retainer, you begin by figuring your labor and materials cost. (Check out the chart on page 157.)

Next you calculate your overhead: all the nonlabor, indirect expenses required to operate your business. Divide this number by your Total Labor & Materials number. Until you have past expenses to guide you, you can figure that overhead will cost you from 35 percent to 42 percent of your labor and materials cost. You can raise or lower the percentage depending on the workings of your own operation.

> ### Smart Tip
> *Tip...*
>
> Your profit factor should always be larger than the net profit you're aiming for. If you want to net an 8 percent profit, for example, make your profit factor 8.7 percent or 9 percent.

Now add your overhead figure (in this case, it's $445.53) to your labor and materials cost, and there's your Total Operating Expenses figure.

Most traders plan on making a net profit of 8 percent to 10 percent from their gross revenues. If you want to net 8 percent before taxes from the self-washing sock sales, you simply

Figuring Your Retainer

	Hours	Rate	Cost
Labor*	40	$26/Hour	$1,040.00
Materials (2% of Your Labor)			20.80
Total Labor & Materials			$1,060.80
Labor & Materials			$1,060.80
Overhead (42% of Labor & Materials)	445.53		
Total Operating Expenses			$1,506.33
Total Operating Expenses			1,506.33
Profit Factor of 8.7%			131.05
Your Net Profit—Retainer			$1,637.38

*Labor cost is based on temporary help. If your employees are part time, add 15 percent for payroll taxes, workers' compensation, and other necessities. If your employees are full time, add 30 percent.

multiply your total operating expenses by a profit factor of 8.7 percent. This produces a profit of $131.05, which is then added to the Total Operating Expenses figure to produce the retainer. If you consult the chart above, you will see that the retainer you should charge is $1,637.38.

Competitive Pricing

How you price your products is extremely important. The price has to be high enough to generate a scintillating profit yet low enough to be competitive in the foreign or domestic market you have chosen. This makes it essential for you to do your market research—finding the typical price range for selected merchandise in your target market and then comparing it against the manufacturer's price. Then you'll need to determine whether that price is competitive in the marketplace. If it's not, then you'll have to do one of the following:

- Ask the manufacturer or supplier for a better price
- Operate on a retainer-only basis with no commission
- Reconsider doing business with that manufacturer or supplier

Once you have determined the normal price range for comparable products and decided that you can add commissions and other markups to the manufacturer's price and still be competitive, you can go buyer hunting. (We will go over advertising and marketing in detail in Chapter 11.)

Keep in mind that pricing is often a case of trial and error. Persevere until you come up with the magic number for both profit and salability. Don't get discouraged. Remember that if one price doesn't pencil in correctly, you can keep changing it until you come up with one that works.

You Be the Judge

The retainer is a smart way to assure yourself of an income on those problem products. But it can also turn into an easy way to shoot yourself in the foot. If you do your job well and the product takes off, generating tons of sales, the manufacturer may start resenting having to pay you merely to arrange sales, which by now is dead easy. (And after all, the manufacturer is supplying the product and paying all the costs to develop the market.) In the end, the manufacturer may decide to ace you out of the picture by selling direct.

If, however, you've been working all along on a commission basis instead of on retainer, the manufacturer will probably view your commissions, which are costing less than the retainer would, as adequate compensation.

This is not to say that such a scenario will occur; the manufacturer may be delighted to pay you until the end of time. But while you're considering which pricing route to take, keep this possibility in mind.

The Distributor Cap

Occasionally, you'll want to, or be asked to, act as a distributor of the merchandise. This means that you'll actually purchase the product from the manufacturer—usually at net wholesale prices, less a percentage for the manufacturer's sales overhead—and sell the merchandise: abroad if you're exporting or in the United States if you're importing.

When you're wearing your distributor cap (the sales kind, not the auto parts kind), every product you purchase from the manufacturer should be priced to cover the following:

- Its wholesale cost
- Handling costs (shipping, cargo insurance, tariffs, freight forwarder fees, sales rep commissions, and any other special costs the project or product requires)

- A proportionate share of your overhead
- A reasonable profit for you

If you've been paying attention so far, you'll have noticed that these are the same things we've talked about with every other form of pricing. Now to accomplish this, you have to apply a markup to the cost of the product, and this gives you your selling price. If the cost of the product, for example, is $5 and your selling price is $10, then your markup is $5 or 100 percent.

Smart Tip

Find a customs broker or freight forwarder you can be comfortable with. Look online (Google is easy), or ask other international traders for recommendations. Then pick someone friendly, knowledgeable, and experienced.

Leave the Light On

Let's say you are working with decorative frog-and-flower porch lights that you have bought from a company in Taiwan. You know they'll sell like crazy all over the United States. The manufacturer is charging you $5 per light, or unit. Check out the chart below, and you'll see that your costs to bring the lights stateside are $6.47 per unit. If you double this, selling each light for $12.94 at a markup of 100 percent, you'll be making $38,820 on the deal. This is good.

Figuring Your Markup

Manufacturer's Cost for 500 Dozen Frog-and-Flower Porch Lights	$30,000
Customs Broker's Fee	280
Inland Freight from Factory to Port	600
Marine Insurance	340
Ocean Freight from Keelung, Taiwan	6,000
Import Tariffs/Taxes	1,590
Total	$38,810

Divide your total costs of $38,810 by 6,000 (500 dozen) units. This gives you a per-unit cost of $6.47.

No One Size

One type of cost you incur is likely to be broker fees. How much can you expect these to be? The customs broker, you'll recall, is the professional who guides your goods through Customs.

There is no one-size-fits-all answer. "It's all based on what's entailed in the shipment," says Dale Wilson of DFM International, a customs brokerage firm.

However, you can expect to pay a base amount of about $130 per shipment, Wilson says, plus about $5 for each $1,000 the shipment is worth.

Expect to pay more if your shipment is subject to restrictions. If you have a food shipment, for example, your broker will have to deal with the Food and Drug Administration; if you're bringing in transmitters, the Federal Communications Commission will be involved. And if your cargo consists of several different types of furniture, like tables and chairs, each distinct piece will have to be categorized.

"If other agencies get involved," Wilson cautions, "the charges increase."

Remember, however, that you'll be selling the porch lights to retailers, who will also need to add their markup to make a profit. And there's no point in marking yourself right out of the ballpark. If you add a 100 percent markup and the retailer does the same, each light will now cost the end user $25.88. And this price might now be too high to be competitive.

So you might want to lower your markup. If you make it 50 percent, your per-unit cost drops to $9.71 and you still make $19,410 on the deal. Still not bad.

That's Illuminating

Now let's leave those porch lights on and illuminate a few more facts about the money you can expect to make. It's much more difficult to determine a set yearly income for an import/export business than for other types of companies. If you're in the car wash business, for example, you're dealing with a predetermined service—cleaning vehicles—and while you can add or subtract waxes, vacuums, and air fresheners, the main thrust of what you're selling is not going to change.

> **Tip...**
>
> **Smart Tip**
>
> Here are good questions to ask prospective customs brokers and freight forwarders: Does the company specialize in these transactions? How long has it been in operation? How many offices does it have, and where are they located? What references can they provide you with? (And make sure you call a couple!)

Feathers or Bricks

The freight forwarder's fees, like those of the customs broker, are not cut and dried. Prices are based on product, origin, destination, size, and weight. Air rates are usually based on either a per-pound or per-kilo weight or on the dimensional weight, whichever is greater. Dimensional weight is figured by multiplying length by width by height in inches and then dividing by 166 to arrive at the number of pounds. Why make it so complicated? The air carrier is compensating for the fact that a 48-inch square box of feathers, while weighing little, will take up more room than a 14-inch box of bricks.

Ray Tobia, president of Air Sea International Forwarding, emphasizes that it's difficult to give ballpark estimates. This is especially true in an era of rapidly-changing freight charges. However, as you can imagine, air charges from Newark, New Jersey, to London will be considerably less than charges for sending the same consignment from Los Angeles to London.

Freight forwarders' ocean rates usually run per 20-foot or 40-foot container or, for loose freight, on a weight/measure basis—per cubic meter or per 1,000 kilos, whichever is greater.

In import/export, however, there are no fixed boundaries. (And isn't this one of the delights of the business?) Like Wahib Wahba, the exporter in Maryland, you can be working with railroads in one country one year and telephone poles in another country the next. You might export coffee go-cups in June and import lawn chairs in July.

Consequently, your profits and expenses will be different for each project. "We're up and down," says Wahib. "It's a long-term cycle. When you bid for a project, your expenses are low. But when you get a project, your expenses become five times higher." These expenses, of course, are offset by your profit, and since you've calculated them ahead of time, you're not likely to be smacked in the noggin by unpleasant surprises.

Baseline Expenses

Now that we've discussed the variable nature of the trader's operating expenses, let's back up a little. You will have some fixed expenses, ones that will form the baseline of your business and that you'll always have, no matter what you're importing or exporting. These, subtracted from your projected gross income, will tell the true tale of how much you'll be making.

▲

We'll assume once again that you'll be homebased, so we won't worry about expenses for office rent or utilities. We do, however, need to consider the following:

- Phone (land line and/or cell)
- Postage
- Stationery and office supplies
- Travel
- ISP (internet service provider)
- Website maintenance (optional)
- Loan repayment

Phone It In

As we discussed in the start-up section of this chapter, phone service of some sort is a must in the import/export business. Whether you'll need, or want, a traditional land line depends on your business.

Email and fax are becoming the methods of choice for communicating with customers. John Laurino in Brazil says those are the options he uses. In Germany, Michael Richter finds email playing a larger and larger role. Jan Herremans, the tire and used clothing trader in Belgium, uses all three phone service methods: phone, fax, and email.

"We used to communicate by fax," says Wahib Wahba in Maryland, "because it was very expensive by phone. Now we use the phone all the time because it's more affordable than it was before. Still, the highest bill I have is the phone."

If you choose the good old-fashioned method of picking up the phone and talking into it for your international dealings, your charges will be much higher than if you send faxes or emails, either of which take only moments.

Sometimes, discussion is required, however. For these occasions, it's smart to have a good, inexpensive plan (or card) for calling overseas. These days you can find rates as low as one or two cents a minute to foreign destinations.

Also, if you haven't already, investigate VoIP (Voice Over Internet Protocol) options. This technology uses the internet, instead of phone lines, to transmit voices. If you download Skype software, for example, you can talk to—and also see—your overseas party, provided that person also has Skype.

Send Me a Letter

Your ongoing postage charges will also vary, depending on how much you rely on mail rather than on phone or email service and where in the world you are sending

▲

material. What kind of material? Requests for catalogs from exporters, your own catalogs, brochures, or price sheets to importers, introduction letters, and pro forma invoices, to name a few.

Take a look at ircalc.usps.gov for an idea of U.S. Postal Service charges for a 1-ounce package or letter by Global Xpress Guaranteed (GXG). The postal service has lots of other options, including Express Mail, Priority, and First Class International letter. Its website comes complete with an International Mail Calculator. All you do is plug in the name of the country to which you want to send mail and the weight of your package, and the calculator comes up with prices for various types of postal services, including allowable size dimensions. And you don't even have to stand in line!

> ## Trader's View
>
> North Carolina trader Sam Nelson exports medical test kits, chemical analyzers, hematology analyzers, and microscopes, among other medical supplies and equipment. Often he sends orders out via the good old U.S. Postal Service.

Paper Tiger

Once you have made your initial outlay for office supplies and stationery, your fixed expenses in this category should be fairly low. Staples last a long time, you can reuse paper clips, and unless you're planning some violent activity with your letter opener and scissors for which the police will bag them as evidence, you shouldn't have to buy another set.

Your main expense will be paper for your printer and fax machine and fine-quality paper for stationery and envelopes. (If you download even a portion of the myriad materials available on the internet, you'll become a paper tiger, ferociously feeding on printed matter.) You can refer to the office supplies shopping chart in Chapter 10 for prices.

Trip Tip

As we have discussed, your travel expenses will be entirely dependent on how you structure your business. Michael Richter travels infrequently since he has built his company around consulting clients in his home country of Germany. In São Paolo, Brazil, John Laurino travels in-country once a month and abroad once a year, spending about ten days on each trip. And across the Atlantic in Belgium, Jan Herremans spends three to four days a week away from home in Europe and takes an average of eight four-day to ten-day intercontinental trips a year. Base your figures on the type of work and duration of travel you'll be doing.

Olé for Online Service

What praises have we not already sung for the internet service provider? As we have said (repeatedly), this is a must for the import/export business. It is also, in most cases, a fixed expense. ISPs generally charge a flat rate of $20 to $25 for unlimited monthly service, which gives you access to the internet and email.

Weaving the Web

North Carolina trader Sam Nelson says many of his clients order medical supplies straight off his website. For him, as well as his clients, this is an efficient transaction method. Although you may decide not to have a website immediately, your decision will probably depend, once again, on what type of business you set up.

If you have a website and need someone to update it regularly, this expense should also be fairly fixed (and dependent on the complexity of your site). You can figure on anywhere from $500 to $1,250 per year. For a discussion of the typical features and associated costs to expect, check out webpagefx.com.

Paying the Piper

We have set aside a fixed expense called loan repayment. If you don't borrow money to start your business, you won't need to bother with this one. If, however, you finance your startup costs through any means, you'll need to repay the piper. Here's where you pencil in whatever your monthly fee is.

Putting It Together

You can use the worksheet on page 167 to pencil in your projected income and estimated operating expenses. You may have many more expenses than the ones discussed here, such as yearly subscriptions to USA Trade Online; trade shows or delegations and the travel expenses that go with them; employees and the workers' compensation and payroll costs that go with them; auto expenses; subscription fees for professional publications; butler and maid service (just dreaming!); and pizza delivery or Chinese take-out costs. We've put in rent, utilities, employee, and insurance costs, but obviously, if these don't apply to you, don't worry about them.

> **Tip...**
>
> **Smart Tip**
>
> Carefully research your markets and products; diligently calculate all shipping tariffs, taxes, and other fees; and keep a close eye on all your documentation. This will give you the best shot at achieving your ideal operating figures.

Once you have calculated your estimated operating expenses, you can subtract them from your calculated earnings and—voilà!—you have a projected income/expense total.

Sailing Straight

You'll recall our introduction in Chapter 4 of the hypothetical trading companies, Cargo Bay Traders and Clipper Trading Service Co. The former is a small, home-based business with a minimum of equipment, no employees, and no website. The latter has rented office space, an administrative assistant, up-to-date equipment, and a professionally maintained website.

These businesses have thoughtfully provided sample projected operating income/expenses statements, which you can check out on page 166. You should keep in mind that although these figures are well in line with industry norms, so are figures that could be much lower (or higher).

The owners of these companies will have to work hard and smart to make sure that their companies' bottom lines stay in shape. And they know that import/export is not a passport to overnight success; they don't expect to achieve these figures immediately.

You can do your own projected operating income/expense statement by using the worksheet on page 167.

A Little Bit of Luck

Now that you have done all the arithmetic, you can determine just how much you will need to get your business up and running. And as a bonus, you can present all these beautifully executed figures to your lender to show him or her that your business is a good risk and that you will be able to repay your loan without difficulty.

Of course, one of the beauties of the import/export business is that its start-up costs are relatively low. So low, in fact, that some traders have let their first projects finance themselves.

Wahib Wahba's business started from scratch. His salary with the mother company, from which his own firm took root, was $25,000. Then he got his first international trade project and his sales, and salary, took wing. "The first project was about $1.5 million," the Maryland trader explains. "The second was [about] $700,000. So that was helpful."

"I don't want to say I'm lucky," he adds. "You have to be somewhere to be lucky; luck doesn't come alone. As far as overhead, you can do export from anywhere you want. Even the phone bills are now cheap."

Sample Operating Income/Expense Statements

	Cargo Bay Traders	Clipper Trading Service Co.
Projected Monthly Income	$6,280.00	$21,200.00
Projected Monthly Expenses		
Rent		2,200.00
Market research/Trade leads	25.00	350.00
Phone service	100.00	200.00
Utilities		125.00
Employee payroll		2,000.00
Advertising	150.00	1,500.00
Postage	40.00	80.00
Insurance	200.00	200.00
Internet service	25.00	25.00
Travel		2,500.00
Miscellaneous Expenses (stationery & office supplies)	20.00	75.00
Loan repayment		225.00
Total Expenses	$560.00	$9,480.00
Projected Income/Expense Total	$5,720.00	$11,720.00

Operating Income/Expense Statements

Projected Monthly Income		$
Projected Monthly Expenses		$
Rent		
Market research/Trade leads		
Phone service		
(include $60 for cell phone service)		
Utilities		
Employee payroll		
Advertising		
Postage		
Insurance		
Internet service		
Travel		
Miscellaneous Expenses (stationery & office supplies)		
Loan repayment		
Total Expenses		$
Projected Income/Expense Total		$

Romancing the Bank

You might want to consider financing through your bank or credit union. In this case, your startup costs and income figures are extremely important. The bank will want to see all this, neatly laid out and carefully calculated. You'll also want to show all the statistics you can gather for the bright future of the particular niche and trading market(s) within which you'll be operating.

Ex-Im Bank

The Export-Import Bank of the United States (called Ex-Im Bank by those in the know) was born in 1934 during the dark days of the Depression, when exports were viewed as a potential boost to our economic rehabilitation. After World War II, the bank helped American exporters in the reconstruction of Europe and Asia, and took on the task of promoting trade between the United States and the Soviet Union.

Now that these missions have been accomplished, the bank has transferred much of its attention to emerging countries whose economies are, Ex-Im says, growing at twice the rate of the industrialized world.

One of the Export-Import Bank's recent goals has been to help jump start the global economy and get it moving again. An additional goal is to increase exports of the environmental goods and services that are in great demand among emerging nations.

Most consistently, however, the Ex-Im Bank is a government agency on a mission to help finance the overseas sales of U.S. goods and services. What this means to you is that the Ex-Im people are standing by to help lend you working capital (assuming, of course, that you qualify). Again, the government is eager to help you sell U.S.-made goods abroad, so if you're exporting, this is another great resource for you.

To help support small-business exporters, the bank has developed several small-business programs:

- *Working Capital Guarantee.* This program guarantees 90 percent of the principal and interest on working capital loans made by commercial banks to credit-worthy small-business people who will use the money to purchase or produce American merchandise or services for export. You apply for a Preliminary Commitment, a sort of letter of credit from Ex-Im Bank, and then take it to your own bank as an enticement to give you the best terms. The guarantee, which usually comes due in six months, can be for a single transaction or a revolving credit line.

> **Tip...**
>
> **Smart Tip**
> Contact Ex-Im Bank online at exim.gov, or call it at (202) 565-EXIM.

- *Export Credit Insurance.* We'll go over this one in detail in Chapter 9. For now let's say that the program provides various policies to guard against a foreign buyer neglecting to pay you.

- *Direct Loans.* But not to you. Here the Ex-Im Bank will lend money to importers wishing to purchase American-made goods, thus indirectly helping your cause. In 2009, in response to the global financial crisis, the Ex-Im bank made a new export financing option available. Foreign buyers of U.S. exports can get 180-day to five-year terms on federally guaranteed loans. What's more, they can get this financing in weeks or even days, instead of the many months previously required. For more details, see sbea.org.

- *Guarantees.* Again, Ex-Im Bank is helping foreign buyers here and indirectly helping you as an exporter by covering the importer of U.S. goods or services against the political and commercial risks of nonpayment.

To qualify as American-made, the product or service must consist of at least 50 percent American content and must not adversely impact the U.S. economy.

In Your Pocket

Most entrepreneurs use a very exclusive source to finance their startup expenses—family and friends. You may choose to go this route yourself. You'll have a lot less paperwork to fill out, and you can let your financier share in the excitement as your business takes off. But remember, you'll still need to figure the repayment of borrowed funds into your costs and you should treat your repayment agreement as seriously as you would any bank loan.

Another route many entrepreneurs take to obtain financing involves an entity as close as your back pocket—the credit card. Before you choose this option, take a look at your available credit balance and—this is important—at the annual percentage rate. Card companies frequently offer low, low rates as an incentive to sign up or use their service. Go with the one that offers the best rate for the longest period.

Now that you've got your financial ducks in a row, it's time to consider employees and insurance.

9

Employees, Insurance, and Other Facts of Life

Depending on how much growth you envision for your business, you may never need employees. Or you may expand to the point where you can't do everything yourself, at which point you'll need to consider taking on assistants.

Employees are one of those entities that seem to bring with them as many cons as pros. When you hire help, you're not a swinging single anymore. You have responsibilities. Suddenly, there's payroll to be met, workers' compensation insurance to be paid, state and federal employee taxes to be paid. And work to be delegated.

Some people are born employers, finding it easy to teach someone else the ropes and then hand over the reins. Others never feel quite comfortable telling someone else what to do or how to do it.

One of the many perks of the import/export business is that you can accomplish a great deal without ever hiring anyone. You can easily start out as a one-man (or one-woman) band, handling all the tasks of your fledgling company yourself. You won't need help immediately. But as your company flourishes, you may one day find that you need: 1) more hours in a day, 2) to make great strides in the field of cloning, or 3) to hire help.

Fun with Filing

A tremendous amount of the work in international trade involves correspondence, invoicing, and preparing documents. And as your company grows, you may discover that you can't have fun with filing and at the same time market your services to clients, arrange deals with representatives and distributors, and promote your clients' products.

When you reach the point where your paperwork and other daily grind tasks are cutting drastically into your marketing and customer service time (and you're walking around with coffee jitters and bags under your eyes from trying to do it all), you'll need to hire an administrative assistant. This valuable member of your new team can work on a part-time or full-time basis, depending on your needs.

You will want an organized, detail-oriented person who can think independently, someone who has a cheerful phone personality and manners, good communication skills, and a knowledge of the computer programs you use.

No matter what position you're trying to fill, the first employees you hire should be as versatile as possible. In small businesses, people wear many hats. Look for someone willing to do whatever is needed, even if an occasional task is outside the comfort zone.

If you can do it, hire your first few employees on a temporary basis first. That way you can see how things go. This strategy saves you from having to let an employee go (which is no fun) if the individual isn't working out or if you

Trader's View

Sam Nelson runs his small North Carolina trading company with the help of two employees. One is an administrative assistant, and the other helps him with accounting and shipping out orders.

can't use help on a continual basis. You can always change positions later to permanent ones.

Equally, it's a good idea to hire part time initially, if possible. As with the hiring of temporary employees, this practice allows you to try out the worker before going to the time—and expense—of hiring full-time permanent employees.

Family members can make ideal first hires. Not only are they usually willing to go above and beyond the call of duty, but they have an immediate loyalty to you and your company. "My daughter, Isabelle, runs the office," says Jan Herremans in Belgium, "and I have three employees grading tires and loading and unloading containers."

Your administrative assistant (or whatever you choose to call the first person you hire) will free you to go out and market and service your accounts. This is good. But as you continue to grow, sooner or later you'll find again that you can't do it all yourself. You'll need to hire another team member, an account supervisor to help recruit and service accounts.

The All-Star

Ideally, your new all-star will have a working knowledge of international trade, but this is not as important as enthusiasm for the sales and services your company offers. For starters, you'll assign him or her an account to service. Then, as he learns how your company operates and what services you offer, he can recruit his own accounts.

Depending on the size of the account, a person with extensive experience in international trade should be able to handle three to five accounts per year. If the accounts are small and don't need a lot of support, the employee may be able to deal with more than that.

Because nobody works for free and salespeople in particular are best motivated by incentives, you'll want to provide your account supervisor(s) with either a draw vs. commission or salary plus commission on the accounts handled.

What's the difference? In a draw-vs.-commission arrangement, you provide your employees with a draw, a set monthly income so that they can be assured of money coming in to pay the rent and feed the dog and cat. Any

Smart Tip

Tip...

You can protect yourself against former employees stealing your accounts by having every account supervisor sign a written employment contract containing a noncompete provision. You should consult your attorney for the finer points, but you can usually limit the competition from a former employee by both geographic area and time period.

commissions they earn are offset against the draw, so they don't get actual money from the commissions until they've gone over the amount of the monthly draw. (If the draw is $500, for instance, and they earn commissions of $800, they receive $300 in commissions with the balance of $500 going to "repay" the draw.)

In a salary-plus-commission arrangement, you pay your employees a set monthly income, but in this case, any commissions they earn are added on to the monthly payment instead of being subtracted from it. So if their monthly salary is $500 and they earn commissions of $800, they get the whole $800 plus the salary.

Draw vs. commission is the best way to motivate your account supervisors to perform at peak efficiency. (The salary-plus-commission method doesn't seem to dangle the same carrot.) Of course, if you have a particularly valuable team member, you might pay her on a salary-plus-commission basis. This will serve not only to express your satisfaction with her performance but will act as a terrific way to ensure that she stays with you instead of going off on her own and taking your accounts with her.

Standing on the Corner

How exactly do you set about finding the right team members? You could stand on the corner and holler until you attract the right person's attention. But here are some more practical suggestions for finding an administrative assistant:

- Recruit from local secretarial schools.
- Try headhunting from domestic companies engaged in products similar to the merchandise you sell.
- Recruit from freight forwarding or customs broker firms.
- Place an ad online.

To find that gem of an account supervisor, try these ideas:

- Recruit salespeople in related fields. If, for example, you export medical supplies, try headhunting in the domestic medical supplies or pharmaceutical sales arenas.
- Post an email ad on the websites of various international trade associations. (See the Appendix for a list of these.)
- Post an ad on your own website. (You do have one, don't you?)

> **Bright Idea**
> Even though English is the "international" lingo for business, you'll have a major advantage if at least one of your team members speaks the languages and understands the cultures of the countries you're dealing with. This strategy can help avoid misunderstandings or breaches of etiquette, not to mention make your communications more effective.

- Recruit at local colleges that offer courses in international trade. You can post an ad on the department's bulletin board or talk to professors about recommending graduating star students.

The Backup Brain

Hiring an employee is one of those take-a-deep-breath-or-hyperventilate steps. You're taking on an extension of yourself, someone who hopefully will become not just another pair of hands but a backup brain, a friend, ally, and member of your business family. How do you choose someone to fill all those shoes?

Beware!
When you schedule work on various accounts, keep in mind not only American holidays, but also holidays in your international trading partners' country. There's no point, for example, in trying to schedule a phone meeting during the Chinese New Year, when all commerce screeches to a halt for a minimum of a week. Foreign holidays are easy to find online.

Your administrative assistant should be not just a desk jockey, a mindless drone at the computer keyboard and telephone, but an integral part of your team. You'll need to rely on him or her to field all the problems that might arise while you're out traveling the world. You'll want someone who scores well on the following skills and abilities:

- *Analytical skills.* Thinks through a problem and arrives at a solution.
- *Oral communication.* Excellent phone manner, good communication skills, with good grammar and vocabulary.
- *Written communication.* Effective writing skills, with good grammar and punctuation.
- *Visual detail skills.* Able to enter correct information on an invoice or lading document without transposing or scrambling it.
- *Feedback acceptance.* Able to accept feedback and follow directions, without getting insulted or defensive.
- *Complementary personality.* Work habits mesh with your own. Some people work better with cheery chatterboxes; others go for the more silent type.

Testing 1, 2, 3

Now test 'em out! Here are a few ideas.

- Provide a typical scenario in which the terms of a letter of credit cannot be completed for a fairly simple reason. (You be the judge.) You might use, for example, a case in which a certificate of origin has not been received from the exporter. Ask your prospects to solve the problem.

- Present a scenario of an importer who's worried because the merchandise your company exported has not arrived. Ask candidates to imagine that you are out of the country. How would they handle the situation? (You can even role play, with yourself as the worried importer.)
- Ask candidates familiar with import/export to fill out a few documents.
- Test prospects on more mechanical tasks, like producing a letter, filing folders, entering checks into an accounting program, or adding numbers on a calculator.

After you have evaluated your tests, read resumes, and checked references, use your own people skills. How do you feel intuitively about your candidate(s)?

Payback

OK, we're actually talking about a positive thing here: Paying your employees and providing benefits.

The amount you pay your employees will depend on many factors, including the job description, your region, the local cost of living, and the employee experience level. In a city or an expensive part of the country, you'll pay more than in other locations. Similarly, an extremely experienced assistant might make 40 to 60 percent more than an inexperienced one.

Although you are required by law to provide employees with workers' compensation and time off to vote or attend to other civic duties, many other benefits are up to you. Optional benefits include the following: retirement, medical, dental, vision, or life insurance plans; paid vacations, holidays, or sick leave. However, in order to attract good workers, most companies provide some or all of these benefits. If you provide employees with benefits that are important to them, they'll be likelier to feel committed to your company.

Accentuate the Positive

Another way to ensure greater employee commitment (not to mention higher morale) is to make a real effort to connect with your employees. As with any relationship, this takes work. Try the following:

- *Encourage communication.* Useful suggestions and feedback, rather than just criticism, are most effective. Also, give your employees the chance to provide feedback about the company, preferably anonymously.
- *Reward creativity.* Workers who provide original, innovative suggestions should be rewarded. The size of the reward is often irrelevant. People simply like to be recognized and appreciated.

- *Avoid micro-management.* Don't breathe down your employees' necks. You hired them, so let them work!
- *Acknowledge your mistakes.* If a problem arises because of your own error, admit it. Everyone probably knows it anyway, but honesty is appreciated, especially when it comes from those in power.
- *See your employees as people.* Employees can tell when an employer appreciates them as people. Interest, as long as it's genuine and nonintrusive, is usually seen as a plus.

Training Again (and Again)

In spite of your best efforts, you may lose some employees just as you've gotten them trained. Wahib Wahba has found this to be the case more than once. "You train them for six to eight months, they work for two or three years, and then they move on and so you have to repeat the whole thing," he says.

Some of this is unavoidable, given the highly mobile society in which we live and run our businesses. But you can keep it to a minimum by careful choice of employees and policies that reward longevity.

Insuring It All

You'll need insurance for many aspects of your business, from employees to cargo. So read on.

Insuring Your Gems

Once you find those gems of employees, you'll need to think about caring for them. Workers' compensation insurance laws vary among states; check with your insurance agent for details in your area. Workers' comp covers you for any illness or injury your employees might incur, from a paper cut gone septic to a back injury from lifting heavy file boxes, to yellow fever contracted while out on a sales trip. (Yes, stranger things have happened.)

If your employees work in your home office and get injured there, your home-owners' insurance may refuse to pay on the grounds that it's actually a workers' comp case. Rather than making yourself a nervous wreck (incurring your own mental health claim) over all this, check with your insurance agent and then make an informed decision.

Thanks, Ex-Im

Thanks to the Export/Import Bank of the United States, you can purchase several types of export credit risk insurance designed specifically for the newbie exporter and the SME (small- to medium-sized enterprise, remember?). These policies protect you in the event that your foreign buyer decides not to pay you for either commercial or political reasons. The Ex-Im Bank (and the United States) hope policies such as these will encourage both you and your financial institution to take on higher-risk foreign markets.

Your menu options at Ex-Im are the following:

- *Small-business policy*. This multibuyer policy requires that you insure all your export credit sales with Ex-Im; it's designed to free you from the "first-loss" deductible of most commercial policies. To take advantage, you must have an export credit sales volume of less than $5 million in the last three years before application, your company must qualify as a small business under the Small Business Administration's definition of the term, and you must have been in business at least one year with a positive net worth. How do you find out if you qualify? Call the SBA's Office of Size Standards at (800) 827-5722 or check its website at sba.gov/size.

- *Umbrella policy*. This policy boasts the same coverage and eligibility as the small-business policy above, but it allows you (as an EMC or ETC) to act as an administrator or intermediary between Ex-Im and your clients.

- *Short-term single-buyer policy*. This one, which covers a single or repetitive sale, is for the exporter who doesn't want to insure everything with Ex-Im. A special reduced premium is offered to small businesses.

Cargo Stronghold

You already know the importance of cargo insurance. To mangle a well-known advertising maxim, "Don't let your merchandise leave home without it." The cost of the insurance usually runs about 1 percent of the insured value, although this varies with the type of goods and method of shipping.

So what do you get for your money? Peace of mind, for one thing, as with all insurance. And, in the event of a cargo misadventure, your insurance coverage should include enough to repay you for not only lost or damaged products, but for your extra time and trouble and those lost profits.

You'll want to purchase all-risk insurance, which covers your cargo against everything except man's inhumanity to man—war, strikes, riots, and civil commotion—and inherent vice in the cargo. What is vice, you ask? It refers to any sort of plague or pestilence that might attack your cargo. Like boll weevils in those gorgeous cotton blankets, for example, or e. coli on your Texas steaks.

You can guard against the battling-humans risk by purchasing war and SRCC (strikes, riots, and civil commotion) riders, and you can also buy riders to protect against whatever form of inherent vice your particular cargo may face.

You might also want to consider general average insurance. This protects you in the event of someone else's cargo loss. Say the ship carrying your containers runs afoul of stormy weather. The captain decides to jettison a portion of the cargo to save the rest, and he dumps

> ### Smart Tip
> Insure an additional 10 percent of the CIF value of your cargo. If your merchandise is worth $5,000, for example, and your ocean freight charge is $400, then you'll want to buy about $6,000 worth of insurance.
>
> $5,000 + $400 = $5,400
>
> $5,400 + $540 (10 percent) = $5,940 (rounded up to $6,000)

somebody else's stuff into the briny deep. Fine, you say. Not quite. According to maritime law, even though your merchandise has made it to port safe and sound, you can't take possession until you've paid for your share of the loss.

The Blanket Policy

Let's look at another scenario. Say the other party in your transaction has purchased insurance—for example, the exporter who's shipping to you CIF (cost, insurance, and freight, remember?)—but you've got a funny feeling that his coverage is not too reliable. Not to worry. You can purchase a contingent policy, which is about half the price of regular insurance and will serve as backup insurance in the event of a catastrophe.

As a newbie trader, your best bet will be to purchase insurance through your freight forwarder, who has a blanket policy, or directly from the air carrier. As you grow, you may wish to purchase a blanket policy of your own, which will cover you for everything you ship over the course of a year.

Ensuring Is Good, Too

Out on the high seas, your cargo may be subjected to rough and stormy weather. On the docks, it can be equally buffeted about by tough longshoremen. What can you do to help ensure your cargo doesn't become a marine insurance claim?

1. Pack with dock loading and unloading procedures in mind. Your cargo may be slung around (or skewered) by anything from a forklift to a sling or net, and then, if it survives that, left outdoors to rot. Often, cargo is "stored" on port

decks or out on airplane cargo tarmacs, without any covering. If you're unfamiliar with overseas port operations and don't have the right packaging, you can lose cargo.

Export Graffiti

The importer usually specifies export marks that should appear on the cargo for easy identification by receivers. These marks include the following:

- Shipper's mark
- Country of origin
- Weight marking in pounds and kilograms
- Number of packages and size of cases in inches and centimeters
- Handling marks using international pictorial symbols (if appropriate)
- Cautionary markings in English and the language of the country of destination (if appropriate)
- Special labels for hazardous materials
- Destination and order number
- Port of entry
- Weight markings
- Country of origin
- Number of containers and size in each

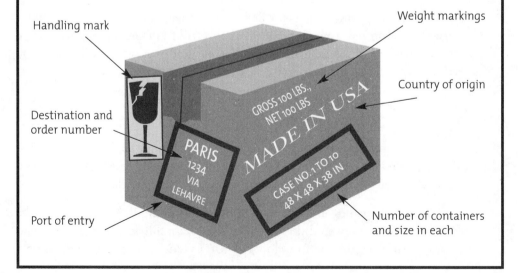

Handling mark

Weight markings

Destination and order number

Country of origin

Port of entry

Number of containers and size in each

GROSS 100 LBS., NET 100 LBS

MADE IN USA

PARIS 1234 VIA LEHAVRE

CASE NO. 1 TO 10 48 X 48 X 38 IN

2. Pack to expect Mother Nature's worst. Container loads can shift during heavy seas and storms. Someone else's cargo can smash into yours—or vice versa. A sea voyage may be good for a human's health, but it can be murder on merchandise. Think heat and humidity, salt air (which is incredibly corrosive), rain, and sea spray. When any or all of this gets into your containers, you can end up with rust, blistering, mold, mildew, and moisture damage.

3. Pack to expect human nature's worst. Some people just can't resist somebody else's goods. Theft can be a problem, especially when containers are left on the docks for a long time.

With all these potential disasters in mind, pack smart. Use adequate packaging materials; make sure your merchandise is cushioned against blows. Waterproof everything possible. Have package exteriors shrink-wrapped. Use waterproof lining on interiors. Coat exposed metal parts on machinery, for example, with grease or some other rust arrester. Use heavy strapping and seals. Discourage theft by eliminating trademarks or content descriptions on container exteriors. (No need to stencil "solid gold bars" on the box!)

Now that we've discussed the employees and insurance you'll need to run your business, it's time to take a look at the equipment that will be vital to its success.

10

Inside the Cargo Hold
Your Business Equipment

Your office will hold your most basic cargo—your computer, fax machine, and other business equipment. With these tools, your operations will run smoothly, speedily, and efficiently; without them, your company would be like a small and rickety biplane trying to deliver merchandise while your competition soared along in jumbo jets.

Similarly, even if no clients see it, your office's location and set-up can have a significant impact on the success of your business. This chapter focuses on equipment and office decisions.

Tools of the Trade

Outfitting an office is a large task. But take heart. We've provided a handy checklist (see page 193) to help you determine what you'll need, what you already have on hand, and which of those in-stock items is up to the job at hand. Die-hard shoppers may want to rush out and buy every item new, but this may not be necessary. Some or all of these things might already be scattered around your home, just waiting to be put to use.

After you've read this part of the chapter, go through the checklist and evaluate your stock. Is your computer trade-ready, or is it an antique that won't be able to keep up the pace? How about that printer? Will it be up to the job?

Now, checklist in hand, let's take a whirlwind virtual shopping spree. Ready, steady, go!

Wait a second. Let's discuss something first. There's always the buy of a lifetime, and there's always the ultimate fancy top of the line. What we're discussing here are the lower-end and middle-of-the-road models.

Computer Glitterati

Your computer will be the luminary of your office setup, coordinating your invoicing, accounting, word processing, and desktop publishing activities—not to mention co-starring in all email correspondence. In addition to any traveling you'll do as part of your market research, it will be your most important startup purchase. If you already own a computer, you'll want to make sure it's capable of handling the tasks you'll assign it.

Your import/export business computer should have the latest operating system so that documents from business partners read in English, not Egyptian hieroglyphics. To run current software properly, you'll need at least 1GB RAM, plus at least a 20GB hard drive. You can expect to pay from $600 to $1,500 for a good name-brand computer/monitor/keyboard, with prices increasing as you add on goodies.

> ## Trader's View
> When North Carolina trader Sam Nelson started his company in 1994, a computer was his only office equipment. His first office location was his home. Now he runs Nelisco Inc. from an office in a commercial area.

Purring Printers

A good printer is a must. Fortunately, really hot-stuff printers are less expensive than ever before, and most models are color-capable. You can expect to pay $90 to $150 for a basic color inkjet printer, $350 to $600 for a basic color laser printer, or $150 to $300 for a basic color printer/copier/fax machine.

> **Bright Idea**
>
> If you plan to travel a great deal, you might want to invest in a laptop computer or a Netbook. Either can do most of the things a desk computer does, with the added benefit of portability.

Just the Fax

The fax machine, as we've discussed, is a must for the international trader. Along with email, it's the method of choice for communicating quickly and clearly with clients, manufacturers, importers, and exporters around the globe. And don't forget faxing lunch orders to that deli down the street.

Fax machines can be purchased as combo fax/copiers, printers, and scanners. Make sure the fax machine you purchase will print on plain paper. Most of the documents you receive will be keepers—correspondence, invoices, and the like that will need to go into your permanent files. The ink on thermal fax paper (that slick gray stuff) fades to near invisibility in a short time, thus negating any archiving attempts.

A basic plain paper fax machine can be found for $30 to $100. As we've already noted, a combination printer/copier/fax machine ranges from $150 to $300 for basic models.

> **Bright Idea**
>
> Purchase a greeting card program. You can customize not only the artwork but also the text or verse and matching envelope. Sending a personalized thank-you card to clients and customers with the addressee's name embedded right in the message makes a terrific impression. You can find professional-quality (and really fun!) greeting card programs in the $30 to $50 range.

Soft on Software

A dazzling array of software lines the shelves of most office supply stores, ready to help you perform every business task: design and print your own checks, make mailing lists and labels, develop professional quality marketing materials, or be your own attorney and accountant.

Most new computers come already loaded with all the software you will need for basic office procedures. If yours doesn't or if you have lucked into a stripped-down hand-me-down, you may want to look into the following

First Impressions

Your business needs a professional image that tells potential clients and customers you're a savvy trader.

You can create this image on your own with desktop publishing. But as with deciding on a business name, be sure that the image you're beaming to the minds of buyers and clients is the one you want. Leave the over-the-top trendy or oh-so-cutesy images for other businesses. A logo featuring dancing skeletons with maracas won't quite cut it (although maracas do lend a Latin beat.)

Your most important goal is to convey the impression of international trade efficiency and expertise. This is what you're selling. Have a friend or family member look over your designs before you commit to a print run of 500 cards or sheets of letterhead. Do they see typos? Amateur design? Or do they catch the gleam of a business riding the waves of proficiency?

programs. You'll need a word processing program, with which you can write correspondence, contracts, sales reports for your clients, and whatever else strikes your fancy. A good basic program, such as the latest Microsoft Word, can be had for $80 to $200.

You may also want an accounting program, such as QuickBooks or Microsoft Money, to track your business finances. These are a sort of checkbook on CD-ROM and make record-keeping a breeze. You assign categories such as office supplies and business travel to the checks you write, and at tax time you print out a report showing how much you spent for what. Your accountant not only thanks you but gives you a discount for not having to wade through all your receipts. You can expect to pay about the same, $80 to $200, for your cyberspace checkbook.

There are also freebie downloadable software programs available online. You can find them at openoffice.org.

You can even get software that will enable you to make free video and voice calls, send instant messages, and share files. As you may already know, we're talking about Skype. This is a leading global internet communications company. Some of the free services require that both

Stat Fact

Founded in 2003 and purchased by Microsoft in 2011, Skype is responsible for a significant percentage of global international calling minutes. According to the Skype website, its users spend more than 2 billion minutes on Skype each day.

parties have Skype software, but you can also call land lines and cell phones for reasonable rates. Skype is available in over 40 countries worldwide. Check it out at skype.com.

Hello, Central

Besides your business cell phone, which you will obviously need, you may want a dedicated office land line and an additional line for your fax machine. If you still have a land line for your home phone, then you'll have three telephone lines coming into your home, two of which will be for your office. Therefore, you'll want a two-line phone so you can put one on hold while you're answering the other. You can divide up the three lines any way you like: You might put your home line and your business line on the two-line phone, leaving the third line for your fax machine. Or you might put the business and fax line on the two-line phone, leaving your home line in the kitchen or den. The idea behind either of these choices is that you can call out on your home or fax line (when it's not in use) and leave the business line for incoming calls.

A speaker is also a nice feature, leaving your hands free to work up financial data on your latest export venture while you're on hold. You can expect to pay about $70 to $150 for a two-line speakerphone with auto redial, memory dial, flashing lights, mute button, and other assorted goodies.

Another way to keep your hands free is to invest in a hands-free headset, usually ranging from $30 to $50.

Automated Answering Service

If you choose not to go with voice mail from your phone company, you'll need an answering machine. Unless you want to put your business greeting on your home machine and take the risk that your kids might erase messages to you, you should buy a separate machine for your office. You can buy a fancy one with caller ID, speakerphones, cordless phones, and 15 kinds of memos, but a good basic model capable of answering your business line can be had for less than $40. For a snazzier model that can answer two lines, expect to pay about $150.

Vociferous Voice Mail

The main advantage to purchasing voice mail with your phone plan is that if you have call waiting and you choose not to answer a second call that comes in, voice mail will take a message for you. Voice mail costs vary, especially because it often comes bundled with other features, but you can expect to pay $6 to $20 a month.

Of course, if you're using a cell phone instead of a land line, you'll already have that voice mail feature.

Laugh at Lightning

You should invest in a UPS, or uninterruptible power supply, for your computer system, especially if you live in an area where lightning or power surges are frequent features. If you're a computer newbie, you may not realize that even a flicker of power loss can shut down your computer, causing it to forget all the data you've carefully entered during your current work session, or—the ultimate horror—fry your computer's brains entirely. With a UPS in your arsenal, you won't lose power to your system when the house power fails or flickers. Instead, the unit flashes red and sounds a warning, giving you ample time to safely shut down your computer. You can expect to pay $125 and up for one of these power pals.

Lightning Strikes Again

A surge protector safeguards your electronic equipment from power spikes during storms or outages. Your battery backup will double as a surge protector for your

---

Read All About It

The written word is a powerful learning tool. One of your first steps in your new venture should be to read everything you can, not just about the specifics of international trade but also about starting a small business and marketing and sales techniques. Blitz the bookstore. Make an assault on your public library.

Your own business library should contain a variety of reference manuals. For starters, check out the following:

- ○ *Building an Import/Export Business* by Kenneth D. Weiss (John Wiley & Sons)
- ○ *Import/Export: How to Get Started in International Trade* by Carl A. Nelson (McGraw-Hill)
- ○ *Export-Import* by Joseph A. Zodl (Betterway Books)
- ○ Any of the Barron's foreign language books, such as *Learn Italian the Fast and Fun Way* by Marcel Danesi (Barron's Educational Series)

Don't stop with these. Immerse yourself in your subject. The more you know, the better an international trader you'll be.

computer hard drive, or CPU, and monitor, but you'll want protection for those other valuable office allies: your printer, fax machine, and copier. They don't need a battery backup because no data will be lost if the power goes out, and a surge protector will do the job for a lot less money. If you have a fax machine, be sure the surge protector also defends its phone line. You can expect to pay $15 to $60 for a surge protector.

Paper Cloning

The copier is an optional item, probably the least important of the large equipment items on the list, but as you grow, you may find it a necessary luxury. Keep in mind that you should never send a piece of paper out of your office unless you've kept a copy. You can always print two copies of every document you generate on your computer, keeping one as a file copy. But some forms, like the Shippers Export Declaration and other government-driven documents that you can't wring from your computer, demand a copier-made duplicate. Copiers come in a very wide price range, with basic ones going for $150 to $300. Also, as we've already mentioned, you can get a combined printer/copier/fax machine of a basic variety in the $150 to $300 range.

Cool and Calculating

What do calculators and telephones have in common? A numbered keypad and an important place on your desk. Even though your computer probably has a built-in calculator program, it helps to have the real thing close at hand. You can even check your work if you have a paper-tape model. Expect to pay less than $15 for a good battery-operated model and $25 to $50 for a plug-in calculator. You can even get a virtual paper tape model for about $18 to $25.

Well Supplied

Although they're easy to forget, small items like pens, paper clips, and sticky notes are inconvenient to be without. Keep your office well stocked with these supplies. Also, don't forget pencils—and a sharpener!

Step Into My Office

Office furniture is another optional item. It's important that your work environment be comfortable and ergonomic, but if you're home-based, it's acceptable to start off with an old door set on cinder blocks for a desk and an egg crate for your files.

When you're ready to make the big step toward real office furniture for that oh-so-professional look, you have a stunning array of possibilities to choose from.

We shopped the big office supply warehouse stores and found midrange desks from $250 to $450, a computer work center for $250, printer stands from $75 to $100, two-drawer letter-size file cabinets (which can double as your printer stand) from $40 to $125, and a four-shelf bookcase for $85.

Chairs are a very personal matter. Some people like the dainty secretary's chair for its economy of space; others want the more up-scale executive model. There are chairs with kangaroo pockets and chairs with pneumatic height adjustments. Prices range from $60 to $350, and up.

Equipment Expenses

To give you an idea of how much you can expect to budget, check out the costs of furniture, equipment, and supplies for our two hypothetical import/export services,

Office Supplies Shopping Mini-List

Computer/copier/fax paper	$_____
Blank business cards	_____
Blank letterhead stationery	_____
Matching envelopes	_____
10 x 13 envelopes	_____
Legal-sized envelopes	_____
File folders	_____
Return address self-stamper or stickers	_____
Extra printer cartridge	_____
Pencil sharpener	_____
Mouse pad	_____
Miscellaneous office supplies (pencils, paper clips, etc.)	_____
Extra fax cartridge	_____
Total Expenditures	$_____

Cargo Bay Traders and Clipper Trading Services Co. (see page 192). Cargo Bay Traders, a homebased newbie with no employees except its owner, so far has made a net profit of $15,000. The fledgling business counts as its equipment resources an inexpensive computer system, an inkjet printer, and the basics in software, as well as a phone and cell phone.

Clipper Trading Services, up and running for three years, makes its base in an office in an industrial park, has one full-time employee in addition to the owner, and has annual net profits of $200,000. Clipper trading boasts a top-of-the-line computer system for its owner, an inexpensive computer for its employee, a laser printer, a combo fax machine/scanner, a copier, and various publishing and marketing software programs that have caught its owner's eye over the years.

Trading Spaces

Whether you're a trader on the move, always flying from one exotic locale to another, or an armchair traveler who conducts most of his or her business from home base, you'll need a business office.

As we've explained, one of the perks of running an import/export business is that it lends itself to the homebased entrepreneur. It doesn't require a high-traffic or high-visibility location and doesn't need to be in a trendy part of town. Although you may have an occasional client stop in, you won't need a mahogany-paneled office with a lobby and conference room. The only real space requirement is an area large enough for your desk, chair, filing cabinets, and perhaps a bookshelf.

It's convenient—you couldn't get any closer to your office unless you slept with your computer. It's economical—you don't need to spend money on leased space, extra utilities, transportation costs, or lunches down at the corner grill.

Lloyd Davidson in Florida has his office at home. So does John Laurino in Brazil. "Of course, when necessary, I rent an adequate [warehouse] space," John says.

The Home Office

If you choose to be homebased, you can locate your office workspace anywhere in the house that's convenient. Ideally, however, you should have a dedicated office, a room that's reserved just for the business. You could locate this room in a den, a FROG (finished room over garage), the garage itself, or a spare bedroom. Keep in mind that whatever space you choose will be your workstation and command center.

If a dedicated office is not an option, you can also station yourself in a corner of the kitchen or at the dining room table. If you have a boisterous family, however, a

Sample Office Expenses

Furniture, Equipment, and Supplies	Cargo Bay Traders	Clipper Trading Service
Computer system (including printer)	$700.00	$3,000.00
Printer/copier/fax	200.00	400.00
Software	300.00	550.00
Phone system	70.00	230.00
Cell phone	100.00	100.00
Answering machine	40.00	130.00
Uninterruptible power supply	60.00	200.00
Surge protector	34.00	34.00
Calculator	10.00	75.00
Desk	250.00	600.00
Desk chair	60.00	200.00
Printer stand	0	70.00
File cabinet	40.00	200.00
Bookcase	85.00	125.00
Printer/copier paper	25.00	50.00
Blank business cards	10.00	18.00
Letterhead	40.00	40.00
Matching envelopes	40.00	40.00
10 x 13 envelopes	20.00	35.00
Legal-sized envelopes	4.00	8.00
Address stamp or stickers	10.00	10.00
Extra printer cartridge	25.00	80.00
Extra fax cartridge	80.00	80.00
Mouse pad	5.00	10.00
Miscellaneous office supplies	100.00	150.00
Total Expenditures	**$2,308.00**	**$6,365.00**

The Trader's Office Checklist

Use this handy list as a shopping guide for equipping your office. It's been designed with the one-person home office in mind. If you have partners, employees, or you just inherited a million dollars from a mysterious foundation with the stipulation that you spend at least half on office equipment, you may want to make modifications.

After you have done your shopping, fill in the purchase price next to each item, add up the total and you will have a head start on the Startup Costs Worksheet on page 67!

- ❏ Windows 8 or higher Pentium-class PC with flat screen monitor and CD-DVD drive $ _____
- ❏ Website   _____
- ❏ Zip drive (if not included with computer)   _____
- ❏ Laser or inkjet printer   _____
- ❏ Fax machine   _____
- ❏ Software:
  - word processing   _____
  - desktop publishing   _____
  - accounting   _____
- ❏ Phones, two or three lines with voice mail, or answering machine   _____
- ❏ Uninterruptible power supply   _____
- ❏ Surge protector   _____
- ❏ Calculator   _____
- ❏ Office supplies (see mini-list on page 190)   _____

Not on the critical list
- ❏ Copier   _____
- ❏ Desk   _____
- ❏ Desk chair   _____
- ❏ Filing cabinet   _____
- ❏ Bookcase   _____
  - **Total Expenditures** $ _____

cubby hole in your bedroom is likely to be much more conducive to quiet, clear thinking than a nook in the family room with kids playing or watching T.V. Besides, yelling into the phone over cartoon KERBLAMs and POWs! will not make you sound particularly professional to your clients.

The Tax Man Speaketh

Another advantage to the home office is the ability to write it off as a home business. The IRS will graciously allow you to deduct money from your income taxes if you're using a portion of your home as your income-producing workspace. You can deduct a percentage of expenses equivalent to the percentage of space your home office occupies. If, for example, you're using one room in an eight-room house, you can deduct one-eighth of your rent or mortgage plus one-eighth of your utility bills.

There is, of course, an *if* involved here. You can use this deduction if you're using this space solely as your office. If you've turned your spare bedroom into your office and you don't use it for anything but conducting your business, then you qualify. If, however, your office is tucked into a corner of the kitchen and you're still feeding people in there, you don't qualify for the home office deduction (unless you can convince the IRS that you order Chinese every night at work and the refrigerator is actually a file cabinet).

Growing Pains

As your business grows or when you find yourself with stock to store, such as when you have your distributor cap on and have purchased merchandise, you may decide that it's time to move up to outside or commercial office space.

Because the import/export business doesn't rely on client traffic or a prestigious address, any area that appeals to you and your pocketbook is up for grabs. Rick Casey, a real estate broker with Bay Properties in Panama City Beach, Florida, recommends going the office/warehouse route in an industrial park. If product storage is your only problem, Casey advises, you might also consider keeping your home office and renting space from a self-storage facility.

If storage is not a concern for you but you want an office away from home, you might look for commercial space in other areas—but not in the retail arena. "You don't want to rent retail space when you're doing a service business," Casey says. "You don't need the high visibility." Or the higher prices.

What's the Alternative?

If commercial office space isn't your bag, you might consider a more unconventional approach. Rent a house or apartment (provided you check the zoning laws first). If you already live in an apartment, you may choose to rent another unit in the same building to use as your office. You can walk to work. And the landlord may give you a package deal—or a finder's fee!

Or you can take a space over a downtown storefront. How about over a coffeehouse or doughnut shop or bagel bakery? What better incentive to get to work in the morning?

Trader's View

Wahib W. advises the newbie trader to focus on a country in which he or she already has direct experience. "I see a lot of [traders] who were in the American military overseas," Wahib says, "or who have an ethnic background from another country and have family or contacts overseas. Personal contact is a very strong [asset]."

Efficiency Expert

If you prefer to have your coffee and croissant—and your office—in your home, make sure your space is organized and efficient. If at all possible, designate a separate room with four walls and a door. Aim for pleasant, quiet, well-lit surroundings. You are going to be spending a lot of time in this space, so you want it to be comfortable.

If you can't carve out a dedicated space, by all means take over a corner of another room. But consider it your permanent office. Choose a desk or table that is large enough to hold your computer, keyboard, telephone, and other desk items and still has enough room to spread out your working papers. A charming 19th-century cherry wood secretary looks great but probably won't allow enough space for your market research, correspondence, and files, plus you and your computer. Don't skimp on elbow room.

Your two main realms of activity will be marketing and administration. Make sure you have enough space to store account records and leads, both client and buyer, as well as reference materials. You can set up separate alphabetical file cards for contacts with suppliers, customers, sales representatives, and distributors, or you can use a system of folders in which you keep copies of all correspondence and replies. Whichever system you choose, remember that you're in the business of matching buyers and sellers as well as producers and distributors, and that you must be able to access this information quickly and easily. It's no fun digging through the back of the clothes closet or running out to the garage every time somebody emails you with a question.

In addition to your marketing materials, you should also carve out enough space for your administrative department. Accurate record-keeping is a must in any business, but even more so in import/export, where documentation rules the day. You'll need at least one file cabinet to start with; you'll probably soon expand to two or more.

You'll also want a bookcase for your reference materials and a comfortable desk chair. If you have enough funds and room, a plump visitor's chair or sofa is a plus for those occasional business guests.

Beware!

Be sure to print and file hard copies of all email correspondence that is sent to you and all missives you send to others. Keeping everything on your computer's hard drive may seem like a swell paper-saving idea, but if your computer crashes, you'll lose everything (including, temporarily, your mind). The same goes for computerized databases of customers, clients, and distributors.

Likewise

If your office is in a commercial space, you'll need the same setup with plenty of room for all those files and your desk, chair, visitors' furniture, and a desk and chair for any employee(s) you may hire.

And let's not forget the electronics. Your computer should occupy a place of honor away from dirt, drafts, and blinding sunlight. Ditto for your printer and fax machine.

In a commercial office, you'll also want that American office altarpiece, the coffee maker, and if you can provide a tidbit or two—a plate of cookies, for example, when you know guests are arriving—you'll go a long way toward cementing ties. Everyone appreciates a treat, and foreign visitors are usually eager to sample anything "American."

No matter where you decide to locate your office, with a little effort you can maximize the productivity of the time you spend in it. Which, of course, will do much to strengthen your business. For more ideas on strengthening your business, as well as increasing your visibility in the trading arena, read on.

11

The Trader's Trumpet
Advertising and Marketing

As an international trader, your mission is sales—in two different but overlapping arenas: 1) selling yourself and your company to clients as an import/export manager for their products, and 2) selling the products themselves to representatives and distributors. Success in one of these arenas will contribute to your success in the other. Once you've established a favorable sales record with one client's goods, you'll have a track record with which to entice other clients. And, of course, each success will contribute to your own self-confidence, which will, in turn, lend that air of confidence to your negotiations with new prospects.

So which comes first, selling the product or yourself? In most cases, you'll need to sell your company first, because until you have a client's merchandise to represent, you're not going to get too far. Marketing your import/export management company involves two steps:

1. Convincing a prospective client that she has a product worth exporting
2. Persuading her to use your company as her export manager

Hunting for Exports

A surprisingly small percentage of domestic producers export their wares. So your marketing goal is to convince the huge remainder that they can increase profits by exporting—with your guidance—to specific target countries. You can accomplish this with direct mail and cold calls. If you're starting with imports, don't ignore this section; you'll work in basically the same manner.

Before you initiate contact with any manufacturer, you'll need to do some basic market research:

- What products are hot sellers in the domestic marketplace? Focus your attention on products that you know well or use yourself, or that are bestsellers in their market niches.
- Are these products hot sellers in your target countries?
- If not, are there situations or markets that would put these products in great demand if the products were available?
- Who manufactures these products?
- What is the selling price of each product, and of competing products or brands, domestically and in your target countries?

Taking the Lead

International traders rarely use print ads to attract customers. Instead, they take advantage of the trade lead sources we've explored in Chapter 7 and throughout this book. But if you live in a trade-rich area, like Miami, you might choose to advertise in your local Yellow Pages, where hopeful manufacturers or vendors can look you up in a snap.

If you decide to go with a phone directory ad, look over the ads of your competitors and then go one better. Make yours stand out from the crowd with clever copy that tells what you do—for instance, products or regions in which you specialize—and why you excel.

Smart Tip

Remember that your job will be easier if you approach manufacturers of products you know and believe in.

Direct-Mail Dazzle

Once you've researched some companies, you're ready to begin your direct-mail campaign. Choose one manufacturer of one of the products you have researched. Then either search online or call the company and ask for the name of the person to whom you will want to write. If the company is small, you will probably want the president or owner. If it's a larger concern, you might want to direct your letter to the vice president in charge of sales or the sales manager. By discovering the proper addressee, you'll be assured of your letter reaching him or her instead of somebody else's wastebasket.

Armed with a name and title, write your letter, taking care to address the following points:

- Introduce yourself and your company.
- Briefly outline the potential of the overseas market.
- Outline the product's potential within that market.
- If possible, explain why and how your company, out of all others, will be able to position the product best. For example, if you have experience with like products, be sure to say so.
- If you already have contacts with foreign distributors, explain that you have foreign reps for overseas sales.
- Ask for a personal meeting to further discuss the possibilities.

Check out the sample letters on pages 200 and 201—one for the newbie with no experience in the product and one for the newbie with a background in the field.

Once your first letter is in the mail, sit down and write another one to another potential client in another product line, and then another, until you've exhausted your first set of preliminary market research products. It's best not to start with two clients that have the same type of products because if they both respond, you'll have to sell in competition with your own

Dollar Stretcher

If you can, target manufacturers within driving distance of your home office. This will keep your initial travel costs to a minimum.

Gum Tree Trading Company

123 Eucalyptus Lane
Sea Terrace, CA 92000, USA

July 5, 20xx

Mr. Murray Mulch
President
Mulch Products Inc.
456 Tea Tree Street
Sea Terrace, CA 92000

Dear Mr. Mulch:

How would you like to exponentially increase your company's sales and expand your market with a minimum of time, trouble, and expense?

Sound impossible? It may not be. As owner of Gum Tree Trading Company, I am currently researching the profitable sales of mulch in the European market. As you may know, organic garden products are very popular in Europe, with sales continuously on the rise. I am familiar with your company's mulches, and after preliminary research, I believe they have tremendous export potential in this area.

To complete my research, I will need pricing information, any brochures and marketing information that you can offer, and a few sample bags of mulch, which I will send on to my foreign representatives.

If we find that we can sell your products profitably in Europe, we will handle all export details from shipping to distribution to securing payment. This is a terrific opportunity to increase your sales with little cost or risk to your firm. I will call you to discuss this exciting program in further detail.

Very best,

Andrea April

Andrea April
Gum Tree Trading Company

AA/ta

(000) 000-1234 (phone)—(000) 000-4567 (fax)
email: GumTree@Holiday.com

Sample Direct Sales Letter #2: Newbie with Experience

Gum Tree Trading Company
123 Eucalyptus Lane
Sea Terrace, CA 92000, USA

July 5, 20xx

Mr. Murray Mulch
President
Mulch Products Inc.
456 Tea Tree Street
Sea Terrace, CA 92000

Dear Mr. Mulch:

How would you like to exponentially increase your company's sales and expand your market with a minimum of time, trouble, and expense?

Sound impossible? It may not be. As owner of Gum Tree Trading Company, I am currently researching the profitable sales of mulch in the European market. As you may know, organic garden products are very popular in Europe, with sales continuously on the rise. I am familiar with your company's mulches, and after preliminary research, I believe they have tremendous export potential in this area.

To complete my research, I will need pricing information, any brochures and marketing information that you can offer, and a few sample bags of mulch, which I will send on to my foreign representatives.

If we find that we can sell your products profitably in Europe, we will handle all export details from shipping to distribution to securing payment. **With more than ten years of experience in garden product sales, I am confident that my company can sell your mulches.** This is a terrific opportunity to increase your sales with little cost or risk to your firm. I will call you to discuss this exciting program in further detail.

Very best,

Andrea April

Andrea April
Gum Tree Trading Company

AA/ta

(000) 000-1234 (phone)—(000) 000-4567 (fax)
email: GumTree@Holiday.com

clients, which is both difficult and unfair. But if you've exhausted your first line of attack (without success), you can go back and try another client in the same product line.

Now wait a week or ten days. If you haven't heard from your first target manufacturer, give him a call. Ask to set up a meeting in his office to discuss your plan. Then call the next manufacturer and the next. If you're not familiar with sales, you may find this portion of the program a white-knuckler. Don't be nervous! You're legitimately

Trader's View

"Never consider that just a letter, a fax, or a phone call is sufficient," advises Bruno C., the French trader. "Follow up regularly."

I Wanna Sell Checklist

When you contact the manufacturer for the first time, you won't know whether you'll be able to handle her merchandise profitably. You'll have to find out its import or export price and then set up additional market research to determine how much sales potential you can realize from the product. So how do you accomplish this?

❑ Take one of the products you've already researched, one you know well and believe in or one that's a bestseller in its market niche.

❑ Contact the manufacturer and explain that you would like to sell her product abroad. Tell her you'll need to conduct some market research so you can find out all you can about the product, including cost, the trade channels she engages in, whether her company can provide any advertising assistance, what size orders she can fill, and how long it will take to fill orders.

❑ Perform a pricing analysis. How much can you sell the product for in a targeted country? What type of commission can you add? Can you keep the price competitive? Don't forget to figure your shipping costs, tariffs, and other operating expenses.

❑ Locate distributors or sales reps. Do they think they can sell the product at this price?

❑ Once you're satisfied that there's a viable market for the product, formulate an initial marketing plan.

❑ Get back to the manufacturer to work out the details and draw up a preliminary contract.

offering these people a terrific opportunity. Not everyone is going to bite (not everyone can recognize a great deal when it jumps up and grabs them), but not everyone is going to turn you down, either. A "no thank you" now and then is part of the game.

(Cold-) Calling All Clients

Cold-calling, so-called because you call a potential client "cold," without any warming up by prior contact, is an alternative to the direct-mail approach. The good news is that if you're calling locally, it's usually cheaper than direct mail. The bad news is that it requires much more perseverance to be effective. The other good news, however, is that, done properly, a cold call can be much more effective than direct mail.

Before you make your first call, be sure you know what you want to say and how you want to say it. Some experts recommend writing out a sort of "script" that you can follow during the course of your call. This is a good starting-off exercise to help plan your spiel, but be aware of the fact that following a script has its drawbacks. The main one is that the person you're calling doesn't know he's supposed to be following the script, too, and when he gets off track, so do you.

A better idea is to discuss your marketing plan with everybody you can get to listen: your spouse or significant other, your parents or children (if they're old enough), your friends, and even your obnoxious neighbor. Each time you tell somebody your ideas and the reasoning behind them, you're rehearsing for that cold call

> **Tip...**
>
> ### Smart Tip
> Pressed for time when it comes to your marketing strategy? Go guerilla with *Guerilla Marketing in 30 Days* from Entrepreneur Press. You'll have all you need to get a marketing plan together in a month, including tips on cross-promoting your products. Hey, wait a minute . . .

to a potential client. And each time someone raises an objection or points out a flaw (here is where the obnoxious neighbor comes in handy), it's an opportunity for you to either overcome the objection or revise your plan to compensate for the flaw. Then when you make your actual cold calls, you're well-versed in all sorts of responses.

Check out the sample cold-call script on page 204. Don't try to follow it to the letter, but use it as a jumping-off point. And don't forget to communicate your enthusiasm!

Desperately Seeking Imports

We've talked about how to find export products to send abroad. But what about imports? How do you go about finding goods to bring stateside? You have several options:

Sample Cold-Call Script

Andrea:	Hi, I'm Andrea April with Gum Tree Trading Company. We've been researching sales of organic mulch in Europe, and we think your products will sell very well there. May I take a few moments of your time to discuss this with you?
Mr. Mulch:	I don't have time now.
Andrea:	I understand. When would be a good time to call you back?
Mr. Mulch:	I am really not interested. Wait a minute. Why do you think our products will sell well? Where in Europe?
Andrea:	Europeans are much more environmentally conscious than we are, and they're also very into gardening, so organic products like yours are big sellers. We are seeing sales increasing by X percent annually, especially in Great Britain. We are also looking at France and Germany as excellent target markets.
Mr. Mulch:	So why are you calling me?
Andrea:	Because we would like to sell your products for you in Europe. We're an export management company. Are you familiar with this type of firm?
Mr. Mulch:	No.
Andrea:	Well, we will handle all the export details, from shipping to distribution to arranging for letters of credit, so you will be expanding your company's sales, your market, and your brand-name visibility at little cost to you.
Mr. Mulch:	So what's the catch?
Andrea:	None. We'll take a commission on our sales, but since this will come out of profits you would not have realized before this program, you'll still be way ahead of the game. And, of course, we'll have to complete our research before we can promise a deal. I will need you to provide me with pricing information, any brochures and marketing information you've got, and a few sample bags of mulch, which I'll send on to my foreign reps.
Mr. Mulch:	You have people in England?
Andrea:	Oh, yes. And in France and Germany as well. How about if I stop by your office later this week? I can show you our preliminary research, and we can discuss the program further.
Mr. Mulch:	Europe, huh? I never thought about it. Sure. Let me have my secretary set up an appointment.

- Travel abroad on an import search mission.
- Wait for foreign manufacturers to contact you.
- Attend trade shows.
- Contact foreign embassies' trade development offices.
- Contact the U.S. Department of Commerce's International Trade Association.
- Track down leads on the internet and in trade publications.

Now, let's tackle these options one at a time.

The Travel Log

Traveling abroad is, in most people's minds, the most delightful of all these options. It's not always practical in terms of time, money, or other commitments you may have, such as your day job or family, but it's not a must, either, so don't fret if you can't manage it.

Dear Manufacturer

Keep these tips in mind when writing your direct-mail pieces:

- ○ Try writing as if you're speaking to a friend. You want your letter to sound professional, of course, but stiff and stodgy doesn't create interest. Keep it peppy!
- ○ Insert a few details about the potential client's product and why the product will sell well abroad. This lends credibility by demonstrating that you've done your homework. You know and understand the field at home and in your target market.
- ○ Have you spelled the potential client's name and his company name correctly? Goofing here will instantly telegraph that you don't know what you're talking about and/or that you don't pay attention to details.
- ○ Do you have everything else spelled correctly, and is your grammar and punctuation fine-tuned? If you're not a whiz at these things, hit your word processing program's spelling and grammar check key. After that, have someone who is a whiz look over your letter. (Electronic spelling and grammar checkers don't catch every error.)
- ○ Remember to stick to the point.

▲

Trader's View

Jan Herremans, the Belgian tire and clothing trader, gets most of his customers from one main source—hard work—which he breaks down into travel, trade shows, business magazines, and the internet.

The big plus is that you can view foreign products in a realistic setting, checking out what sells where, why, and for how much. You may know here at home, for example, that Swiss watches and Japanese electronics are top sellers, but so does everybody else. This knowledge is not necessarily going to shoot you to the top with a new and exciting product. But if you travel in Mexico, for example, you'll see that everybody on every street corner is savoring paletas, frozen Popsicle-type treats made with fresh fruit and cream. If you put this person-on-the-street observation together with your own domestic observation that smoothies—fresh fruit and yogurt frozen drinks—are the rage, you might decide that paletas could be a good import.

If you're interested in general merchandise, traveling in search of goods can be the best way to garner immediate results. As in domestic exporting, there are many manufacturers out there who have never considered selling their products in the United States, even though the market may be extremely profitable. And the most effective way to find these companies is through field research.

But keep this caveat in mind: Don't limit yourself by looking only at what products you want to import. Consider also what kinds of strategies you'll use to make your profits. Are you more interested in importing products with brand-name identities, or do you lean toward low price and high volume?

If you're going the low-price/high-volume route, you'll want to focus on countries that are low-cost-goods producers, like China, India, and Mexico. Because these countries usually have emerging economies, your importing mission (indeed your entire trip) may be a little more complicated and require a little more patience. But don't be daunted. This is the stuff of adventure. And if you're not the adventurous type, think about this: The potential profits in these types of ventures are often much greater for the newbie importer than going the brand-name route.

Just Call Me

Traveling in search of products to import is fun and lucrative, but experienced importers also rely on manufacturers contacting them. This method has two important bonuses: 1) You don't have to go anywhere to search for merchandise, and 2) you don't have to persuade anybody to export their merchandise. If

Smart Tip

Tip...

Access the International Trade Administration's website at trade.gov for contacts in your field. These people are ready to help you export.

Bright Idea

Trade shows, held for every industry from bridal planning to building supplies, are a good way to scope out products. You'll get a rep's-eye view of what's hot and what's new in the market. North Carolina trader Sam Nelson has attended trade shows from the beginning. "I go to network," he says.

they are contacting you, you know they are interested.

If you're brand-new to international trade, of course, this option is probably not going to do you much good because no one knows you're out there to contact. But as your company grows, as you make contacts all over the world, you'll find that other companies will come to you—often sooner and more frequently than you might imagine.

Not all your calls for help will come from manufacturers with a product to export. You'll also receive calls from importers seeking a particular U.S. product—sometimes merchandise with which you have no familiarity. Where do you go to fulfill their requests? One terrific source is the Thomas Register of American Manufacturers, a database of products and companies that boasts more than 700,000 manufacturers and distributors from 28 countries with 11,000 product categories. Access the register for free at thomasnet.com.

Singles Dances

Trade shows are a terrific way to meet foreign manufacturers, distributors, and representatives. Like church-sponsored singles dances, everybody there is in attendance for the purpose of attracting somebody else. So get out there and mingle!

Foreign trade shows or fairs, set up by foreign governments to showcase their own manufacturers, are held to tempt you, the potential importer. You'll have to travel abroad to attend some shows. Others come to you (or rather various locales in the United States). Call the embassy or consulate of the country you're interested in to find out when and if they have trade shows scheduled and where.

Toothpicks to Tires

While you're making those calls to consulates and embassies, ask for their trade development office. Many countries and geographic regions sponsor offices where you can find specific information on manufacturers of everything from toothpicks to truck tires to fur coats.

Smart Tip

Tip...

How do you convince potential clients that your company is the one to go with? Impress them with your knowledge of the product or the field, your sales contacts, and your sales track record. If you don't have one yet, substitute your enthusiasm for the product.

Often a single phone call is all it takes to get a long list of suppliers eager to do business with American importers. Don't be shy. These people are on the job just to match you with a supplier back home. Let them get to work!

The U.S. government's International Trade Association can also help you locate various trade groups and development agencies that will help you find specific kinds of manufacturers or suppliers.

Bounty Hunting

Like a good bounty hunter, you'll want to explore every avenue. Don't forget the many terrific online trade lead sites. For starters, check out:

- Tradenet at tradenet.com
- WTN-DE Business Center at wtn-de.com
- TradeKey at tradekey.com

If you find something you like, send a letter expressing your interest (see page 209).

Selling Yourself

You've located foreign manufacturers or suppliers whose products have U.S. sales potential. Now you have to sell them on the idea of entering the American marketplace and convince them that you're the person to usher them in. How do you do this? Basically, the same way you'll pitch domestic manufacturers, with a direct-mail campaign. Only in this case, you'll do better to think of it as a direct fax letter. Although many traders rely on international mail, unless you're sending to regions or countries with highly developed infrastructures, such as Western Europe or Canada, you'll be much more assured of your missive reaching its destination if you send it by fax.

In your letter, outline the various opportunities available in the United States for the product and highlight that you'll handle all import logistics with little cost to the manufacturer. Check out the sample letter on page 213. Notice that this letter is very similar to the domestic one, with two exceptions:

1. We've addressed the owner of the company as Monsieur (abbreviated M.) instead of "Mr." Even though the letter is in English, this little touch shows that you know something about the French

> **Trader's View**
>
> "Don't think having a good product alone will boost sales!" cautions Michael Richter. "You have to do marketing and set aside a corresponding amount of time for that [task]."

Sample Trade Lead Response Letter

Treasure Bay Traders
789 Seekers Cove
Sea Terrace, CA 92000, USA

July 5, 20xx

Mr. Nigel Owens
Managing Director
Sterling Frames Ltd.
62 Gosham Street
Chipping Huntbridge, Sussex, England

Dear Mr. Owens:

We are responding to your trade lead, which we viewed with great enthusiasm on the International Trade Data Network. We are very interested in importing fine English interior design products such as your sterling silver frames. Our research shows a great demand for this type of product in the American market, and although we are a newer trading company, we are positioning ourselves as a leader in European interior design imports.

Please send us your current catalog and best export prices, along with any samples you feel would help us promote your products. Please feel free to contact me to discuss any questions you may have.

Very best,

Eric Williams

Eric Williams
Treasure Bay Traders

EW/ta

(000) 000-1234 (phone)—(000) 000-4567 (fax)
email: TreasureBay@Holiday.com

language and that you've taken the care and courtesy to address M. Picard in his own tongue.

2. We've checked to make sure we've eliminated any slang that may be confusing to non-native speakers.

International Call

Follow up in a few days with another fax. Think of the follow-up as a firm but gentle nudge, an opportunity to strengthen your position and demonstrate real interest in importing the merchandise. Check out the sample follow-up letter on page 214. Remember that part of your task is to convince the potential client that your company is the best one for the job, so you have to supply a reason for this. If you can't claim, as Andrea does in the sample letter, that you're experienced in interior design (or mulch or whatever) sales in the United States and Europe (or wherever), then come up with something else. Maybe you're only experienced in the United States so far. That's fine! That's where you'll be selling. Maybe you're not experienced yet, but you've done a great deal of research. Fill that in instead. Use your creativity!

If you know the potential client speaks English or if you speak his language, try a phone call instead of a fax. Just remember: When calling non-native English speakers, talk a little slower and a lot more clearly. Most people tend to mumble or slur speech, which makes it difficult for foreign ears to comprehend.

The Marketing Plan

Whether you're planning on exporting or importing, be prepared to present your prospective client with a marketing plan. If the manufacturer is close to home, you'll naturally present it in person. If she's overseas, you may still have to (make that get to) arrange a personal visit to close the deal. If you feel strongly enough about the product's U.S. potential, the trip will be worth the time and expense.

To prepare your marketing plan, you'll need the information you've already asked for: pricing, product brochures or literature, and samples. If your prospect balks at supplying these materials, tell her that you'll need them to further explore the market potential and develop a presentation for her, outlining the market strategy you plan to pursue.

Once you have the materials in your office, sit down and figure out every possible expense you'll have so that you can arrive at your sales price. (Take another look at Chapter 8 for a review of how to do this.) Then, if you've already been in contact with distributors or representatives, find out if this price will sell in their market. If you don't have any reps yet, you'll need to locate one (see "Pursuing the Perfect Rep" section) and determine if he can work with that price. Assuming the answer is yes, you've got a viable product.

Now write out your marketing plan, which should include the following:

Smart Tip _Tip..._

To make sure you're not calling clients in the middle of the night, check out time zones for hundreds of international cities at world timeserver.com.

- *Target.* Which country or countries will you or your representatives sell in? Why are these markets viable? Include positive market research information and be sure to assemble it in a clear, concise, easy-to-digest format. This is where your desktop publishing programs will shine; you can make charts, graphs, and tables interspersed with facts, figures, and text.
- *Sales.* Explain at what price you'll sell the product. Give your annual sales forecast, your fee structure, and the profits the manufacturer can expect.
- *Marketing.* Briefly touch on any special marketing or promotions for the product, for example, foreign or domestic trade shows or any local advertising your reps will do.

Money Talks

If the merchandise you're interested in isn't branded (doesn't carry a brand name), copyrighted, or otherwise restricted in some way, perhaps your best profit potential lies in acting as an import merchant. You'll purchase the goods outright and then sell them to your own distributors. Provided you have the necessary capital and marketing power, your contact with the foreign supplier will be geared more toward negotiation. Ask that all relevant information, such as price and terms of quote and financial requirements, be in written form.

If you're serious about buying, most foreign suppliers will be eager to talk. But make sure the price quoted will give you enough room to make an acceptable profit. And when you're ready to buy, be prepared for a letter of credit. Virtually every overseas supplier will want one, especially if you're a first-time customer.

We Now Present

Your presentation package must look professional. Use those desktop publishing programs and your own creativity to develop the following elements:

- Your marketing plan
- Your company brochure with a current client list (when you have one)
- A personal resume highlighting any background relevant to the product or to sales or international trade

Beware!
Your exact distribution and marketing plans are your trade secret. Don't give your prospect anything but a general outline. Let him rely on you!

Now make up a cover page with the title Export Marketing Plan for Mulch Products Inc. (or whatever company) centered about one-fourth of the way down the page. A few inches below it, center your company name. You can put your logo below this if you've designed one. Put this package in a folder or binder. You'll find several styles to choose from at just about any office supply store. Make sure the one you go with looks stylish and professional. A good choice would be the kind with a black plastic and metal slide and a clear plastic cover through which your cover page will be visible. It's equally important to ensure that everything in your marketing plan is spelled correctly and is grammatically correct. Typos and grammar goofs will make you look amateurish and inattentive to detail.

Take a Meeting

Arrive at the presentation looking as sharp and professional as your marketing plan. Even if you live in a casual area where shorts and T-shirts are the norm, put on a power suit. Be prompt. Tardiness is a sure way to jeopardize your chances for success. It demonstrates that you don't have a lot of respect for your prospective client and that you're not very efficient, neither of which is going to make you a golden boy or girl in the eyes of your target person.

Once behind the target's office door, you'll present your pitch. Be sure to cover:

- how cost-effective exporting the product can be
- the potential returns the manufacturer will realize
- any costs involved to export the product, i.e., any special labeling or marking, export packing
- your fee structure

Remember that your angle is:

Gum Tree Trading Company

123 Eucalyptus Lane
Sea Terrace, CA 92000, USA

July 5, 20xx

M. John Pierre Picard
Picard & Fils et Cie
456 Rue des Matins
75007 Paris, France

Dear M. Picard:

How would you like to exponentially increase your company's sales and expand your market at almost no cost?

Does this seem impossible? It may not be. As owner of Gum Tree Trading Company, I am currently researching the profitable sales of European mirrors in the United States. As you may know, these interior design products are very popular in America. I am familiar with your company's high quality mirrors, and after preliminary research, I believe they have tremendous export potential.

To complete my research, I will need pricing information, any brochures and marketing information that you can offer, and a few sample mirrors.

If we find that we can sell your products profitably in the United States, we will handle all export details from shipping to distribution to securing payment. This is a terrific opportunity to increase your sales with little cost or risk to your firm. I look forward to hearing from you soon to discuss this exciting program in further detail.

Very best,

Andrea April

Andrea April
Gum Tree Trading Company

AA/ta

(000) 000-1234 (phone)—(000) 000-4567 (fax)
email: GumTree@Holiday.com

Sample Foreign Sales Follow-Up Letter

Gum Tree Trading Company
123 Eucalyptus Lane
Sea Terrace, CA 92000, USA

July 5, 20xx

M. John Pierre Picard
Picard & Fils et Cie
456 Rue des Matins
75007 Paris, France

Dear M. Picard:

I am writing to follow up on the fax I sent last week. My company is very interested in representing your fine mirrors in the United States. I would like to repeat that this is a terrific opportunity for your company. We would purchase directly from you and handle all export details ourselves.

We are experienced in interior design product sales in the United States and in Europe. I will call you to discuss this exciting program.

Very best,

Andrea April

Andrea April
Gum Tree Trading Company

AA/ta

(000) 000-1234 (phone)—(000) 000-4567 (fax)
email: GumTree@Holiday.com

- Exporting opens additional markets to the manufacturer at very little cost to him.
- You'll handle all logistics, from shipping through documentation to the securing of payment and documentation.
- All he has to do is fulfill the orders you'll bring in and prepare them for shipment.

Representative or Distributor?

Keep in mind that if, as a new trader, you pitch yourself as a sales representative who's working on commission, you probably won't be able to close a deal on the first or even second call. Without a track record, you'll have to be both persuasive and tenacious.

As an alternative, you may want to offer yourself as a distributor. The good news here is that it's easier to convince the manufacturer to go with you. He doesn't have to put out money for commissions or anything else except a few samples. The bad news is that buying the product yourself will add a sizable amount to your startup costs. If you strongly believe in the product, however, and you have the funds (or can get a loan for them), this is one way to position yourself in the trade channel.

Shake on It

After your brilliant sales presentation, your prospect is anxious to shake on the deal and get exporting. Close the deal by having him sign a sole representative contract, which you've already had your attorney draw up and which you've cleverly brought along. This contract should cover the various guidelines of the agreement, including:

- Responsibility for promoting the product
- Territory
- Method and times of commission payments
- Handling methods required for letters of credit
- Any necessary product modification
- Annual sales forecasts

Marketing to the World with One Click

Look beyond your own storefront for successful online trade marketing. After all, just hanging out your online shingle does not mean business will just walk in the virtual door. Like personal investing, you must build a diversified portfolio of online marketing and advertising to generate positive results.

Count Me In

The first marketing ploy is the easiest and cheapest. Participate in online import/export communities. Whether you post frequently on Q&A message boards or record the online minutes for your local international business club, be a presence. There are points to be gained by simply "showing up." Remember, though, that you are representing your company at all times, so type accordingly. Some tips:

- *Project the positive.* You are the public face of your trading company, so act like it. If you feel the need to post something negative, think on it first, then do so in the most professional manner possible.

- *Become an expert exporter.* Offer quotes for news articles, write in to message boards as a professional exporter/importer with XX years in the business. Soon, you'll find yourself at the top of the Google listings.

- *Check that grammar.* You don't need to be Shakespeare to have good, solid, basic grammar skills.

- *Offer an exchange.* Provide a free online course to a group or association in exchange for online marketing to its constituents.

What You See Is What You Get

Website or no website? That is the question. And, for all but the tiniest trading businesses, the answer is increasingly *yes*. John Laurino in Brazil and Michael Richter in Germany both have their own websites. "To be present on the web is a key point for any small business," says John—and with good reason. In the years since he launched his site, the Brazilian trader has signed on many clients who found his company through a web search.

In Germany, Michael went with a web presence for two reasons. "I wanted to be found worldwide," he says, "and to give others general information so as not to answer every question again and again."

And it worked. The following year he made about 40 percent above the turnover of a normal year.

Sam Nelson, exporting from North Carolina, does a significant portion of his sales via his website.

Luckily, website creation and maintenance today are cheaper than ever. For the price of a

> **Smart Tip**
> You can search for domain names and receive alternate choices if your number-one pick is taken at register.com. The site also provides links for web hosting, design, and other useful services.

Netflix membership, you can create and manage an online presence that will be available to possible clients all over the world. And no, you don't need to know a lot about web design or maintenance to make it happen.

Most website design sites offer a "What You See is What You Get" (WYSIWYG) approach to design. Using templates created by the hosting company, you can simply enter text and post photos or images to your site and change these as often as you like. You can choose colors, graphics, and fonts that best express your company and what it stands for. If you want a simple site, with a few pages that tell who you are, what your company does, and how to reach you, this is the fastest, easiest, and most polished-looking approach for the absolute beginner. Check out website hosting companies Network Solutions (networksolutions.com), Go Daddy (godaddy.com) and Verio (verio.com).

While this option is great for beginners, keep in mind that it may not offer all the features of your favorite online sites: visitor counters, encryption, or e-biz capabilities. You do, indeed, get what you pay for. If you want those features, you can get a professionally designed website. For a monthly fee, most design companies can also arrange for hosting and online or phone tech support 24 hours a day, seven days a week. You will need to provide all images and logos, as well as a script for each proposed site page and some guidance on buttons and links.

No matter what route you choose, you will have to pay to register a domain name for your company site. So make it count. If the name of your company is already taken by another registered domain, try tweaking it a bit. For example, bobsafrican imports.com may already be taken, but try bobsafrican.com or another permutation. You can also try adding on a different site type on the end, like .biz.

Hello, Neighbor: Advertising on Import/Export Friendly Sites

Remember what your parents always told you: It doesn't hurt to ask. This is the case, too, with advertising. If an online site includes advertising, find out how you can jump on the bandwagon.

Smart Tip

An effective online marketing tool is having your own online newsletter. It can be created in a professional program, such as Quark Xpress or Adobe Photoshop, or be a simple email of information. Creating a blog is also a potentially effective way to market your company. Your blog could focus on any number of possible topics, either related to the items you import or export or to world news, or even to transportation. Be creative! Consider Blogger (blogger.com), Typepad (typepad.com), Wordpress (wordpress.com), among many others.

▲

If you have any money in your budget for advertising, set some aside for online marketing in the form of purchasing email lists and sending blasts, sending out press releases to trade news sites, and buying selective ad space.

Information firms abound on the internet, and they are all willing to sell you lists of possible contacts and clients. Beware, though, and do your research before you fall for a pyramid scheme that will only result in you losing $500 of your hard-earned coin. Instead, consult your trusted government business and trade sites and contacts to find out who's reputable and who's not in the information selling business.

Press releases are free to create (minus your personal labor cost) and free to send out to any organization, be it professional or news-oriented. Consider taking time once or twice a month to compile a press release about big news in your own company or about an industry trend on which you can comment as an export/import expert. Create an address list within your email management program so you can fire off that release with one click. Boom! You've accomplished several tasks—positioning yourself as an expert, reaching a free audience, saving time—in one shot.

Howdy, Pardner: Co-Op/Partner Marketing and Advertising

Another way to reach the same markets is to find co-op avenues for marketing and advertising. In other words, find some reciprocity in your efforts.

Many sites, whether those of groups and associations or of your foreign counterparts, advertise online. Rest assured that not all of (or even a majority of) this advertising is paid for in full. Rather, much of it appears thanks to a cooperative effort on the part of the advertiser and venue.

Perhaps an ad is paid for partially, and the balance of the bill is offset by offering reciprocal advertising on another site. Or perhaps you can score an ad on a website for 30 days from a trade partner if you offer him the same courtesy. Maybe your currency for advertising is free or discounted shipping on products, reduced fees, or an overall price break. There are many ways to handle co-op advertising and marketing. You are only limited by imagination.

Several websites offer guidance in your online marketing and advertising efforts. Good old export.gov is a solid starting point for basic marketing info. Trade Easy's website (tradeeasy.com) offers marketing solutions to sellers in a buyer's market. And importexporthelp.com offers over 873 tools for trade marketing solutions.

Getting the Product Out

You've successfully landed a client with a perfect product to sell and you've determined which countries you're going to sell it in. Now comes the next phase of the game—getting your product into the marketplace and generating those sales. This is a biggie. Even if your business organization is rock-solid, you're not going to earn a cent if the product sits on the proverbial shelf.

While import sales are essentially a hands-on affair, including cold-calling and meeting with retailers and wholesalers, export sales are much more difficult to organize. After all, you're dealing in foreign territory. This is why exporters often rely on foreign sales representatives or distributors. How you decide to set up your distribution network depends on what you're selling and how closely you want to be involved with sales.

You don't have to hire anybody. Lots of exporters run the whole show themselves. But if you do decide to go with a rep, remember that these people will represent your client and his product to everyone in the trade channel down to the end user. And since you are the manufacturer's representative, your rep's performance will be a direct reflection on not only the client and the product but also on you and your company as well.

So, assuming you're going to hire sales help, which specific conduits in the trade channel will be most effective for you? The three most common options for the export management company are:

- Sell direct to foreign markets. (Hire your own people to work in the country as sales representatives.)
- Hire a commission representative or representative company.
- Work with a distributor.

The best trade channel options for the importer are:

- Manufacturer's representatives
- Distributors
- Retailers

Selling Nozzles

Before we go any further, let's slip back into the trade channel and review the various conduits:

- *Representative.* This is a person who can work alone or as part of a company with various reps on board; she makes sales calls for you to wholesale or retail buyers.

When she's solicited a sale, she passes it on to you. In most cases, you then send the merchandise directly to the buyer. A typical representative's commission is 5 percent of the cost of the goods, but this varies slightly from one part of the world to another and from product to product.

Smart Tip

Tip...

Distributors should be placed under contract with specific clauses ensuring that they maintain adequate facilities and personnel to service the product.

- *Distributor.* A company that buys your goods and resells them to a retailer or other representative for further distribution through the channel until the product reaches the end user. A distributor, who determines his own sales price for your product, may wait until sales have accumulated before buying the merchandise, or he may purchase the merchandise up front and warehouse it, thus acting as a wholesaler. You won't have as much control as you would with a representative, but you will not have as many worries because the distributor handles all advertising, promotions, returns, and customer service. A distributor acting as a wholesaler, buying your imported merchandise and warehousing it before accumulating sales, is sometimes called an import house.

- *Manufacturer's representative.* This is a salesperson who specializes in a specific product or line of complementary products, for example, home electronics (televisions sets, radios, CD players, and sound systems). He often provides additional product assistance, such as warehousing and technical service. He can work alone or as part of an agency or "stable" of reps, in which case each rep divides his selling time among the various products promoted by the agency. This allows you to field a regional or national sales force without expending any capital. The downside, however, is that because these people carry a variety of product lines, yours may end up at the bottom.

- *Retailer.* The ultimate distributor who sells to the end user.

- *Direct sales.* An anomalous offshoot of the trade channel. Direct sales can work for products with a very limited market in which each sale is substantial. If you're selling jet engine nozzles, for example, you can easily send out your own reps to pitch jet engine manufacturers. There aren't all that many out there. When you make a sale, you'll probably be assured of repeat business. There aren't too many nozzle suppliers either. But for most products, the markets are so large and complex that this method is just not feasible.

Pursuing the Perfect Rep

Finding the perfect sales rep is just as important as finding that perfect manufacturer and product. Because some reps are better than others at pitching different types of products, the trick lies in choosing one who best complements your particular type of merchandise and, preferably, already has experience and contacts. If you plan to sell in more than one corner of the world, you may need to locate several representatives. If your target countries are all in close proximity, however, you'll do better to find a distribution company or rep that can handle them all.

So where do you find these perfect people? If you're talking exports, for starters, go back to Chapter 7 and take another look at the wonderful services offered by the ITA's Commercial Service, including the Agent/ Distributor Service and the NTDB. Other foreign rep sources include:

- Freight forwarders and customs brokers
- Trade associations in the countries you are targeting
- Foreign consulates, embassies, and trade offices
- American chambers of commerce abroad
- International Yellow Pages (which you can find on the internet)
- International trade publications

Sources for domestic distributors and representatives include:

Trader's View

In North Carolina, Sam Nelson finds freight forwarding companies convenient for exporting medical equipment like microscopes and medical scanners. "I call, and they come and pick it up," he says.

Exclusively Yours

In your negotiations with the manufacturer, ask for exclusive distribution rights, at least for the area you'll be selling in. Many companies look for three-year exclusive rights at first, with the stipulation that this right is renewable each year thereafter. If you're selling products for a manufacturer who doesn't have any U.S. sales yet, you may think this is not a problem, but it can be. Once you do your job and the product is selling like mad, another importer may come along, approach "your" manufacturer and undercut your prices. So ask for an exclusive contract right from the beginning before you have competition to worry about.

If the manufacturer is afraid to give you a three-year exclusive, try negotiating. You can sign an agreement, for example, stipulating that if you sell X amount of product within a specified time period, you'll retain exclusive rights.

- Domestic trade associations, publications, and journals that cover your product's industry
- Referrals from your international banker
- Manufacturer's Agents National Association (see the Appendix for contact information)
- Your local phone directory or directories for target cities all over the United States
- U.S. and state trade centers

Interview Kit

After you've compiled a list of reputable distributors or representatives, the real work begins: choosing the best one for your company and products. Interview your prospects with as much care as you'd take to interview prospective employees. A good place to start is with a sort of interview in a kit, a three-part packet consisting of a one-page fact sheet, product literature, and a questionnaire. You should prepare a packet for each client and have enough printed so that you can pop them in the mail or pass them out as the need arises.

The fact sheet should outline your client's commission structure, agreement policies, and company information so that each prospective rep has a snapshot of who he'll be dealing with and what he can expect as compensation. The questionnaire, which you'll ask prospects to fill out and return to you, is designed to elicit as much pertinent information as you could possibly need. Check out the sample on page 223.

Once you receive a prospect's questionnaire, make sure you check references. Find out if other companies that deal with this rep are satisfied with the relationship. Delve into what size territory the rep is most capable of covering. You don't want one with a tendency to bite off more than he can chew.

If a prospect doesn't return the questionnaire, call or fax him with a friendly nudge. If you still don't receive a response, cross him off your list. A person who doesn't take the time to respond to a potential associate is probably not going to take the time to do a good job, either.

You should now meet your prospect in person. You can find out if you really click, and you can size up the way he handles himself in a one-on-one situation rather than on paper. If you're in two different countries, however, and your budget simply won't stretch for an in-person meeting, be sure to conduct a phone interview. Another alternative is an electronic video call, via Skype or similar software.

Sign on the Dotted Line

When you've decided which reps you want on your team, it's time to sign on the dotted line. You need a written agreement or contract to clarify their responsibilities

Product Representative Questionnaire

Name _____

Company name _____

Address _____

_____

Phone number _____

Email address _____

1. What import products do you handle? _____

_____

_____

2. What export products do you handle? _____

_____

_____

3. Where do you make the majority of your sales? _____

_____

_____

4. How do you prefer to work (as distributor, sales rep, manufacturer's rep)?

_____

5. What territories do you cover? _____

_____

6. What commission would you feel comfortable with? _____

_____

7. Do you work on your own, or do you have a company? If so, how many branches and salespeople do you have? _____

_____

_____

_____

▲

Product Representative Questionnaire, continued

8. Please list pertinent bank references, including address, phone number, and contact person. _____

_____

_____

_____

9. Please list at least three client references, including address, phone number or email address, and contact person: (Use reverse for more, if necessary.)

   a. _____

   _____

   b. _____

   _____

   c. _____

   _____

10. May we have some details on your professional history (if you work on your own) or on your company history?

    Number of employees: _____

    Years in business: _____

    Annual sales: _____

    Assets: _____

    Liabilities: _____

    Net worth: _____

11. Please list any other information you feel would be helpful to us in considering you to represent our client:

    _____

    _____

    _____

and duties as well as yours. We strongly advise that you consult an attorney familiar with international law, especially as a newbie, because you might overlook details that could turn into migraines down the line.

The specific details of each agreement will vary from one situation to another, but they should all include these types of basics:

- *Responsibilities of the distributor or representative and your responsibilities.* Make sure these are clearly delineated and spelled out. This will be a legally binding contract.

- *Term of contract.*

- *Compensation.*

- *Any bonus or incentive programs.*

- *Territory.* Does the distributor or rep have exclusive or nonexclusive rights to the territory? This is an important consideration. Most reps prefer to have exclusive rights to market your product in a given territory. Furthermore, granting the rep exclusive rights is a good way to give her a start-off perk and develop that winning relationship.

- *Pricing.* This is often the most significant variable determining sales success. Price your product carefully, neither too high nor too low. Remember that your representative will earn a specific percentage, while a distributor will buy at the prevailing wholesale market price.

- *Warranty and returns.* Who's responsible for returns or repairs? What is the policy? This can be a critical section of your agreement depending, of course, on what you're selling. Also consider whether you'll need product liability insurance.

- *Does the rep have the right to use trademarks, patents, and copyrights in advertising?* Make sure the product doesn't require or infringe on any of these intellectual property rights.

- *Marketing and advertising.* Spell out who's responsible. Remember that you or the manufacturer may have to defray some of these costs.

- *Record-keeping.* Both parties should keep sales and other pertinent records and reserve the right to examine each other's documents.

- *Language.* What language in the agreement is legally binding?

- *Contract termination.* Give yourself an out. If the rep fails to meet certain requirements, for example, a minimum number of sales within a specified period, you can terminate the contract.

- *Arbitration.* Make sure your agreement contains a clause outlining what happens if you and your rep disagree in interpretation of the terms of the contract. Most such contracts stipulate arbitration by the International Chamber of Commerce.

At 'Em Advertising

Although your main concern is finding buyers to distribute the product abroad or domestically, you don't want to drop your responsibility for further promoting the product. Ultimately, your success depends on how well the product sells to the end user. Some products may not require advertising, for example, imported handcrafts that sell in specialty stores and boutiques. Others, such as certain food products or even organic mulches that may face stiff competition in the marketplace, may benefit from advertising campaigns.

Advertising is a major expense. The distributors you deal with and their distributors or reps along the trade channel may not have much in the way of advertising budgets. These people will also probably be dealing with several product lines in addition to yours, which means they may not be spending the ad dollars they have on your merchandise. In such a scenario, you may want to initiate a cooperative advertising program with the manufacturer.

Co-op advertising will not only reduce your distributors' advertising expenses but will also promote your client's product. It's a cost-efficient and effective way for both the manufacturer and retailer or distributor to reach their target markets.

Although co-op advertising policies differ among manufacturers, most are written so that the manufacturer pays a portion of the advertising costs and supplies the retailer with material to include in the ad whether it's print, radio, or television.

Banana Peels

You may need to give your manufacturer some major guidance in his advertising campaign. An ad blitz that takes this country by storm may fall flat or even backfire in another country. The annals of international trade are filled with horror stories of novice (and even major-league) companies who lost millions of dollars because they didn't understand the cultures of the countries they were selling in.

Make sure you, your manufacturer, and his advertising agency take these kinds of issues into consideration:

- *Language.* Don't try to translate things literally. Some slang and colloquialisms have

> ### Bright Idea
> Clever, consumer-friendly tags add to the buyer's perception of a product's value. Artisans who sell at crafts shows and gift boutiques, for instance, have found that a piece that carries a tag describing the artist and the craft will sell for a higher price than one with no tag.

no direct translation; others transmute into something ridiculous, rude, or both. When you translate, make sure your grammar is correct.

- *Cultural taboos.* In many countries, particularly Islamic ones, states of undress that we may think look alluring in advertising art will come across as lewd, lascivious, and possibly even illegal.
- *Colors and gestures.* As we mentioned in Chapter 3, colors mean different things to different cultures. White is the color of mourning in China; in some tropical countries, green implies danger. Gestures also vary by culture. The thumbs-up sign is rude in Australia, and in Argentina, the OK sign (thumb and index finger inscribing a circle) has lewd connotations.
- *Educational levels.* In emerging countries where literacy levels are low, print ads are not going to get you very far. Try another media instead.

Look for the Label

Another way to either slip on a banana peel or tap dance to the top is through labeling. Although almost every product imported into the United States by law requires a "made in wherever" label, not every product needs a fancy or informative one. Those French mirrors, for instance, may not need any supplemental verbiage, while the organic mulch will probably benefit from a bag that extols its environmental virtues.

You'll have to decide how important labeling is based on each product and the country it's being sold in, although it can always be a benefit. You'll want to impress upon your clients that this is a terrific way to build goodwill and additional advertising among both dealers and consumers. You'll have to let them know that they may need to have their labels translated and reprinted into the target language. They may also have to convert sizes and measurements to the metric system so local consumers can understand them.

Labels also serve to let the consumer know how to use and care for the product. Informative labels increase sales of better-quality products. And this helps small manufacturers with a superior product overcome some of the effects of extensive advertising by larger competitors.

Public Relations Patter

Once you land your first clients, you should continue to promote yourself to them and to new prospects and your community through public relations. You can use materials garnered from your brochure, your copious market research, and your own

▲

Hand in Glove

Don't forget that your manufacturer will have to do some specific marking and labeling to meet government and shipping regulations, ensure proper handling, and help receivers identify shipments. Also remember that certain products that fall under regulatory guidelines must be clearly marked as such.

If you're importing latex gloves, for example, that have not been approved for medical use, you can't use the description "exam gloves" in any way. If you do, the Food and Drug Administration folks will hold your shipment until you change each inner box and outer carton to read "industrial use" or "general purpose." Your customs broker will be able to tell you about these sorts of regulations, but it's your responsibility to forward the information to your supplier.

---

import/export experiences to publish articles in pertinent industry association journals or to give talks for local business associations. Remember that word-of-mouth is a powerful advertising tool. Each person who reads your article or hears you speak is a potential client.

Join industry organizations. This is always a good idea.

How about going live on the air? Volunteer yourself for a local radio station's "business time" chat show. Listeners can call in and ask questions about international trade.

If you are aware of a promotional event in town where you think industry manufacturers or suppliers might show up, say, at an industry-specific charity event, offer to help. If the event is in aid of an environmental cause and your services are green—you are selling or distributing environment-friendly products, for example—you can point this out. The main benefit of attending these events is that you can meet potential clients, shake their hands, and become a familiar face. Then when you call on them, you will have a common ground. You can say, "Remember me? We met at the Save the Spotted Owl Charity Picnic."

Market By Educating Your Customers

One of the most efficient and effective ways to promote any business is through content marketing, defined by the Content Marketing Institute as "a marketing technique of creating and distributing relevant and valuable content to attract, acquire, and engage a clearly defined and understood target audience—with the objective of driving profitable customer action." Some people refer to content marketing as education marketing. The idea is to provide information that has value to your audience through your online content. You can share and promote that content through a variety of ways, and one of the most popular is social marketing. But if you're going to do it, you need to do it right.

The two primary components of social marketing are media and networking. Social media are websites and applications used for social networking. Social networking is the use of dedicated websites and applications to communicate informally with other users or to find people with similar interests to oneself.

Perhaps the biggest challenge of social marketing is the number of platforms available and the rapidly-changing popularity of those platforms, which is why we're not going to give you how-to lessons on specific social media sites. It's not necessary for you and your company to be active on every social network. A smarter strategy is to pick the two or three networks that are most popular with your market and establish your presence on them, and not worry about the others.

It's important to keep in mind that social marketing should be only one component of your overall marketing strategy. You've probably heard plenty of stories about companies that have thousands or even millions of fans and followers, and thought that you should try to do the same. The reality is that you should do what's best for your company and what matches your strategy. These steps will help you get started:

1. Set clear goals for your social marketing efforts. Be specific and keep those goals in mind with everything you do.

2. Dedicate the human resources to social marketing. You need someone on your team (and it could be you) who understands social marketing, is comfortable with the platforms you'll be using, and has the time to manage your social marketing program.

3. Be prepared to produce sufficient content. Content is the fuel for your social marketing vehicle, and without it, your efforts will stall.

4. Prepare your website for social media attention. Be sure your website is ready for the increased traffic social marketing could generate.

5. Remember that it's a conversation. Don't simply talk at your audience, engage with them.

6. Create a social media policy for your employees. Employees need to know what they can—and can't—say about the company when they are online.

Stat Fact

Of marketers surveyed by *Social Media Examiner,* 89 percent said that increased exposure was the number one benefit of social media marketing.

7. Be realistic in your expectations. Don't anticipate monumental results for a minimal investment.

Service That Customer

In international trade, your customer service procedures fall into three categories: representatives, retailers, and end users. Like everything else in import/export, these categories overlap. By servicing one, you'll be helping the others. And the best way to do this is through dealer assistance programs. Here you supply your representatives with a variety of informational aids and materials. One set is designed to help the rep land the account:

- Catalogs
- Price lists
- Sales letters
- Any perks you can think up, like in-store posters or sample merchandise give-aways

The next set of materials is designed to help the retail customer sell to the end user:

- Product management aids
- Display aids and ideas
- Stock control plans
- Sales promotion kits

Aside from these kinds of materials, your customer service program should emulate that of any domestic program. Your reps need to know that if they or someone further down the trade channel has a problem with the product, the manufacturer will take care of it. If you're acting as a distributor and you've purchased the product outright, you'll either have to handle after-market problems and servicing yourself or write some kind of servicing into your contract with the manufacturer.

Making sure your clients are satisfied with their service from your company is a good step toward ensuring the financial health of your business. Coincidentally, finances are the focus of the next chapter.

More Trade Dollars
Effectively Controlling Your Finances

Whether you are a chronic number cruncher or one of the finance-phobic, you'll want to give your company periodic financial checkups. "Why?" your obnoxious neighbor may ask. "You already did all that math stuff in the startup chapter."

Just tell him that was the preflight exam for the wonderful cargo carrier that's your business. When your fledgling operation is in full flight, you'll want to conduct periodic safety checks to make sure your business is as healthy as you imagine.

If there's a problem, you'll find out before it becomes critical. For example, if you discover that your commission fees barely cover your travel expenses, you can change gears and raise your commission rate before signing another client at the same too-low rate. You can also take measures like changing your phone plan or cutting back on travel.

Financial checkups don't have to be negative. They can give you a rosy glow by demonstrating how well you're doing, possibly even better than you expected. If you've been saving for a new printer or a market research trip, or if you're hoping to take on an employee, you can judge how close you are to achieving that goal.

Making a Statement

An income statement, also called a profit-and-loss statement, charts the revenues and operating costs of your business over a specific period of time, usually a month. Check out the income statements on pages 233 and 234 for two more hypothetical import/export services, Fair Trade Imports and Trade Winds Exports. Fair Trade handles $810,000 worth of business annually, while Trade Winds breezes along with $2,193,600 of annual business.

Fair Trade, a one-man band, is owner-operated and has its home base in the guest bedroom. Trade Winds has one full-time employee, an administrative assistant, and makes its base in a 900-square-foot downtown office. Neither owner draws a salary; they both rely on a percentage of the net profit for their income.

Both companies operate on a commission basis, with the owners taking their compensation from pretax net profits.

You'll want to tailor your income statement to your particular business. To make the statement really right, you'll need to prorate items that are paid annually, such as business licenses, tax-time accounting fees, or Export.gov subscriptions, and pop those figures into your monthly statement. For example, if you pay an annual Export.gov fee of $200, divide this figure by 12 and add the resulting $14.58 to your subscriptions expense. Use the worksheet on page 235 to chart your own income statement. You'll be surprised how much fun finances can be!

Credit Me This Much

One issue that can vitally affect your finances is the extension of credit to your customers. Virtually any business beyond the level of street vending is forced into making

Fair Trade Imports Income Statement

Income Statement
For the month of April 20xx

Monthly Income

Gross sales	$67,500.00	
Cost of sales	59,150.00	
Gross Monthly Income		**$8,350.00**

Monthly Expenses

Rent	$ 0.00
Phone/utilities	168.00
Postage/delivery	33.00
Licenses/taxes	339.00
Employees	0.00
Benefits/taxes	0.00
Advertising/promotions	410.00
Legal services	148.00
Accounting services	220.00
Office supplies	115.00
Transportation/travel	550.00
Insurance	157.00
Subscriptions/dues	26.00
Miscellaneous	170.00

Total Monthly Expenses	**$2,336.00**
Net Monthly Profit	**$6,014.00**

Note: Cost of sales refers to the cost of the product as well as all documentation required to complete all trade transactions.

Trade Winds Exports Income Statement

Income Statement
For the month of April 20xx

Monthly Income

Gross sales	$212,400.00	
Cost of sales	182,380.00	

Gross Monthly Income   **$30,020.00**

Monthly Expenses

Rent	$1,850.00
Phone/utilities	320.00
Postage/delivery	80.00
Licenses/taxes	805.00
Employees	2,213.00
Benefits/taxes	378.00
Advertising/promotions	1,160.00
Legal services	246.00
Accounting services	425.00
Office supplies	166.00
Transportation/travel	1,480.00
Insurance	376.00
Subscriptions/dues	45.00
Miscellaneous	360.00

Total Monthly Expenses   **$9,904.00**

Net Monthly Profit   **$20,116.00**

Note: Cost of sales refers to the cost of the product as well as all documentation required to complete all trade transactions.

Income Statement Worksheet

Income Statement
For the month of _____

Monthly Income

Gross sales   _____

Cost of sales   _____

Gross Monthly Income $_____

Monthly Expenses

Rent   _____

Phone/utilities   _____
   (add $60 cell phone charge)

Postage/delivery   _____

Licenses/taxes   _____

Employees   _____

Benefits/taxes   _____

Advertising/promotions   _____

Legal services   _____

Accounting services   _____

Office supplies   _____

Transportation/travel   _____

Insurance   _____

Subscriptions/dues   _____

Miscellaneous   _____

Total Monthly Expenses $_____

Net Monthly Profit $_____

Note: Cost of sales refers to the cost of the product as well as all documentation required to complete all trade transactions.

credit term decisions early on. As an international trader, you'll find yourself faced with those same decisions. As you start out, however, a large part of the problem will be lifted from your shoulders by virtue of the letter of credit. Because the tried-and-true L/C is an intrinsic part of the import/export world, your customers will take it for granted. This is how they pay you—upfront through the international bank.

But as your company grows and you and your customers get to know each other, they may begin to ask for credit terms. Sometimes it's difficult not to extend credit. Your customer may want to purchase exactly what you want to sell in an amount that's too sweet to resist. But he also wants 60 days credit before he pays. How you respond is up to you. In Belgium, Jan Herremans accepts only L/Cs and one other form of payment. "Due to many, many sad experiences," he says, "[I take] cash or irrevocable letter of credit only!"

In Germany, Michael Richter accepts several different payment forms. "If the customer is buying merchandise, we agree for [starters] on a secure payment by L/C and/or bank draft," Michael explains. "Later we take payment as per an agreement or contract to be made. With bigger businesses, we may take financing in various percentages."

If you choose to extend credit, remember that any time you do, you're allowing your customer to use your money interest-free. This can be a good way to extend goodwill and build customer loyalty, but it can also be a good way to lose your shirt. Make sure that your cash flow can cover the credit period before you say OK. And make as sure as you can that your customer can come up with the funds when due.

How do you do this? By any one of several means:

Beware!
According to U.S. Customs and Border Protection, many new importers are surprised by bills for duty tariffs, merchandise processing fees, and broker services charges. Don't be one of them! Make sure you do your homework.

- Ask your banker to investigate.
- Order a report from a service like Dun & Bradstreet, which has more than 100 million business records on file.
- Request a World Traders Data Report from your local U.S. Department of Commerce district office.

Keep It Flowing

There are numerous ways to ensure you have enough money available when you need it. Vigilance is the name of the cash flow game. Watch what you spend, look hard for ways to save money, and make sure clients pay you on time. If you take on a distributor function, keep a close eye on inventory. Don't overbuy. Research thoroughly and be conservative. If you think you may eventually need to borrow money, take steps ahead of time. Opening that line of credit before you need it can save you from high interest rates. (And if you don't need it, no harm done. Just open a credit line that carries no penalties for not using it.)

Hanging in There

During economic downturns like the recent global recession, keeping an international trading business in good fiscal shape can become increasingly challenging. Fortunately, most recessions are not global. So chances are, some countries will be unaffected, or at least substantially less affected, by the downturn.

Even the recent global recession did not have an adverse effect on all sectors of international trade. "We haven't really been affected," says Wahib Wahba, New Jersey trader of railroad and telephone equipment. "Our clients are governments, and during recessions, governments often increase their spending."

Taking Inventory

OK. You've found some really terrific merchandise and decided to take it on wearing your distributor cap. You've taken title to the stuff—actually purchased it yourself—and are working with reps to sell it around the country. Great! Except that now you have inventory, stock that has to be stored somewhere and accounted for.

What to do? First, remember that your capital is tied up with your inventory. If you don't move your stock quickly, you're liable to run into that old business nemesis, the cash-flow problem. So try to have buyers lined up before you purchase the goods.

If you don't, start up an inventory system to ensure that you have enough stock on hand to supply your buyers but not so much that you're paying through the nose for storage space. Keep careful track of how quickly items are moving, determine how long it will take to replace them, and order new shipments accordingly. Do this at regular intervals so you can develop a better feel for how quickly items are selling and how long shipments take to arrive.

Sam Nelson, exporting medical equipment from North Carolina, also found his business not dropping off nearly as badly as he expected. "I was surprised myself," he says.

In both fair and foul economic times, traders need to be able to switch gears, if necessary, and look for other opportunities. "You can be selling a good product this month, and then maybe it doesn't sell so well and something else will come along. You have to be flexible," notes Sam.

Banking Buddies

From your first import/export venture, you should get used to thinking of your bank as a buddy—after all, you're going to be working with the folks down at the branch a lot as you fulfill letters of credit. Your international banker should also be able to help you do the following:

- Locate new overseas markets
- Develop data on the business climate in the country to which you're planning exports
- Secure introductions to banking and trade contacts abroad
- Secure letters of introduction and letters of credit when you're traveling abroad
- Find credit information on potential overseas buyers
- Establish your good credit when someone checks up on you
- Stay current on export regulations
- Exchange currencies
- Secure financing for exports
- Collect foreign invoices, drafts, letters of credit, and other foreign receivables
- Transfer funds to other countries
- Lend credit assistance to your foreign buyers

Bankers are extremely important in the import/export industry. Add finding a compatible banker to your startup list of projects; then start interviewing, either by phone or in person.

Interviewing bankers gives you the opportunity to establish a relationship. And the closer your relationship with the bank manager

> **Bright Idea**
> Consider a bank with a home office in a country you will be working with. If you're exporting to Japan, for example, you might go with a bank like Sumitomo. If you are exporting to Germany, how about Deutsche Bank? Foreign banks with U.S. branches can often speed the opening of L/Cs and sometimes offer better lending terms.

or other executive, the better your chances of getting loans and special favors when you need them.

The fact that you're a newbie with a small startup account is not a drawback. You're offering the bank the prospect of major future transactions; it doesn't hurt to cite examples from your projected income statements and market research. And don't forget the inherent glamour and adventure of international trade. If you were a banker, wouldn't you find your business more interesting than, say, dry cleaning? Choose a banker who's excited about your company; then let him share in the excitement of developing it.

Oh, Pick OPIC!

The Overseas Private Investment Corporation, affectionately known as OPIC, is a self-funded U.S. government agency that provides project financing, investment insurance, and a variety of investor services to 150 emerging-economy countries around the globe. OPIC encourages American overseas private investments to generate domestic exports and create jobs. With assets of over $6.3 billion, OPIC concentrates heavily on SME projects.

As with any government entity, paperwork abounds, but if you're thinking of exporting services or working on large projects, you should give OPIC an electronic jingle at opic.gov or call the agency at (202) 336-8400.

Play Money

As an international trader, you'll often deal in other currencies besides U.S. dollars, so you'll need to develop an awareness and appreciation of world currencies. Anyone who has traveled outside the United States finds out almost immediately that a dollar isn't always worth a dollar. Its value changes from country to country and from day to day according to U.S. and other national economies.

Whenever you discuss prices with your clients, customers, or anyone else in your trade channel, you'll need to think about the currency exchange rate. Since this rate constantly fluctuates, and since you may have to alter your prices to reflect the current rate, this adds an exciting tactical aspect to the import/export game.

Let's say, for instance, that you are working with Egyptian goods and the dollar goes down in relation to the Egyptian pound. If you're importing from Egypt, you will groan because you'll now have to pay more in dollars to purchase the merchandise. But if you are exporting to Egypt, this same news will put a smile on your face.

The devalued dollar will cost less in the land of the Nile, so you can either lower your price, which will please your customer, or you can maintain your price and take a higher profit.

So as an international trader, it behooves you to keep your eye on currency rates. When the currency rate swings one way, you might want to import; when it swings the other, you can think export. Or you might make it a general rule to import goods from emerging-economy countries whose currencies are always weak in relation to the U.S. dollar (you can buy more for less), and export goods to countries with economies that are generally stronger than ours, such as those in Western Europe.

See Spot Transact

Sometimes you'll be responsible for exchanging foreign currencies into U.S. dollars, which is generally done two ways:

1. *The Spot Transaction*. This involves the sale of U.S. dollars and the purchase of foreign currency (or the reverse) for immediate delivery, or on-the-spot delivery. For instance, if you sell merchandise to a company in Japan, you'll quote your price in either U.S. dollars or yen. Now the exchange rate may change before the deal is complete, but you've already set your price. This is where your tactical ability comes in (or a crystal ball, if you have one). If you quote the price in dollars, the Japanese company assumes the risk of a change in rates because it will have to pay the dollar value no matter what, and this change may or may not be to its benefit. If you quote the price in yen, you're the one assuming the risk. On the date of payment, you have the bank change the yen to dollars (or buy dollars with the yen). If the yen is weaker, you lose a percentage of your profits, but if the yen is stronger, you gain profits.

2. *The Forward Transaction*. If you don't have a crystal ball and don't want to sit around worrying about whether the exchange rate will go up or down, you can purchase the foreign currency at the time you

> **Smart Tip** *Tip...*
> When changing money, the larger the amounts, the better the rates. Often credit cards get the best exchange rate, so charging could cost you less. (As long as you pay off the charges right away, of course.) Sneak a peek at foreign exchange rates at x-rates.com.

> **Smart Tip** *Tip...*
> It's sometimes easier to find a buyer if you agree to accept payment in her currency.

Money by Another Name

Country	Name of Currency	Code
Belgium	European euro	EUR
Brazil	Brazilian real	BRL
Canada	Canadian dollar	CAD
China	Chinese renminbi (ren)	CNY
Egypt	Egyptian pound	EGP
France	European euro	EUR
Germany	European euro	EUR
Hungary	Hungarian forint	HUF
India	Indian rupee	INR
Indonesia	Indonesian rupiah	IDR
Japan	Japanese yen	JPY
Mexico	Mexican peso	MXN
Netherlands	European euro	EUR
Philippines	Philippine peso	PHP
Poland	Polish zloty	PLN
Russia	Russian ruble	RUB
Saudi Arabia	Saudi Arabian riyal	SAR
South Africa	South African rand	ZAR
South Korea	South Korean won	KRW
Taiwan	New Taiwan dollar	TWD
Turkey	Turkish new lira	TRY
United Kingdom	British pound sterling	GBP
United States	U.S. dollar	USD
Venezuela	Venezuelan bolívar	VEB

make the deal. If you quote your price in yen, you immediately purchase the yen from the bank at the rate that coincides with your price quote. This way both parties are free of risk. But don't dismiss that crystal ball. If the foreign currency increases in value, you'll have lost an extra percentage point of potential profit.

▲

The Tax Man Cometh

When you earn all that bounty from your impeccably run trading business, someone will be queuing up for a piece of the action: Uncle Sam. If your budget allows, you should engage an accountant. You probably won't need him or her for your daily or monthly concerns, but it's well worth the expense to have someone in the know at the reins when April 15 comes around, or for those panic-enducing questions that come up now and again.

If you are exporting, be aware that tax breaks for exporters are sometimes available. (They appear to go in and out of style.) You or your accountant should investigate whether there are any current advantageous tax laws in effect.

Your tax deductions should be about the same as those for any other small or homebased business. You can deduct a percentage of your home office so long as you are using it solely as an office. These deductions include all normal office expenses plus interest, taxes, insurance, and depreciation (this is where the accountant comes in handy). The IRS has added all sorts of permutations, including that the total amount of the deduction is limited by the gross income you derive from the business activity minus all your other business expenses apart from those related to the home office. (And you thought that new board game you got for Christmas had complicated rules!)

Basically, the IRS doesn't want you to come up with so many home office deductions that you end up paying no tax at all. If, after reading the lowdown, you're still confused, consult your accountant.

The Foreign Tax Man Cometh, Too

Many countries have taxes that will affect the import and export prices of goods headed into and out of the country. These taxes include, but are not limited to, the Value Added Tax (VAT) in the European Union and the Goods and Services Tax (GST) in Australia, New Zealand, Canada, Hong Kong, and Singapore. Make sure you have taken foreign taxes into account.

Trader's View

Indonesia, the world's top producer of crude palm oil, recently levied a 3 percent palm oil export tax, which raised the base export price of the oil.

Brilliant Deduction

What else can you deduct? Business-related phone calls, the cost of business equipment and supplies (again, so long as you're truly using them solely for your business), subscriptions to professional and trade journals, and auto expenses. These accrue when you drive your trusty vehicle in the course of doing business or seeking business. In other words, you're chalking up deductible mileage when you motor out to your clients' offices to pick up samples or present marketing plans, or when you take a spin to the bank, the freight forwarder's office, or down to the docks with documentation.

It's wise to keep a log of your business miles. You can buy one of several varieties at your

Bright Idea

Index Mundi (index-mundi.com) provides statistics and other information, including everything from demographics to the economy, on a country-by-country basis. The source for most of the information is the CIA World Factbook.

Innocents Abroad

Traveling is half the fun of international trade. But make sure you're not an innocent abroad. Plan your itinerary carefully to make your trip as personally and professionally profitable as possible. To make every moment count, combine several business activities:

- ○ Find new clients and reps.
- ○ Reinforce your relationships with current clients and reps.
- ○ Evaluate your competition.
- ○ Update your market research.

Set up meetings before you leave home so you're assured that the people you want to see will be available. And, as always, do your homework. Will you be arriving in a country during a holiday or festival when offices will be closed? Research local customs.

Several websites can give pointers: Check out Executive Planet at executive-planet.com for extensive information on 30-plus top U.S. trade partners. Going Global (goinglobal.com) has great tips on 24 of the countries you'll most likely trade with. Similarly, The Internationalist (internationalist.com) provides terrific information by country. And don't forget the Country Commercial Guides at export.gov. These sites will let you know country-specific "intelligence" on anything from which gestures are improper to how fashionably late to arrive for dinner to tips on small talk.

local office supply or stationery store, or you can make one yourself. Keep track as you go. It's no fun to have to backtrack at tax time and guesstimate how many miles you drove to see how many clients how many times during the year.

Let Me Entertain You

You can deduct entertainment expenses, such as wining and dining a client during the course of a sales pitch or hosting potential reps at a coffeehouse. Hold onto your receipts and keep a log of all these expenses as well. (If you're entertaining at home, have your clients or prospects sign a guest book.)

You must have a business-related purpose for entertaining, such as a sales presentation. General goodwill toward your fellow professionals doesn't make it, so be sure your log contains the reason for the partying.

Planes, Trains, and Automobiles

When you travel for business purposes, you can deduct airfares, train tickets, rental car mileage, and the like. You can also deduct hotels and meals. And you can even, under certain circumstances, deduct recreational side trips you take with your family while you're traveling on business. Because the IRS allows deductions for any such trip you take to expand your awareness and expertise in your field of business, it makes sense to take advantage of any conferences or seminars that you can attend.

While we're on the topic, if you don't already have a U.S. passport, apply for one now. Processing can take weeks. And keep your passport ultra-current. Some countries will deny you entry if you have six months or less left until your passport expires.

Tally-Ho

When you tally up all your moneysaving strategies and your care in watching your bottom line, these should add up to significant savings for your business—and, correspondingly, added health for your company.

Fair Winds or Foul Seas

Most people succeed in the import/ export business by following the tried-and-true business methods of persistence and plain old-fashioned hard work, with a healthy dose of optimism liberally sprinkled throughout. All the raw talent in the world doesn't change the fact that becoming an international trader involves a lot of work. Rewarding and sometimes exhilarating work, but darn hard work nonetheless.

Sam Nelson mentions the need to be flexible. "And you have to have patience," he adds. His other advice? Don't be constantly worried about the competition, especially from big trading companies. "These are huge companies, and that's intimidating," he says. "I try not to pay attention to that."

Industry expert Wendy Larson notes that building strong ties is crucial to success in the trade industry. "There is no substitute for face-

> **Beware!**
> Researching the customs and culture of your trading partner countries is important. It's also a good idea to check with a native speaker. That way you can avoid little glitches like Microsoft's Vista, which in Latvian translates as "frumpy woman." Or the German backpacks exported as "Body Bags."

to-face relationships." She also stresses the importance of familiarity, both business-wise and culturally, with the part of the world in which you're trading. "Really knowing your market is very important. An export to Asia is different than an export to Europe." Her suggestion is to consider the problem that businessperson is trying to solve. "After the problem is identified and the possible solutions are developed, match the output to the country, and that potential exporter will have great success. The key is to style it right for their culture."

After reading this book, you should know that what you suspected before is true: becoming an international trader is not the same as becoming an overnight success. It takes lots of market research, loads of planning, hours of financial calculations, sore knuckles from knocking on virtual doors, and the abundant application of creativity to land that first client, and more of the same to land the ones that follow.

Ring of Contacts

When the international traders interviewed for this book were asked about their best and worst experiences in the business, they gave, not surprisingly, some very honest responses.

"There are many [best] experiences," says Jan Herremans in Belgium, "but I have a nice feeling in my 30 years in business of having built a ring of contacts around the world, many of whom are personal friends, all business put aside."

In Germany, Michael Richter tackles the question from two angles: his 24-plus years as a trader and his 16-year tenure as an international trade consultant. "Everything always went smoothly," he says, "and from the [standpoint of] my consultancy, my system of looking at markets simply works perfectly and has brought most clients between 30 percent and 80 percent rise in turnover per year."

The Right Reputation

How are U.S. products viewed abroad? How do they stack up against similar goods produced in other countries? Questions like these are important to those traders looking to export American products.

Sam Nelson, trading in North Carolina, has many clients who consider American medical equipment to be high quality. "They say it's expensive but the quality is good," he notes. "Chinese equipment is cheaper but not made as well."

Lloyd Davidson agrees. "The United States overall has a good reputation for its products. Foreign companies like to deal with us." Products the United States is particularly noted for include aircraft, medical and scientific equipment, and agricultural products.

If you export, you'll want to be known as a trader who reliably supplies high-quality goods. Choosing your export products carefully with a constant eye toward quality as well as price will serve your business well. This is true both now and in the future. Your business is one of many U.S. companies contributing to the United State's future reputation for its products. A continued positive reputation for U.S. goods will help your company continue to grow.

Wahib Wahba sums it up well. "People overseas like when a product says 'Made in USA.'"

But the import/export life doesn't always flow smoothly. Michael's worst experience involved a letter of credit from a customer in Thailand. "We were about ten days late in supply due to unforeseen circumstances," the German consultant recalls. "Although the contractual agreement said the customer had to change the date, he refused. So we had to fake the documentation to be presented to the bank in time for getting the money from the L/C. Then we shipped afterward, having the money already."

In São Paulo, Brazil, John Laurino ran into a similar case of a customer not keeping his word. "My worst experience," John says, "was one that did not happen! It's a joke. My worst moment happened when I had to get some television tube replacements from a Chinese maker. We had agreed on a 1.5 percent defective rate. In reality, the rate was 4 percent. So the maker was supposed to refund me the difference. After six months of negotiations, I had to lie, saying that if he would refund me, I would place another order."

But not everything went badly. "My best experience was in the pet shop field," the Brazilian continues. "I located a source of aquarium supplies for a Brazilian company. The profit margin for my client was more than 600 percent."

For Lloyd Davidson, as well, his best experiences come from being able to hand his clients golden eggs. "[It's] fulfilling our commitment with our principal to convert a simple inquiry into an actual sale," the Florida-based export manager says. A worst-case experience is the opposite. "[It's] when a prospective buyer, after several months of back-and-forth, suddenly disappears from the radar screen, without explanation, while we assume he has probably gone to a competitor."

Trader's View

"Try not to be discouraged too fast or by a setback," Bruno Carlier counsels. "Practice sports and try to go out from time to time to [get away] from all your preoccupations."

And in France, Bruno Carlier relates, "So far, I haven't had a worst experience. Nonetheless, nearly every week I have very bad experiences when I get an answer from a potential client who says they are not looking for the product any more, or that they just need very small quantities, or that they possibly [won't] need our products [for another] three or more months. Since our products sometimes act as a complementary part of a finished product, this can occur because they haven't finished installing the production line.

"The inexistence of a 'worst experience' is certainly due to my short experience [in the business]. Anyway, I have got plenty of time. I'm in no hurry to live such an experience.

"Every significant contract is a best experience. A very best experience, for example, is when you have been working from three months to a few years on a really important contract. You haven't received any news from your potential client for a few months and then, suddenly, you receive an order."

When You Believe

If you are the type of person who can handle these sorts of highs and lows, you will probably thrive in the world of international trade. If not, you may discover during your company's first year of life, or later, that the business isn't for you. You may feel that instead of being blown along by fair winds, you're at peril in foul seas.

Whether or not you're earning money, the success of your business is contingent on a happiness factor. Because it's a lot of work and a lot of responsibility, you may discover that you'd be just as happy, or more so, working for someone else. And that's OK. With everything you have learned you'll be a great job candidate.

None of the people interviewed for this book, from a green-as-can-be newbie to a veteran with more than 30 years' experience, seem to have any intention of packing it in. Rather, they have a sense of being a part of the world, a philosophical outlook that lets them see all of us on this globe as part of a whole.

Michael Richter in Germany sums it up best. "Do not just rely on a given home market," he says. "We are living in the world, but we all need the other ones. Be open to people, but don't lose your own thoroughly prepared idea. Cooperate with others. Don't just rely on yourself; others can open markets that you will never have reached on your own."

And Wahib Wahba, the native Egyptian, says, "Work on [doing your job] all the time. It's a continuous process, doing it every day with the belief that you're going to succeed."

This seems to be the common denominator of all the international traders who so generously helped with this book: winning attitudes. If you go into this business with the right stuff—a willingness to work hard and learn everything you can, the confidence to promote yourself and your business, and the drive to succeed—chances are you will.

Appendix

International Trade Resources

They say you can never be rich enough or young enough. While these points could be argued, we believe you can never have enough resources. Therefore, we present a wealth of sources for you to check into, check out, and harness for your own personal information blitz.

These sources are tidbits, ideas to get you started on your research. They are by no means the only sources out there, and they should not be taken as the Ultimate Answer. We have done our research, but businesses do tend to move, change, fold, and expand. As we have repeatedly stressed, do your homework. Get out and start investigating.

Associations

The American Association of Exporters and Importers, 1050 17th Street NW, Suite 810, Washington, DC 20036, (202) 857-8009, aaei.org

The Federation of International Trade Associations, 172 5th Avenue #118, Brooklyn, NY 11217, fita.org

International Chamber of Commerce, 38 cours Albert 1er, 75008 Paris, France, 011-33-1-49-53-28-28, iccwbo.org

The International Federation of Customs Brokers Associations, 55 Murray St., #320, Ottawa, Ont. K1N 5M3, Canada, ifcba.org

International Organization for Standardization, iso.org

International Small Business Consortium, 1001 Bayhill Drive, #300, San Bruno, CA 94066, (650) 260-3170, allbusiness.com

Long Island Import Export Association, 2652 Dorothy Street, Bellmore, NY 11710, (516) 783-1369, liiea.org

Organization of Women in International Trade, 1707 L Street NW, #570, Washington, DC 20036, owit.org

Small Business Exporters Association, 1156 15th Street NW, #1100, Washington, DC 20005, sbea.org

The Southern U.S. Trade Association (SUSTA), 701 Poydras Street, #3725, New Orleans, LA 70139, (504)568-5986, susta.org

Western U.S. Agricultural Trade Association (WUSATA), 4601 NE 77th Avenue, #240, Vancouver, WA 98662, (360-693-3373, wusata.org

World Trade Centers Association, 120 Broadway #3350, New York, NY 10271, wtca.org

Books

Building an Import/Export Business, by Kenneth D. Weiss (John Wiley & Sons Inc.)

Exporting, Importing, and Beyond, by Lawrence W. Tuller (Adams Media Corp.)

Export-Import, by Joseph A. Zodl (Betterway Books)

Import/Export: How to Get Started in International Trade, by Carl A. Nelson, (McGraw-Hill)

Importing into the U.S., available at customs.ustreas.gov

Selling to the World, by L. Fargo Wells (McGraw-Hill)

Any of the Barron's foreign language series, such as *Learn Italian the Fast and Fun Way*, by Marcel Danesi (Barron's Educational Series)

Customs Brokers and Freight Forwarders

Air Sea International Forwarding Inc., 1320 West Blancke Street, Linden, NJ 07036, (732) 607-0600, airseaint.com

Serra International Inc., 75 Montgomery St., #300, Jersey City, NJ 07302, (201) 860-9600, serraintl.com

Credit Reports

Dun & Bradstreet, (855) 992-2594, dnb.com

Forms

Unz & Co., 333 Cedar Avenue, Building B, Suite 2, Middlesex, NJ 08846, (800) 631-3098, (732) 667-1020, unzco.com

Helpful Government Agencies—Import/Export

Bureau of Industry and Security, Outreach and Educational Services, 14th St. & Pennsylvania Ave. NW, U.S. Department of Commerce, Washington, DC 20230, (202) 482-4811, www.bis.doc.gov; Check BIS' website for Western regional addresses and phone numbers.

Canine Enforcement, cbp.gov/xp/cgov/border_security/port_activities /canines/canine.xml

Export Assistance Centers around the country can be found on the Commercial Service website at sba.gov/cs or by calling (800) USA-TRADE.

Export-Import Bank of the United States (Ex-Im Bank), 811 Vermont Ave. NW, Washington, DC 20571, (800) 565-EXIM (3946) or (202) 565-3946, exim.gov

The Export Legal Assistance Network (ELAN), exportlegal.org

Foreign Agricultural Service, U.S. Department of Agriculture, 1400 Independence Ave. SW, Washington, DC 20250, fas.usda.gov

International Trade Administration, 1401 Constitution Ave. NW, Washington, DC 20230, (800) USA-TRADE, trade.gov

Overseas Private Investment Corporation (OPIC), 1100 New York Ave. NW, Washington, DC 20527, (202) 336-8799, opic.gov

Shipper's Export Declaration (U.S. Census Bureau, Foreign Trade Division), census.gov

Showcase Europe, export.gov/europe

Small Business Initiative (Export-Import Bank), www.exim.gov/products/special/small bus.cfm

▲

U.S. Census Bureau, Foreign Trade Division, U.S. Department of Commerce, U.S. Bureau of the Census, 4700 Silver Hill Rd., Suitland, MD 20746, mailing address: Rm. 2179, Bldg. 3, Washington, DC 20233-6700, (800) 923-8282 or (301) 763-INFO (4636), census.gov/foreign-trade/www/abtftd.html

U.S. Commercial Service, International Trade Administration, U.S. Department of Commerce, 1401 Constitution Ave. NW, Washington, DC 20230, (202) 482-2000, trade.gov/cs or buyusa.gov

U.S. Customs and Border Protection, 1300 Pennsylvania Ave. NW, Washington, DC 20229, (877) 227-5511, cbp.gov

U.S. Department of Commerce, 1401 Constitution Ave. NW, Washington, DC 20230, (202) 482-2000, commerce.gov

Helpful Related Government Agencies

Agricultural Marketing Service, 1400 Independence Ave. SW, #3071-S, Washington, DC 20250-0201, (202) 720-5115, ams.usda.gov

Animal and Plant Health Inspection Service (APHIS-USDA), 1400 Independence Ave. SW, Washington, DC 20250, (202) 720-3861, aphis.usda.gov

Bureau of Alcohol, Tobacco, Firearms, and Explosives, Import/Export, Office of Public and Governmental Affairs, 99 New York Avenue, NE, room 5S, Washington, DC 20226, atf.gov

Center for Biologics Evaluation and Research, 1401 Rockville Pike, #200N, Rockville, MD 20852-1448, (800) 835-4709, fda.gov/cber

Center for Devices and Radiological Health, Food, and Drug Administration, 10903 New Hampshire Avenue, W066-5431, Silver Spring, MD, 20993, (800) 638-2041, fda.gov/cdrh

Center for Food Safety and Applied Nutrition, Food and Drug Administration, 5100 Paint Branch Pkwy., College Park, MD 20740, (888) 723-3366, fda.gov

Centers for Disease Control and Prevention, 1600 Clifton Rd., Atlanta, GA 30333, (800) CDC-INFO (232-4636), cdc.gov

Drug Enforcement Administration (DEA), Mailstop AES, 8701 Morissette Drive, Springfield, VA 22152, (202) 307-1000, justice.gov/dea

Environmental Protection Agency, Ariel Rios Building, 1200 Pennsylvania Ave. NW, Washington, DC 20460, (202) 272-0167, epa.gov

Federal Communications Commission, 445 12th St. SW, Washington, DC 20536, (888)225-5322 (CALL FCC), fcc.gov

Federal Trade Commission, 600 Pennsylvania Ave. NW, Washington, DC 20530, (202) 326-2222, ftc.gov

Food Safety and Inspection Service, U.S. Department of Agriculture, 1400 Independence Ave. SW, Washington, DC 20250, (402) 344-5000, fsis.usda.gov

International Mail Calculator, ircalc.usps.gov

ISO 9000 Information, ts.nist.gov (click on "search," then type in ISO 9000)

National Center for Import/Export, (301) 734-8364

National Institute of Standards and Technology, 100 Bureau Dr., Stop 1070, Gaithersburg, MD 20899, (301) 975-NIST, nist.gov

Office of Engineering and Technology, 445 12th St. SW, Washington, DC 20554, (202) 418-2470, transition.fcc.gov/Bureaus/Engineering-Technology

Office of Regulatory Affairs, 10903 New Hampshire Ave, Silver Spring, MD 20993, (888) INFO-FDA, fda.gov/ora

Pipeline and Hazardous Material Safety Administration (PHMSA), U.S. Department of Transportation, East Building, 2nd floor, 1200 New Jersey Avenue, SE, Washington, DC 20590, (202) 366-4433, phmsa.dot.gov

U.S. Consumer Product Safety Commission, Office of Compliance, 4330 East-West Hwy., Bethesda, MD 20814, (301) 504-7923, cpsc.gov

U.S. Department of Agriculture, 14th St. & Independence Ave. SW, Washington, DC 20250, (202) 720-2791, usda.gov

U.S. Department of Energy, 1000 Independence Ave. SW, Washington, DC 20585, (800) DIALDOE, energy.gov

U.S. Department of Health and Human Services, Secretary's Office, 200 Independence Ave. SW, Washington, DC 20201, (877) 696-6775, hhs.gov

U.S. Department of Justice, 950 Pennsylvania Ave. NW, Washington, DC 20530, (202) 514-2000, justice.gov

U.S. Department of Transportation, 1200 New Jersey Avenue SE, Washington, DC 20590, (202) 366-4000, dot.gov

U.S. Department of the Treasury, 1500 Pensylvannia Ave. NW, Washington, DC 20220, (202) 622-2000, treasury.gov

U.S. Fish and Wildlife Service, 1849 C St. NW, Washington, DC 20240, (800) 344-WILD, fws.gov

U.S. Food and Drug Administration, 10903 New Hampshire Avenue, Silver Springs, MD 20993, (888) 463-6332, fda.gov

U.S. Nuclear Regulatory Commission, 11545 Rockville Pike, Rockville, MD 20852-2738, (301) 415-7000, nrc.gov

U.S. Postal Service, (800) ASK-USPS, usps.com

U.S. Small Business Administration, International Trade, 409 Third St. SW, 8th Fl., Washington, DC 20416, (800) 827-5722, sba.gov

Industry Experts

Wendy Larson, Manager/CEO, Big Tree Organic Farms, P.O. Box 736, Turlock, CA 95381, (209) 669-3678, bigtreeorganic.com, email: wlarson@bigtree organic.com

International Trade Directories

Croner Publications, 10951 Sorrento Valley Rd., #1D, San Diego, CA 92121-1613, (858) 546-1894, croner.com

Magazines and Publications

Export America, offered through the Department of Commerce, thinkglobal.us

The Journal of Commerce, The JOC Group, 2 Penn Plaza East, Newark, NJ 07105, (877) 675-4761, joc.com

World Trade Magazine Online, worldtradewt100.com

Market Research

Foreign exchange rates from x-rates.com

Index Mundi, indexmundi.com

International Trade Data Network, itdn.net

The U.S. Commercial Service, export.gov

The World Bank, data.worldbank.org

The World Trade Organization, stat.wto.org

Thomas Register of American Manufacturers, Thomas Publishing Co., 5 Penn Plaza, New York, NY 10001, (800) 699-9822, thomasnet.com

Marketing Associations

American Marketing Association, marketingpower.com

Direct Marketing Association, the-dma.org

eMarketing Association, emarketingassociation.com

Promotion Marketing Association, pmalink.org

Miscellaneous International Business Websites

AT&T Phone Service, General Business Resource Center, (800) 661-2705, att.com

The Electronic Embassy, embassy.org

Executive Planet, executiveplanet.com

FedEx, (800) GOFEDEX, fedex.com

Going Global, goinglobal.com

The Internationalist, internationalist.com

Skype, skype.com

Seminars and Workshops

The American Association of Exporters & Importers, 1050 17th St. NW, #810, Washington, DC 20036, (202) 857-8009, aaei.org

The Federation of International Trade Associations, 172 5th Avenue #118, Brooklyn, NY 11217, (888) 491-8833, fita.org

Unz & Co., 201 Circle Dr. N, Suite 104, Piscataway, NJ 08854, (800) 631-3098 or (732) 868-0706, unzco.com

(*Note*: Check with your local community college or university. It may sponsor seminars and workshops, too.)

Successful International Trade Businesses

Global Partners Inc., Wahib Wahba, 303 Second St., Suite D, Annapolis, MD 21403, (410) 626-1515, globalpartnersusa.com

Intyre, Jan Herremans, Veldstraat 21a, B-9220 Hamme, Belgium, 011-32-52-481136, intyre.com, email: info@intyre.com

▲

LND Export Management, Lloyd N. Davidson, 749 SW Watson Pl., Port St. Lucie, FL 34953-6340, (561) 336-0139, email: lnd@lndexportmanagement.com

Marketing-und-vertriebsberatung international, Michael Richter, MBA, HauptstraBe 27-88422 Seekirch, Germany, 011-49-(0)7582-933371, marketing-und-vertrieb-international.com, email: michael.richter@marketing-und-vertrieb-international.com

Nelisco Inc, Sam Nelson, 10911 Raven Ridge Road #103 Falls of Neuse Rd., Raleigh, NC 27614, (919) 217-3948, nelisco.com, email: sam@nelisco.com

Trade Leads

National Trade Data Base, trade.gov

TradeNet, tradenet.com

(*Note*: The Federation of International Trade Associations has a trading hub web page with links to most international trade lead sites. Check it out at fita.org/trade hub.html.)

Glossary

Abatement: reduction or discount given as a result of damage to a shipment or overcharge in bill payment.

Absolute quota: limit on the amount of a product that can be brought into a country during a specified time period.

Adjustment: changes in information submitted to U.S. Customs.

Ad valorem: according to value.

Advising bank: the seller's or exporter's bank in a letter of credit transaction.

Acceptance draft: see *sight draft*.

Advanced emerging market: a nation with good export potential due to its relatively strong combination of income and infrastructure.

AES: see *Automated Export System*.

African Growth and Opportunity Act (AGOA): U.S. legislation offering special tariff rates and other advantages as incentives to African countries to open their markets.

Agent: salesperson who pitches a product to wholesale or retail buyers but does not take title to the product.

AGOA: see *African Growth and Opportunity Act*.

Air waybill: bill of lading from an air carrier.

All-risks clause: insurance provision for extra coverage (but despite the name, it doesn't cover everything).

Andean Trade Preference Act (ATPA): legislation granting duty-free product entry for designated Andes-mountain region nations.

Anti-Dumping Act: U.S. legislation designed to counteract the practice of dumping.

APHIS: acronym for Animal and Plant Health Inspection Service, a division of the Department of Agriculture.

Applicant: the buyer or importer in a letter of credit transaction; also called an opener.

Assist: a tool, mold, engineering drawing, artwork, or other item that assists in the assembly and sale of the product.

ATA carnet: an international customs document allowing duty-free entry for goods, such as product samples; also called a carnet.

ATPA: see *Andean Trade Preference Act*.

Automated Export System: electronic process used to file export information directly to Customs.

Available at sight: letter of credit term meaning the funds will be paid as soon as the conditions of the L/C are met.

Backhaul: return of transport vehicle from the destination to the point of origin, with cargo picked up at destination or elsewhere, usually resulting in a favorable freight rate, since the vehicle is not returning empty.

Balance of trade: balance between imports and exports.

BEM: big emerging market; in other words, an emerging nation with great export potential.

Beneficiary: the exporter or seller in a letter of credit transaction.

Bill of exchange: see *Draft*.

Bill of lading: a receipt from the ship, air, or trucking line showing that it has the merchandise.

BIS: see *Bureau of Industry and Security*.

BISNIS: International Trade Administration's acronym for its Business Information Service for the Newly Independent States.

Bonded warehouse: warehouse or other storage area within customs territory where imported goods can be stored without paying a duty.

Branded product: one that carries a brand name.

BRIC countries: Brazil, Russia, India, and China—emerging market countries with especially large, mostly young populations.

Bureau of Industry and Security (BIS): U.S. government agency that administers exports.

Caribbean Basin Initiative: a plan under which designated Caribbean countries are granted duty-free entry for certain products.

Carnet: see *ATA carnet*.

Carrier: transportation line that hauls cargo.

Cash against documents: see *Collection draft*.

Cash in advance: payment term meaning the importer pays for the goods before they are shipped.

CBI: see *Caribbean Basin Initiative*.

Certificate of manufacture: document verifying that the merchandise has been manufactured and fulfills the general product requirements.

Certificate of origin: form verifying the product was manufactured in the country of origin.

CFR: see *Cost and freight*.

CIF: see *Cost, insurance, and freight*.

CIP: see *Cost, insurance, and freight paid to*.

Clean bill of lading: one in which no discrepancies or problems with the goods have been noted.

Clean draft: draft to which no documents are attached.

Clean on board bill of lading: see *Clean bill of lading*.

Collection documents: shipping documents or records.

Collection draft: agreement in which buyer takes title to the shipment once it reaches its final destination and pays for it there.

Commercial invoice: finished version of the pro forma invoice.

Commercial service: see *US & FCS*.

Commission agent: an intermediary commissioned by a foreign firm searching for domestic products to purchase.

Commission representative: foreign independent sales representative.

Commodity control list: a listing of potential export items subject to BIS export controls.

Compact of Free Association (FAS): legislation granting duty-free entry to certain products of the Marshall Islands and the Federated States of Micronesia.

Conference line: association of ocean freight carriers with common shipping rates and conditions; also called ocean freight conference.

Confirm: letter of credit term meaning the bank guarantees payment as long as the conditions of the L/C are met.

Consular invoice: document demanded by a country, along with a fee, before it will allow entry of merchandise.

Consularization of documents: practice of paying a fee at import to have entry documents stamped as legal; also called legalization of documents.

Consumption entry: customs entry for goods intended for immediate resale.

Contingent policy: an insurance policy that backs up the regular policy in the event of a catastrophe.

Cost and freight (CFR): shipping term meaning the exporter has the goods transported to the port or airport and loaded onto the carrier, and pays the shipping charges to the destination.

Cost, insurance, and freight (CIF): shipping term meaning the exporter pays all costs, including insurance and freight, to the product's destination.

Cost, insurance, and freight paid to (CIP): same as cost, insurance, and freight, except that the exporter pays for delivery to the importer's door and retains title up to that point.

Country-controlled buying agent: foreign government agency or quasi-governmental firm charged with locating and purchasing products.

Customs broker: individual or company licensed by the Department of the Treasury who acts as the importer's agent for the product's entry into a country; also called customhouse broker.

Customhouse broker: see *Customs broker*.

DAF: see *Delivered at frontier*.

Date of expiry: the date the letter of credit expires.

DDP: see *Delivered duty paid*.

Dealer assistance program: a program in which the importer or exporter provides sales representatives with product information aids and materials.

Delivered at frontier (DAF): shipping term meaning the exporter pays ground transport freight costs to the border, where the importer takes title.

Delivered duty paid (DDP): shipping term meaning the exporter takes on all costs, including customs duties, to have the goods delivered to the importer's door.

Dimensional weight: a value of the cargo that considers its weight and volume.

Discrepancy: letter of credit term meaning a problem in fulfilling the L/C's conditions.

Distributor: a company that buys an imported product and then sells it to a retailer or other agent; also called a wholesale distributor.

Dock receipt: document verifying that the merchandise has arrived at the dock.

Documentary credit: see *Letter of credit*.

Draft: banking term meaning the buyer's order to pay the seller.

Drawback refund: a refund on duties paid on imported merchandise that is processed or assembled for re-export.

Dumping: the practice of flooding a market with an imported product that's far cheaper than a comparable domestic one.

Duty: import tax.

EAR: acronym for Export Administration Regulations.

EBB: Economic Bulletin Board, a trade service of the U.S. Department of Commerce.

ECCN: see *Export control classification number*.

ECU: see *European currency unit*.

ELAN: the Export Legal Assistance Network, developed the Federal Bar Association and the Small Business Administration.

EMC: see *Export management company*.

Entry for consumption: see *Consumption entry*.

EU: see *European Union*.

Euro: see *European currency unit*.

European currency unit: a standard monetary unit for the 15 nations of the European Union; also called an ECU or a euro.

European Single Market: another name for the European Union.

European Union (EU): a single nontrade barrier marketplace formed by 27 Western European nations.

Evidence of right to make entry: a bill of lading or air waybill submitted to the portside customs office.

Ex Dock: shipping term meaning the importer takes title to the product at the export dock.

Ex Ship: shipping term meaning the importer takes title to the product at the ship before it departs.

Ex Works (EXW): shipping term meaning the importer takes title to the product at the exporter's or manufacturer's "works," or factory.

Ex-Im Bank: the Export-Import Bank of the United States.

Export control classification number: number given by the Bureau of Industry and Security to all U.S. exports and that must be listed by the exporter.

Export management company (EMC): a business that handles export operations for a domestic company.

Export trading company: a business that exports goods and services or provides export-related services.

FAS: see *Compact of Free Association*; can also be a shipping term. See *free alongside ship*.

FCA: see *Free carrier*.

FOB: see *Free on board vessel*.

Foreign distributor: a foreign merchant, similar to a wholesale distributor in the United States, who buys for his or her own account, then distributes the product.

Foreign trade zone (FTZ): a warehouse or other storage facility in which imported goods can be stored or processed without having to pay duties.

Formal customs entry: one in which the merchandise is valued at more than $2,000.

Forward transaction: term used when foreign currency is purchased at the time an export price is quoted.

Foul bill of lading: one in which a problem with the goods has been discovered.

Free alongside ship (FAS): shipping term meaning the exporter will have the goods loaded onto the ship or air carrier, where the importer then takes title.

Free carrier (FCA): shipping term meaning the exporter loads the goods onto the truck or other carrier at his works, where the importer takes title.

Free on board vessel (FOB): shipping term meaning the exporter loads the goods onto the ship or vessel, where the importer takes title.

Freight forwarder: individual or company that acts as the exporter's agent for product export.

FTA: see *United States-Israel Free Trade Area*.

FTZ: see *Foreign trade zone*.

Full set: shipping term referring to the three original bills of lading traditionally issued and signed by the captain.

GATT: see *General Agreement on Tariffs and Trade*.

GDP: see *Gross Domestic Product*.

General Agreement on Tariffs and Trade (GATT): international agreement designed to reduce trade barriers between countries.

General average insurance: covers the holder against general cargo loss on board ship as opposed to covering only the holder's merchandise.

General order (G.O.): goods considered abandoned by customs and put into a bonded warehouse.

Gross Domestic Product: total value of all goods and services produced within a country in a year.

Harmonize: to develop a single or matching system of tariffs.

Harmonized Tariff Schedule of the United States: listing of all U.S. tariffs.

Immediate transport entry: customs entry for goods to be shipped to another location for customs clearance.

Import/export merchant: a businessperson who purchases goods directly from a domestic or foreign manufacturer, then packs, ships, and resells the goods.

Import quota: a limit on the quantity of a particular product that can be brought into a country over a specified period of time.

Importers security filing: electronic filing required of importers and shipping lines to provide Customs with information about the contents of shipping containers well before the goods arrive in the United States.

▲

Incoterms: International Chamber of Commerce terms that are a worldwide standardization of shipping terminology.

Independent line: shipping line not allied with an ocean freight conference.

Informal customs entry: one in which the imported goods are valued at $2,000 or less.

Inherent vice: damage that could arise due to the nature of the goods being shipped.

Inspection certificate: document certifying the quality, quantity, or conformity of the product.

Insurance certificate: document confirming that marine insurance has been provided and indicating type of coverage.

Intellectual property: a product that has been patented, trademarked, or copyrighted and is protected by law.

In-transit entry: official customs entry designating import goods moving from the port of unloading to the port of destination.

Irrevocable letter of credit: a letter of credit that cannot be rescinded by the buyer, or importer.

ISF 10+2: see *Importers Security Filing*.

ISO: International Organization for Standardization; organization composed of representatives from many nations that decide worldwide industrial and commercial standardization.

ISO 9000: international quality management certification.

ISO 14000: international environmental management certification.

Issuing bank: see *Opening bank*.

ITA: International Trade Administration; a division of the U.S. Department of Commerce.

Joint venture: a partnership between two or more companies.

KORUS: see Republic of South Korea and U.S. Free Trade Agreement.

Lading: freight or cargo.

L/C: see *Letter of credit*.

Legalization of documents: see *Consularization of documents*.

Letter of credit (L/C): document issued by a bank per instructions from an importer authorizing the exporter to draw payment after fulfilling terms set out in the document; also called a documentary credit.

Liquidate: to complete a customs entry.

Mail entry: official customs entry designating import items sent via another country's mail system.

Manufacturer's representative: an independent salesperson who operates out of an agency that handles an assortment of complementary products.

Median age: age at which half of the population is younger and half older than that age.

Most favored nation: see *Normal trade relations.*

NAFTA: see *North American Free Trade Agreement.*

Negotiable bill of lading: same as "To order of shipper," meaning the bill is not consigned specifically to the importer.

Normal trade relations: trading partner status with the United States allowing standard duties on goods (formerly known as most favored nation).

North American Free Trade Agreement (NAFTA): agreement among Canada, Mexico, and the United States to phase out all trade barriers over a 15-year period beginning in 1994.

NTDB: National Trade Data Bank; a world trade database available through the U.S. Commercial Service.

Ocean freight conference: see *Conference line.*

OEM: original equipment manufacturer.

On board bill of lading: document that confirms the cargo has been placed on board the vessel.

On consignment: payment term meaning the importer pays for the goods after he's sold them.

On deck bill of lading: document used when the goods must be transported on deck, as with livestock.

Open account: payment term meaning the importer sends payment to the exporter or seller when he receives the goods.

Opener: see *Applicant.*

Opening bank: the customer's, or importer's, bank in a letter of credit transaction; also called an issuing bank or an originating bank.

OPIC: the Overseas Private Investment Corporation, a U.S. government financing agency.

▲

Order bill of lading: negotiable bill that must be endorsed by the shipper before it's handed over to the bank.

Order notify bill of lading: similar to an order bill of lading except that the importer and sometimes the customs broker must be notified when the ship reaches port.

Originating bank: see *Opening bank*.

Packing list: document detailing the number of items in shipment, how they are packed, serial numbers, weight and dimensions; also called a packing slip.

Packing slip: see *Packing list*.

Per capita GDP: the value, per citizen, of the total goods and services produced within a country in a year.

Personal baggage entry: official customs entry designating import items arriving in a passenger's luggage.

Pro forma invoice: a price quotation in the form of an invoice.

QS 9000: international quality management certification for the automotive industry.

Republic of South Korea and U.S. Free Trade Agreement (KORUS): Free trade agreement currently in discussion between the United States and South Korea that, if passed, would bilaterally reduce or eliminate tariffs on many products.

Retailer: the last conduit in the trade channel that sells the product to the consumer.

Revocable letter of credit: a letter of credit that can be rescinded by the buyer, or importer.

Shipper's Export Declaration (SED): document required by the U.S. Census Bureau for all export shipments in excess of $2,500.

Sight draft: a draft payable when the merchandise arrives at the dock.

Sight letter of credit: letter of credit paid immediately upon fulfillment of the terms.

SME: small or medium enterprise.

Spot transaction: the sale of domestic dollars and the purchase of foreign currency, or the reverse, for immediate delivery, or on the spot.

SRCC: marine insurance term meaning strikes, riots, and civil commotion.

Standby letter of credit: an L/C that's set in motion if the buyer doesn't pay within a specified period of time.

State-controlled trading company: foreign government-sanctioned and controlled trade agency; often deals in raw materials, agricultural machinery, manufacturing equipment, and technical instruments.

Straight bill of lading: a non-negotiable bill that prohibits release of the goods to anyone but the person specified on the shipping documents.

Strategic alliance: an agreement between domestic and foreign companies to work toward a common goal.

Tariff: trade barrier in the form of a tax.

Tariff-rate quota: a time period during which a specific product can be imported at a reduced tariff rate.

Temporary entry under bond (TIB): customs bond posted for goods, such as product samples, temporarily entering the country.

Terminal receiving charges (TRC): fees charged by the shipping line to load the goods.

Three-level channel of distribution: a trade channel that uses a middleman who resells to the consumer.

Through bill of lading: used when several carriers are involved.

TIB: see *Temporary entry under bond*.

Time draft: draft payable within a specified time period after the importer has received the merchandise.

To order of shipper: shipping term meaning the goods are consigned to the steamship line rather than the importer; also called a negotiable bill of lading.

TOP: Trade Opportunities Program; a trade leads program available from the U.S. Commercial Service.

Trade barrier: checks or hindrances on international trade set up by national governments to protect domestic industries from foreign competition.

Trade channel: the means by which merchandise travels from manufacturer to end user.

Trade preferences: privileges of being a trading partner or having normal trade relations with the United States and therefore paying standard duty rates.

Trading partner: favorable trading relationship with another country.

Tramp vessel: cargo ship that doesn't operate on a fixed schedule.

Transportation and exportation entry: official customs entry designating items arriving at a nondestination country's port and passing through to the destination country.

Transship: to ship a product into one trade region or country, offload it, and then reload and ship it on to another.

TRC: see *Terminal receiving charges*.

▲

United States-Israel Free Trade Area (FTA): an agreement that provides duty-free entry for certain Israeli products.

USD: U.S. dollars.

US & FCS: the U.S. Foreign and Commercial Service, also called the Commercial Service, a division of the U.S. Department of Commerce.

Validated export license: license required to export U.S. goods on the Department of Commerce's Commodity Control List, such as articles of war, advanced technology, and products in short supply.

Value-added tax (VAT): a tax tacked onto domestic and imported products in European Union countries.

VAT: see *Value-added tax*.

Warehouse entry: customs entry for goods to be stored in a bonded warehouse and then withdrawn in portions.

Wholesale distributor: see *Distributor*.

Wire transfer: procedure in which funds from the importer's bank are wired to the exporter's bank account.

Index